D0455086

*A Man and
his Mountains*

NORMAN CROUCHER

A Man and his Mountains

Kaye & Ward

KINGSWOOD

Photographs

All photographs are copyright of the author except:
North Wales on page 59 by courtesy of Malcolm Creasey
White Edge on page 60 by courtesy of Gordon Stainforth
Pisco on pages 62–3 by courtesy of Glenn Albrecht

Copyright © 1984 by Norman Croucher
Index compiled by
Isobel McLean
Published by
Kaye & Ward Ltd
The Windmill Press,
Kingswood, Tadworth, Surrey

Printed in Great Britain by
Butler & Tanner Ltd
Frome and London

ISBN 0 7182 2000 5

Contents

You need not be a country dweller to appreciate a book on
country life, nor a climber to enjoy tales of mountain adventures. So this book is not written exclusively for mountaineers,
and though it has not been possible to avoid climbing terms
entirely, the few which are used are explained in the short
Glossary, which is followed by a simplified description of
climbing techniques.

I

In the Alps

In the sunny days of 1978 and in the early Eighties came the blessing of some of the finest mountain adventures of my life, in China, the Andes and the Himalayas. But we should begin in the Alps in 1975, where and when first stirred the emotions that were to lead me there.

On lush Swiss mountain pastures and silvery glaciers we wandered contentedly above Saas Fee, a delightful village of timber chalets and bright flower boxes and jingling, clip-clopping horse-drawn carriages, all sheltered in a broad valley. In every direction, fields and forests and pastures lifted from the valley floor, gently at first, then more and more steeply until they met the white hems of peaks where the snows always lay. A fat glacier snout poked down the head of the valley and in some lights threatened to thrust its way right into the village and crush it all. Judy found complete enjoyment in walking but I burned to climb, so I talked with a mountain guide, a local man, who agreed to do the south south west ridge of the Egginer. Though short, the ridge was supposedly harder than any I had tried, and it was wise to be with an expert. Camillo, big-limbed, heavy-featured, ruddy-faced, about six feet tall, could get along quite well in English so it was easy to explain what was on my mind. His pleasure at learning this prospective client was a fairly experienced climber was in no way diminished when a shortage of legs was mentioned, so I began to wonder if his command of my language was as good as we had mutually and tacitly accepted from the start. It seemed better not to labour the point too far. He would find out soon enough and perhaps by then it would not matter much.

'I'll take the cable car with you when you go tomorrow and wait at the bottom of the mountain,' Judy announced. Hopes of training my wife as a climber had never borne fruit, though for a while she had tied the rope on and I had dragged her around, an unwilling puppy on a lead. She managed a thin semblance of enthusiasm over some years but there was no point in trying to fool ourselves. It's simple enough to understand what was wrong: she carried the burden of reluctance all the time. She wanted to climb because she did not want to be left behind but she had no love for the sport itself. There's no shame in that; maybe she had too much sense. Sometimes we walked together on the easier slopes, so mountains were half bond, half wedge between us, though not strongly so in either sense. She was not so fast uphill, but on the way down and headed for home she moved like a camel that has smelt water.

From the way he bubbled full of cheer on the fine, fresh morning of our climb, and chatted amiably to total strangers on the path to the cable car, it was clear the prospect of a shortish climb with a mountaineer of some experience appealed to Camillo. Poor Camillo. While we sat to wait for the first car of the day, the unusual outline of my trouser legs caught his eye; straps and metal created unnatural bulges at the knees. His brow folded into two vertical furrows above his nose and a finger pointed.

'Vat is this?'

So he had not understood. What on earth had he thought I was saying as he nodded and said, 'Yes, yes,' the day before?

'The leg is artificial, Camillo.'

From Camillo there came a long, uncomfortable pause, then he made a statement just to end the awful silence.

'You must be very careful.'

'That took the bounce out of him,' was Judy's observation afterwards. Camillo's bounce had deserted him right enough, and his already long face seemed stretched another two inches by jaw-drooping misery. Battling with indecision, he teetered uneasily on the very brink of changing his mind about going until, like a delivering angel's chariot from my point of view, a hearse in Camillo's eyes, the cable-car drifted quietly down and I got in, fast. Camillo followed, leaden footed.

Fifteen awkward minutes of silent ascent crawled by and from the isolated upper cable-car terminus we headed for the mountain. I could have done with a straightforward walk on even, compacted snow, but nature had decided shortly before that it was time to have an avalanche there, so we had to pick a way through a jumble of ice chunks up to tea-chest size sprawled in our path. A long ice axe helped me balance in a walking stick manner, but this was tough going and Camillo saw me waddling along at my worst even before we had reached the ridge. Once at the ridge's bouldery foot I squatted on a rock to tuck my trouser legs out of the way in socks, and in order that Camillo should realise properly what he was taking on, and to give him some encouragement, I bared one beige-painted metal leg, hairless of course, with an ankle sufficiently slim to be coveted by the ladies.

2

'Strong enough for climbing,' I said, hammering the limb, clunk, clunk, with a fist. Camillo brightened a little and I deceived myself into believing, because I wanted to, that I had won his confidence, until his next question arrived.

'But zee other one is all right?'

It had the ring of a prayer.

'No. It is the same.'

'Ah.'

Poor devil. I felt for the miserable man who stood before me, but found myself unable to generate sufficient compassion to let him off the hook.

'They're off below the knees so it's not so bad. I climb a lot,' came out in a rush. Might just as well have said, 'I don't fall off *every* day.'

'I've done much longer routes, Camillo.'

That was better. Despite his grey gloom a retreat was not suggested. For a while Camillo seemed prepared to accept me rather like an iron ball on a chain that would follow him everywhere if it could and pay the fee at the end of the day. It's not quite the relationship you expect between guide and client, but it would do.

So we got on with it. The south south west ridge rose at first as an intimidating jut of cliff several hundred feet high, though one could assume from its grade (3, 1 being easiest and 6 hardest) that it could not be as hard as appearances suggested. It swept up steep and gigantic.

Having roped ourselves together we called goodbye to Judy and set off through higgledy piggledy boulders strewn about the base of the ridge. Judging from the look on Camillo's face we might never meet her again; he possessed a kind of 'We're going to die with our boots on' expression and held his head high.

First the ridge presented a short chimney as high as a two-storey house; a chimney is simply a crack wide enough to get your body in. This was an easy one. Subsequent rock sections had helpful holds just where I would have asked: sharp ledges an inch wide for the toes, or large as window sills, prows of rock big as a fist to grasp or stand on, cracks that would take fingers or a hand, a deep hole which admitted the toe of a boot, and a thin flake with a tombstone resemblance over which a hand could be hooked.

So good and so numerous were the cracks and protrusions that we could move quickly, and quite soon we passed the only others out to enjoy the route that day, three in all. It was rare for me to pass anyone. My word yes, rare. Camillo's face was easily read, and radiated growing surprise and relief. Was he relieved! Misery had evaporated with the humpy white morning mist of the valleys below. Camillo smiled again;

3

some of the bounce had come back. Perhaps the Englishman was not mad after all.

'I am happy now I have seen how you can climb,' he informed me.

He would go ahead and find a ledge to stand on so he could hold me on the rope if I fell, and from eighty feet or so above he would call, 'Coming now,' and when I caught up he would say, 'Stopping now.' Ahead again, he would order, 'Coming now,' once more.

'Always we must make the safe,' he repeated many times as he flicked the rope behind a rounded spike of rock, a bollard against which the rope would run and buzz if I tumbled.

On that day, on the Egginer's firm rock, rust-red and lichenous, even the steepest parts felt safe, though very occasionally with a tentative touch, like a cat pawing its way carefully around a strange room, I found a loose hold and rejected it. So, steadily we gained hundreds of feet up the cliff and within an hour and a half were ploughing ankle deep across a clean, level, fresh snow plateau, a distinct step in the sharp angle of the ridge. Camillo's happy yodels darted and echoed around. His bounce was definitely back to normal and he said, 'We will make all the difficult pieces on the way. There are some steep pieces we can go around but we will go over. There is more snow than sometimes and that makes it harder but we will make them.'

A thin cloak of snow masked the holds here and there and had to be brushed away with a hand, but mostly the climbing was agreeably straightforward. Camillo bellowed down to three people far off on the easy route to tell them the way, but for some reason we could not fathom they retreated when no great distance from the top. I basked in the warm pleasure of being for once on a harder way up, though we had not reached the top yet.

Let's go back briefly and fill in a few gaps. Whether child or shy, confused, unconfident young man, I was an inveterate climber-up of anything that could be climbed: trees, houses, rocks, farm buildings, quarries were my mountains. One January, when I was eighteen, I spent two days on a rock climbing course on the sea cliffs of my home county of Cornwall. 'The Cornwall Youth Committee has kindly agreed to subsidise the cost of the course; the charge for those attending will therefore be 12/6,' the leaflet said. The subsidy was welcome for our family was periodically badly off; at the time my parents were receiving a small grant each year from the local authority to help keep me in a school uniform, so you will understand that there was not much money to spare. The outcome of that course was that I was addicted irrevocably to climbing, and introduced to other addicts.

Not long ago I revisited the scenes of my childhood and adolescence. Meadow Cottage, where I was born, a neat little whitewashed cottage standing on its own in a walled and hedged garden at the end of a lane, on the edge of Mount Hawke village, is much as I remembered it, except like all buildings from the past it has shrunk. We had moved away when I was four and I can recall little of what happened there, though I do remember picking oakapples in the lane and seeing a traction engine at the end; and also being taken to a little railway halt in a pushchair which cast a wheel on the way; standing on a chair to escape our new Alsation dog; riding a rocking horse in my sister's school; running home in terror from the stone wall around a mine shaft because an air-raid siren wailed and the Germans were going to bomb us; and last I remember people running and climbing over hedges to take a look at a crashed aeroplane. One hedge was too high for me so I went home, morbid curiosity unsatisfied. The Germans did bomb our village, my parents said, though they had been aiming for an aerodrome three or four miles away. The bombs fell in a line up a road and none exploded except the last, which landed in a field and killed a cow. There's one more memory: the look on my mother's face when someone brought to the door our pet rabbit, limp as a dead eel. 'Sorry, thought 'twas but a wild one an' we shot it.'

On that recent return to Meadow Cottage nostalgia was honeylike and warm and bright cornflower blue, but at Carn Brea, at the isolated farmhouse where I suffered the searing loneliness of adolescence, memory was hurtful. Somewhere along the same path to adulthood I had gone astray and become distant, detached from my fellow travellers. They always seemed to be coping, adjusting; perhaps they felt as befuddled as I, and many probably believed I was getting along all right. Those tender teenage times were a trial.

Going back to a quarry close to the farm, to look at where I had climbed alone, untaught, in Wellington boots, I was pleased to see the steep brown wall above the green water quarry. Quite hard, by the look of it. So, there really had been a budding climber inside me back in the days when legs were real. The wall was at the same time a harsh reminder of the agility, the physical ability, which was gone forever, snatched by drunkenness, and I did not want to look for long.

On that first rock climbing course I began to find myself. Not long after, when I was nineteen, I lost my legs below the knees (if you look at a climber in breeches, I end approximately where his breeches do, and it's hollow metal from there down) and always on my mind during convalescence was the question, can I climb again? Pretty soon, on two peg legs, I did climb a scruffy little tree near the convalescent home,

5

and concluded that a bit of easy climbing would be all right. That was comforting. As soon as I had artificial legs, scrambles on easy rock on the coast near home cheered me even more, and then an instructor from that first climbing course took me on. He helped a great deal, largely because his attitude from the start was, 'We'll see how much you can do,' rather than, 'I don't think you can do it.' For nearly ten years I climbed occasionally on very short sea cliff routes, in quarries and on moorland outcrops, but it was mountains I was after. Rock climbing is all about getting up rock from several feet to a few hundred feet high. It is not, like mountaineering is, about climbing ice and snow as well, trekking across glaciers and alpine pastures, and reaching summits. At first, for two years or more, I suffered a nagging pain in my right stump, a pain which brought with it tiredness and irritability, and hindered adjustment. When after two grey years the pain eased, it seemed so easy by comparison to get about. So in a way the pain did me good, though only when it was finished.

In 1969 I struggled up a small mountain in North Wales, finishing like a pilgrim, crawling on my knees through the snow. The mountain demanded too much energy in return for standing on its top; I was not good enough. The mountains would never be mine. But hope sprang up again in the notion that more training might help so the same year saw me walking 900 sore miles from John o'Groats in the north of Scotland to Land's End in the south of England. For the first three weeks or so the stumps of my legs were rubbed raw in patches and badly bruised. 'Stumps in bad state, bleeding in five places,' said my diary on the second day. Day after day the winter rain or spray thrown up by vehicles soaked me to the skin, headwinds made the going very hard, and once a gale picked me up in the air and dropped me in the path of traffic so I had to crawl out of the way. Many a time a day's rest was the only easement for a stump which had been cruelly treated. The early days of the walk are in part lost to me, clouded in a veil of physical pain. But other times remain and most of it was great fun. I managed eleven miles a day on average, and once having set out it would have been harder to have given up than to have carried on. Down the ribbon of road I trundled my rucksack on a golf trolley day after day, and as darkness approached it was time to look for somewhere to stay: a transport café, an inn, a guest house, a farm house, a chalet, someone's house, even a castle once. Sometimes accommodation was easy to come by, sometimes it was not, but I never had to spend a night out.

One of the hardest features of the journey was the recurring question, 'I hope you don't mind me asking, but how did you lose your legs?' Understandably, strangers wanted to know, and I was obliged to face

6

them and explain I was run over by a train as a drunken pedestrian. Being unfamiliar with drink, I had become very drunk one night and had taken a short cut through a wood to where I was sleeping out; next day I was due to start work in a piston ring factory. It was all part of the process of breaking away and looking after myself after the sheltered life of school. I did not do very well, falling down a railway embankment and getting hit by a goods train. I came to and something within me said, even in my befuddled state, that though I did not know what was amiss something was wrong and I should call for help. I was found on the track and taken to hospital. Intermittently I came to before dawn, and at times had a dream-like idea that my legs were gone and at other times I thought nothing at all was wrong; this hazy confusion was a blessing for the truth came gently. One of my first reactions was, thank God I didn't hurt anyone else; and I thanked God too that it was my own fault, for had someone else caused me such severe injury I would have faced the risk of being very bitter. The blame was mine and I just had to get on with living. What I would have given for it to have been the result of a respectable industrial accident or a sporting injury. But no, it had to be lived with. Adjustment, acceptance, were based partly on the thought that in a way it was fortunate that no one else was to blame, for bitterness would have been a great hindrance. I had my fair share of depression but I simply could not feel bitter or self-pitying because my mind rejected these feelings and put the blame squarely with me. Before long I recognised I would have to come to terms with *how* it happened; that it had happened was not so difficult to accept. The challenge to get on with living was greater because of the circumstances of the accident, and someone helped a great deal by saying, 'No one can make you feel inferior without your consent.' That took a long time to sink in, and I can't even remember who said it, but those words were a shield carried from John o'Groats to Land's End and by the end I had no more need of the shield. I had had a small bit of limelight and survived. I had crawled out from hiding. So the stern three-month training walk was a success in more ways than one.

As soon as the weather allowed, the following summer I went to Switzerland and climbed the Mönch (13,449 feet, 4,099 m) twice and the Jungfrau (13,642 feet, 4,158 m). Though these are relatively easy ascents started from high up at a mountain railway terminus, I did not find them at all easy. They taught me a lot.

Next year it was Mont Blanc (15,780 feet, 4,807 m) in France. That took two and a bit days up plus a day stranded in a high hut by ferocious winds. Prolonged movement resulted in quite a lot of injury to one stump, the weather caused mildly frostbitten fingers, the extreme effort of climbing brought on vomiting, headache and nose-bleed, and the strain on my back muscles was so great that they ached for days. But it was *fun*. I wanted more, had to have more. So I attempted the Eiger; the Mönch, Jungfrau and Eiger are neighbours, inseparable from each other, and having done two of them it was natural enough for the eyes to wander towards the third.

The Eiger by the west flank was a different matter from the other two: we had to begin from a lower starting point, so bivouac equipment was essential. The first attempt ended half-way up when the guide with me reckoned the wind was too high and that there was nowhere convenient for a bivouac above us. The more experience I acquire the more I would disagree with the opinion he expressed, but I knew that scepticism from guides was going to be just one more obstacle to be overcome. Sometimes they made me feel like I was trying to sell them a three-legged racehorse, but if I persisted, no matter how many of them made excuses or sniggered about my aspirations, in the end I found someone to climb with. A second try on the Eiger with two friends from South Wales ended two-thirds of the way up on the second day, because the avalanche risk was too great and I was very slow. In hindsight, turning back was a good decision. Defeat number two. I was prepared to wait and try again but the weather had other ideas and turned nasty, never relenting for long enough for conditions to become suitable. Staying in Switzerland for week after week would have been too expensive, were it not for my good fortune in finding a washing-up job in a hotel which furnished my bed and board.

Attempt number three commenced at three o'clock one fine, chilly morning after a six-week wait, and I got to the summit and back again in nineteen-and-a-half hours of climbing, broken only by short rests. The two guides with me were determined to show that not only could I climb the route but that I could do it up and down in one day, so they kept me at it. To expend such energy for so long! It was tiring enough for the guides, and to me it felt as hard as cross-country running, if not harder, and who does that for nineteen-and-a-half hours? Towards the end there came a tiredness which could have put me to sleep standing up if I had allowed it, I believe. Shortly before we finished the guides confessed that they were motivated by more than the desire to show that I could cope; in addition to announcing that I would be up and down in a day, they had backed their judgement by betting a bottle of champagne on my success! Oh, so tired, oh, so sore, and oh, so pleased. We had seen only two other Eiger aspirants, who did not quite reach the summit, so we had the mountain almost to ourselves. That was the best way to do it.

A couple of Swiss peaks, the Wellenkuppe (12,800 feet, 3,903 m) and the Breithorn (13,660 feet, 4,165 m) came next, and then the Matterhorn (14,690 feet, 4,477 m). That brings us up to 1974. I had not been particularly interested in climbing the Matterhorn *until* I saw it. The first glimpse of this superb peak standing seemingly aloof above Zermatt, and I was trapped. Line and shape are two strong influences on my choice of routes, and seen from Zermatt the Hörnli is a fine ridge line up one of the most impressive mountains in the Alps. And when we came to do it in September the five other people who tried that day turned back, leaving five of us to enjoy the mountain solitude and summit. We spent thirteen-and-a-half hours on that beauty, up and down. Half-a-dozen other alpine ascents, lots of rock climbs and a few mountains in Britain brings us up to date. There it is; now, the Egginer again.

The summit came in sight sooner than I expected. A couple of pitches (see Glossary) on rock, a short scramble, and there we were, after three hours on the go. The climbers behind conferred sincere congratulations when they arrived, for Camillo explained my circumstances.

'We have done everything, all the hard pieces, and I am happy,' he told them.

The descent of the easy way, a monotonous clamber down loose stones, was tolerated rather than enjoyed. At the bottom where Judy waited, Camillo stopped hikers on the trail to tell them proudly of his unusual client. Each would listen for a while, nodding Germanically, seriously, very slowly, and saying something like, 'Is that so?' and then they would ask the whereabouts of this man. The image they had could not have matched the real thing, for each time Camillo pointed me out I was leaning limply against a boulder and retching noisily, like an unhappy donkey braying. It lasted three hours or more; sometimes I could not eat for twenty-four hours. The nausea barrier, I called it, and on some alpine climbs I felt as if I had volunteered for a bad dose of 'flu; continuing to climb while in this condition could be a terrible hardship. What I did not realise in those early days was just how much each climb was taking out of me.

A grade 3 ascent. A quiet pleasure came over me later in the day, but that feeling was soon rudely dismissed for in a Saas Fee bookshop I came across an up-to-date guide-book in English, and, picking it up to read the route description and gloat a bit, I learned that the route had been demoted to the grade below. Some rat had downgraded my route! Grades of alpine routes are not subject to much alteration but I had managed to pick one which was. Tucked away was one more package of mountain memories to look back on and enjoy, and at least I had begun to break away from the easiest routes, but I was deeply dissatisfied that this short route, no more than a trainer for most alpinists, was not grade 3. Perhaps I was too concerned about grades at the time, but it's a stage most of us go through and some never get through. Having wrung as much joy from the mountains as anyone I knew, I greedily wanted more, and somehow it seemed right to attempt harder routes. Not very enlightening that, but it is the only way I can express it: it *felt* right to climb harder. Having got thus far it seemed proper to stand on the shoulders of experience and reach higher; I would try again on another mountain.

With unreliable weather skulking around and dangerous snow conditions high up, it would have to be one of the lower peaks. The Jagihorn above Saas Grund village fitted the bill: 3,206 metres, or about 10,500 feet. The South Rib was grade 3; a sneaky look at the guide-book in the bookshop confirmed that. And the route was short. An American climber, Jon Ryder, needed hardly any persuasion to go, and on foot we followed a meandering trail climbing steeply through a forest towards our objective.

Our journey was broken conveniently for the night at the Weissmies hut at 8,900 feet (2,720 m). After three hours on the mule trail at my plodding pace we drew near the wood-shuttered building and there was the mule itself, chewing at short grass. A doleful St Bernard lay outside, then padded up to be patted. Not far away the pale terracotta Jagihorn, a cathedral arch in outline, rose sharply to a humpy summit. It was only slightly snowy, where isolated specks of white had survived the sun.

On a short, sound and snowless route there was no need for the usual sleepy zombie-walk into the biting cold at three or four o'clock in the morning, so we waited until seven o'clock before emerging from the hut. A faint scratch of rarely trodden path took a direct way across moraine (see Glossary) and two shallow streams towards our mountain. The steep pull up the lower grass and earth flank took perhaps twenty puffy minutes before we scrambled over broken rock to the foot of the South Rib.

'Looks like where we join the rib and the real climbing starts,' Jon remarked.

'The rib must be very short. Takes about an hour and a half to the summit. Still, I reckon I'll be pushed to get up so we could take a long time.'

On rock lying back a little from vertical, a horizontal ledge, at its narrowest half the width of a boot sole, invited us along a wall without difficulty on to the rib. Jon muscled up the steep first pitch. He had left his home in America and slogged all winter clearing snow on a Swiss mountain railway, saving his pay and reserving the whole summer for a climbing holiday. His age I put at about twenty-five years and his muscular physique and short-cropped fair hair gave him the appearance of a typical fit and strong American sportsman. Apart from climbing, fanatically keeping fit and playing chess, he would explain with a mock Noel Coward accent he 'took a certain interest in the popsies, too.' With the same accent English friends were addressed as 'You bloody rotter.'

The mood was right and I threw myself at the rock, savouring each sight, smell, sound and touch. There was a delightful pitch of 3 (about Very Difficult in the most common British grading system) and we moved together rather than one at a time; only rarely did either of us feel the need to stop alternately to belay, another climbing term which means to attach yourself to the rock so you don't get pulled off if someone else takes a tumble. We relied instead on slipping the rope behind natural gateposts or spikes of rock as we went, 'making the safe' as Camillo would say. The mountain gave us more rock of about grade 3: a short wall rising almost straight up but with an abundance of holds. My lack of leg muscles resulted in staccato movements: jerk, jerk, jerk, too much jerk, so after moving one boot I often had to look down to make quite sure its partner was behaving itself, staying on the hold where it was supposed to be. Compared with the usual climber, power came more from the arms, and I resorted to using rubber knee pads to gain any extra holds I could. Progress was hard, a sweaty business, spasmodic, punctuated by animal grunts and pauses to work out what move would come next. Lack of bend at the knees was a handicap, lack of ankle mobility an even greater one. You need ankles as flexible as a gymnast's to be a good climber.

Whenever I put a boot in a narrow vertical crack on the Jagihorn I had to be careful not to put too much weight on it; the boot would go in all right but it didn't always want to come out again, so quite often I had to miss out a hold other climbers would use. More than once I had got a foot stuck. Another useful method of climbing, by jamming a leg or a knee in a vertical crack, does not always work for me because a metal leg just slips out; but I cannot emphasise too much that the biggest problem stems from those rigid feet.

A steep corner, like two walls meeting in the corner of a big room, bulged where we would have preferred not on the right and forced me to hug the rock close like someone scared, to press past the bulge. I had to be extremely cautious and avoid that dreaded fall which, even if of only six or seven feet, was too dangerous to risk, almost too frightening to contemplate, for someone who would land on metal legs. What would the impact do to spine or hips? And, my mind kept asking, if I landed from a great height, would my knee caps be torn away as I sank into the metal legs? Falling and not striking the rock below was a different matter; I'd had one or two falls of ten feet or so in circumstances where the stretch of the rope merely cushioned the fall and prevented me hitting the ground. In reality the thin red rope offered great security against death, and serious permanent injury was improbable as long as we took the trouble to climb as we should. However, I could never forget that one bad fall could mean the end of climbing, perhaps of walking too. Buckled legs could be hammered back into shape but real bones might not mend so easily. Perhaps I was over-concerned and over-cautious, but I remembered an acquaintance of mine who fell from a horse, landing on her one artificial leg, had severe long-term problems through damage to the stump.

The route followed the crest of the rib more or less, with air on either side.

'Want to keep goin' fairly fast so we don't get stormed on. Would be tricky if it got wet,' Jon said as he moved on.

There was angry weather headed our way but we expected to be up and down well before it caught us. Where Jon skipped nimbly across like a competent tightrope walker, I straddled a short, sharp horizontal ridge and worked across in little bumps. *A cheval* the French say: on horseback. On either side the rib fell away, precipitous and exciting, inducing the enjoyable state of mind in which alertness was not spoiled by too much fear.

Jon started up a vertical wall. Soon the rope hung straight down from his waist, clear of the rock for twenty feet, and I wondered why I wanted to follow. Why did I enjoy all this? No answer came but I realised what an important place climbing had seized in my life. The restless urge to be in the mountains surged through me with increasing strength as years went by.

'Mountains are dangerous. You could waste your life if you go on climbing,' a friend once advised, but I could not agree with that. Life could be wasted by climbing *carelessly* and it could be wasted in another sense by not climbing at all.

The rib gave almost continuous climbing connected by short bits of scrambling, and gradually and surely we gained hundreds of feet. An hour and a half winged by.

'Wait until you see what's ahead,' Jon shouted down.

'What is it?'

'I don't like to tell you, you bloody rotter.'

'What?'

'I think it's the summit.'

'There must be more.'

'No, there's a big stone man here.'

I'd never heard that expression for a cairn. But he was right, and in a couple of minutes we ambled over the last bit of easy scramble to the jagged summit, where twenty people could have stood at once. We were the only ones there.

'We should have looked for some harder bits to do on the way. It was too easy,' Jon said.

'Speak for yourself, buddy. But it did all go surprisingly easily.'

It had been easier than expected. Formerly I had had extreme trouble walking on soft snow. On that same holiday I had started practising on snowshoes; it required care to avoid stepping with the giant feet on the rope to the man ahead and the resemblance of my gait to that of an elderly cowboy was remarked upon, but hours of snow-muffled steps confirmed that my old mountain enemy, soft snow, could be defeated with these ancient weapons. Once more the mists of confusion rolled back and the way ahead was clear: where necessary I could avoid floundering in soft snow by wearing snowshoes but, provided they were not too long, some harder rock routes were more attractive than easy snow routes. Though there was still much to be learned the harsh days of mountain initiation were at an end. Now I was on the right track. And if I could go on some slightly harder routes, how about some really big mountains, with a few bivouacs? It was worth thinking about.

We wandered down the easy way and Jon headed straight back to the valley. I took some time off at the hut because I liked it there, and the afternoon was whiled away in dozy contemplation of the peaks.

That evening, dim gaslamps left dark shadows untouched in corners of the warm hut and under tables and benches. Hammering rain, with us at last, made the building more cosy. I ate a meal which had the fantastic flavour only a hard-earned appetite can impart, and dreamed of future climbs. That was the nice thing about climbing: there was always something to look forward to as well as something to look back on.

The weather throughout Switzerland deteriorated and it was time to head for home. In a way I had accomplished little in two weeks: a few walks, one peak of 11,000 feet and another of 10,500. Yet I felt profound satisfaction; admittedly it was short, but there was one grade 3 behind me, and I had learned a lot besides. Now I could just get on with enjoying climbing without bothering too much about grades.

2

On British Rock, the Alps again, and a Breakthrough

Frequent visits to the Roehampton limb centre were necessary when I climbed, and this was one of many reasons which pushed me towards being self-employed, so I could go as often as was required. Everyone at the centre was helpful, particularly my doctors, Doctors Tiwari and Fletcher, and my fitter, Brian Campbell. We often discussed possible adaptations to my legs for climbing, and for a while we even contemplated using some form of cloven foot; mountain goats manage well enough, was the basis of our argument. However, Judy was not impressed.

'I know you're a bit of a devil but that's going too far.'

From a practical point of view, as yearnings turned more and more towards mountaineering rather than rock climbing, the idea was not so good because it would mean carrying yet more weight in the form of a pair of feet and a spanner or two, but I did regret a little the lost opportunity of leaving a very interesting set of tracks in the snow. Or getting on a bus to go climbing would have been amusing.

Climbing at home never brought such delectable thrills as the Alps, but was still good in its own way and was, additionally, essential training for the big peaks to come. I should therefore tell you something about climbing in Britain – just a few pages to give you a better idea of what climbing is like for me.

My friend Des Turner bought a car, hand-painted, bright lilac and for that reason christened Lilac. We often took her for weekends to climbing areas. I had the advantage that if we arrived late at night and slept in Lilac, with my legs off I fitted comfortably along a seat. Des had given up his mathematics degree course several years before and turned to taxi driving because he felt he did not fit in at college, which is not surprising because he summed up the course as 'a waste of time'. He was something of a cynic and the sort of son mothers worry about. I met his; she did. On his best behaviour he was very helpful and good-natured, though there lurked in him a moody character who was seen less often.

In the summer of 1977 I began to feel increasingly tired and exceedingly bad tempered. Soon afterwards the cause became apparent: I had shingles. If you've not suffered from shingles you probably won't know how painful and tiring the ailment can be. A shooting pain jerked frequently down the left side of my chest and down the left arm, for about two weeks. And I felt awful for some weeks afterwards.

The illness did bring with it one bonus: for many years previously I had experienced a pain in the left side of my chest whenever I became very tired, and though this pain increased a great deal during the outbreak of shingles, it disappeared at the end of the attack. Naturally enough a pain in that region had caused me some concern, and though some tests had not revealed anything amiss, I did wonder for many years if I was negligent in ignoring it. But, though the symptom had seemed worthy of attention, I was reluctant to fuss about it.

When I got back to climbing, Des and I discussed whether I would ever manage a Very Severe (VS) route. That's no great thing if you have legs, but for anyone like me it was an amibitious prospect.

(In Britain one system of grading rock climbs runs: Easy, Moderate, Difficult, Very Difficult, Severe, Very Severe, Extreme. Though I had completed many climbs in the lower five grades I was hard pressed sometimes even to second (see Glossary) Difficult, Very Difficult and Severe routes, let alone lead them.)

Five days later Des and Colin, a gypsy-looking man with a mop of dark hair, stood with me below Pharoah's Wall, high up on the north side of Llanberis Pass.

For twenty feet the climb runs direct and easy so we all went that far, to a ledge as big as two car roofs at the base of the steep wall. Colin belayed (see Glossary) while Des climbed and slotted in three runners (see Glossary). For a while he rested, twenty feet above, allowing the top runner to bear his weight; it occurred to me that I would have to be very, very spent to put trust in such a tiny runner.

Light drizzle started to drift down and with that disappeared any slender chance there might have been of my getting up. The rock was too slippery, and now Des had to choose to go up or down. My vote was for down, taking everything, including his ability, into account.

'You can always use the excuse that I wouldn't be able to follow,' I offered, because he was wavering. 'I'd have no chance in the wet.'

He rejected the way out and inched above the top runner. He tried tentatively to get higher and backed down, tried again and backed down once more. That was his style, yoyo-ing nervously up and down in cautious little forays until he did it. Or didn't. Suddenly, as he stretched for a handhold, he gasped a short, 'Ah!' and his feet slipped off. Hands alone could not keep him up and he fell. Colin held on to the tightening, stretching rope from below but the top runner was plucked out by the force of the fall. From Des's lips crept a quiet, strangled cry which continued as he fell.

'Aaaaaaaaaaaa!'

We all knew the bottom runners were too low to save him from striking the ledge where Colin and I stood, and he would accelerate in a fall of twenty feet before he hit rock. In an upright position Des flew down, a dummy with arms flapping pathetically, and all the time he plaintively uttered his quiet wail. He shot past, so far out from the wall that he missed our ledge. Now the low runners and rope might cushion him. As he dropped from sight there came a nasty sound, a stomach-tightening slap and a crack as some part of his body struck the lip of the ledge. His jaw or head, I thought. Or perhaps an arm. Colin was pulled tight on his belays as Des went ten feet below us, and then the rope buzzed by no more. He had gone as far as he would go. Thirty feet in all.

Silence. We would not be able to see him until we unclipped from our belays. I freed myself while Colin stayed where he was to hold the rope. He called:

'You all right Des?'

Two or three tortoise seconds went by and a reply drifted back on a croaking voice.

'My arm's broken. Think my leg's busted too.'

So a stretcher was fetched and he was ferried down sliding scree to the road and an ambulance took him to hospital.

When we visited Des in hospital the score was one broken arm and a broken bone in his foot. Prior to being trundled away to the plaster-room, true to form he insisted he would not stay in hospital overnight, though the doctor advised this.

'Want to go down the pub,' he said, cussed to the end. We thwarted him by stranding him without transport.

Des feared his mother would hear about his accident but managed to keep it from her.

'She rang to ask if I was going home to the Lake District for the weekend,' he said a few days later. 'I told her I couldn't because I was broke. It was true, in a way.'

Colin gave up climbing for marriage. I suppose an accident like that would make some people think twice about climbing, but it had no such effect on me.

A few weeks went by before another Very Severe started the craving again. This time my partner was Gordon Stainforth, whom I had met through the South Wales Mountaineering Club. From Pen y Pass, at the top of the long uphill haul out of Llanberis, we ambled in half an hour through lovely Cwm Dyli, past little Llyn Teyrn to the Teyrn Bluffs. Yes, this was the slab we sought, where Via Media ran up the centre. Without clumps of purple heather, a gorse bush dotted here and there, and thick moss, the grey and brown rock mass might have looked dull, but it was a colourful display. Rock and adornments, and pleasing.

'Magnificent slab!' Gordon praised with great enthusiasm as he got a runner on twenty-five feet up. 'Beautiful rock.'

By the time he stopped almost all of the 150 feet of rope had run out.

'When you're ready, Norman.'

The first few finger holds turned out to be small, enough only for the tips; with knee pads to help it was possible. But they slipped up my legs to come to rest uselessly on the thighs. Ten feet up and another failure stared me in the face.

Back on the ground I resorted to tying each pad in place with thin rope, and went at it again. In short bursts ten feet were grabbed back, then ten more, twenty more, thirty. Sometimes the rock had little more than slight ripples on its surface, but that was enough. Pad, pad, pad, on the knees.

'Superb!' Gordon shouted. 'You're going very fast.'

Fast for me, that was. Using knees, or boots where the configuration of the rock permitted, I pulled up on any tiny knob or ripple, on any edge of thin crack, or dent. Every fifteen feet or so there was something big enough to stand on comfortably, for a rest.

'Now look down,' my companion called a couple of times. 'Nice, isn't it?'

In twenty minutes the hard 130 feet were behind and I led the last easy bit. You can argue about grades, but I had seconded either a VS or a good Severe. Whichever it was, another memory had been collected, another day spent well, another itch satisfactorily scratched.

VS aspirations stirred again, in the Lake District, two weeks later. My partner was Jim Morgan, a local man and a member of Cockermouth Mountain Rescue team. At Shepherd's Crag in Borrowdale, a cliff peeping out of the trees close by the road three miles south of Keswick, someone was struggling up a route near the one we were on.

'What's that one, Jim?'

'Brown Slabs Crack. VS.'

'Any chance I could get up?'

How was he to know?

'Don't think it's a good one for you, lad. It's savage. But if you want to give it a try...'

I did. Yes indeed. The third of a party of three hauled himself up the crux with considerable difficulty, then Jim went ahead. With every subtle movement of his feet the route seemed to confirm itself to be too hard. I was short on leg strength but most of all it was foot mobility which was lacking.

Lashed securely to a tree ninety feet above, Jim called, 'Made me sweat a bit. Now, you.'

The first thirty-five feet held no difficulty. The job in hand then was a smooth slab no steeper than a climb we had done earlier, close by, but much harder on account of a lack of holds. It was angled at seventy degrees, and on the right the slab was bounded by a slightly overhanging wall. For several feet where the wall met the slab there was a crack, big enough for a hand. Apart from that crack neither the wall nor the slab offered much to grip or get a toe on.

'The corner groove can be climbed direct and is Very Severe,' was the brief guide-book description. For quite a long time I just stared, half believing there was a certain arrogance or foolishness in contemplating even seconding a route which climbers of the two-legged variety described as Very Severe. Eventually I had to launch out from the haven of the good holds, or back down. There was no compromise.

'Right, Jim. I'll give it a try.'

The right hand slid into the crack and arched to wedge fingertips, ball of thumb, bottom of palm on one side and the back of the hand on the other, tightly against the rock like a crab wedged in. As I heaved up a little and tried to work out what to do next, sweat made the hand slippery and less secure.

What now? Knee pads helped upward progress inches at a time and I got into a position where my knees, hands and boots were on the slab and my back was pressed hard against the overhanging wall. Now it was the whole body imitating a crab. With hands low down I pushed upwards to gain half a dozen sweet inches for the right boot to come to rest on a toehold the size of a small Brazil nut. For minutes at a time, with knees and hands forced exhaustingly in opposition to my back, I pretended to push the overhanging wall back, to separate it from the slab, and that action squeezed enough friction from the rock to keep me up. Another hand jam and a frantic burst won ten more inches. It was so smooth! Every inch was fought for and I made more racket than a bag of grumpy baboons. Despite all the noise some moves gained no more than two or three inches.

There was a runner now, and I hung on to rest. Among the purists that is not done, but it was that or back down with arms limp as a string of sausages.

'Having a breather, Jim.'

'Fine, lad.'

How high am I now? Fifty feet? Is that all? It's only a hundred feet altogether, so is it worth bothering about? Only half-way up and the hard part is to come. The other climbers had to turn their feet this way and that.

'Climbing again, Jim.'

'Right, lad.'

My mind tried to squeeze out sufficient will to move. For a minute, reluctance to plunge once more into an area almost devoid of holds bound my hands invisibly to the runner, but in the end I tore myself free. The crack was climbed by laybacking, that is, by gripping an edge of the crack and leaning back, taking much of the weight on the arms. Laybacking was the only way and for a few feet I managed with the knee pads rather than boots on the slab. Breath hammered in and out, loud as any runner's, and my arms didn't like it. The crack faded to almost nothing and died muddily away. No more laybacking. From the bottom this had looked like the end of the hardest bit, but when he reached there Jim had shouted, 'It's not over yet by a long way.'

He advised, 'Now you have to get your left foot out on that hold.'

Whether it was a small shallow scoop or a bit of a bump I cannot remember, but it was tiny. To get a boot on there would require a wide bridging movement; in other words, I had to do the splits.

I took stock. The right boot rested rather awkwardly in the main crack, poised ready to slip out if I moved jerkily; even if I made no movement it looked as if it might go. The hands could not find anything to hold but could be rested flat against the slab for balance. The left knee pad helped prevent me sliding down and was also keeping me in balance, and it was this leg which had to be moved. While the leg moved, only the unreliable right foothold in the crack would prevent gravity having its way. So with nothing to hang on to, and with one dodgy foothold, I had to stretch a leg out leftwards and finish up doing the splits on two dodgy footholds!

High up on the wall on the right I discovered a hold. Not a good hold, but better than just pressing a hand to the rock.

'Well, Jim, I'd better make the move.'

As I did so, I talked to myself. Talking seemed to aid concentration.

'Let's see if the right boot's where it should be before I start. Well, that will have to do. Now, the left hand ... gently does it ... move it leftwards a little ... careful ... left hand out a little more ... caterpillaring along the slab ... careful ... my word, careful ... now the left pad ... lift ... ever so gently ... stretch ... oh, my ... streeetch ... be a good boot and go where you're supposed to ... bit further, my little darling ... steady ... hell, careful Croucher ... falling's not nice ... doing the splits is hard ... falling and doing the splits at the same time can't be fun ... slowly does it ... right boot, stay put ... please stay put ... oh my ... mama mia ... stretch a bit more ... steady ... mama bloody mia ... *done it!'*

'Great!' from Jim. A nervous giggle from me.

The slab allowed something small for the hands and Jim was only a few feet away. I slithered and grovelled up to the tree as fast as possible and we went up the last comparatively easy thirty feet to the left of an easier groove.

'Well, you did it lad!'

Very glad to have finished, even more pleased to have succeeded. An agreeable tingle spread through the belly region, chasing out the slightly sick sensation of nervousness. Hadn't led it, didn't do it in good style, took nearly an hour for a hundred feet, but I did a real VS. How wrong were the people who said climbing was not for me; how wrong if they would deny me this. I looked at my world through the rose tint of success and liked what I saw, and ambition lay for a while as calm as Derwentwater below. We quit the crag as it faded in the dark.

'To tell the truth, I wouldn't have put any money on your getting up that,' Jim said.

'Nor would I.'

I did not deceive myself. As VS's go, this was not an impressive one, and it would be only on rare occasions that I could find in myself what it took to get up that grade of climb. And relative novices have seconded VS climbs with no trouble. Leading can be even more frustrating because seldom do I come across a route which I am competent to lead. I had led up to Severe but there are a great many easier climbs which I would be able to lead only by taking a very great risk.

Yet climbing would for me be blighted if ever I became infected with a feeling that grades were everything. There has been many a memorable day on easier climbs, like one I remember with Dave Parsons, an ebullient Welsh jester, beginning to expand around the middle but still agile and strong, a man who patiently taught me over several years. One weekend we were in North Wales when hurricane force winds tore up trees, ripped off roofs and blew over vehicles; it was a fiend that hunted for weaknesses and found many. All over the country storms caused the deaths of over twenty unfortunate people in the worst winds recorded for three decades. The wind and rain eased somewhat and we grabbed a climb. With a 'Hee! Hee! Hee!' every so often, like a wheezy accordion, Dave headed up. Far below in a lake we could see a battered lorry trailer that had been blown into the water being hauled out by crane. Dave had made 150 feet up the rockface when he yelled happily, 'The wind's colossal up here.' While he hesitated, hunched up for a few seconds, the wind gusted as if deliberately, devilishly trying to tug him from the rough, grey rock.

'Beautiful'.he roared, and made another move in defiance of the wind. 'Beautiful!'

Dave's friend Huw took second place and I third up a crack big enough to squeeze a leg in, which we all did to make progress, then up another steep crack and left along an exposed wall we went, beneath a bulge as big as an elephant. Where the bulge met the wall below it, a horizontal crack, like a letterbox ten feet across, let us hook in fingers and hang on to the lower lip whilst stepping leftwards along the wall for several moves on tiny, tiny footholds. The longer the fingers clutched, the more they were robbed of warmth and though they ached with cold inside they were numb outside.

'Felt a bit sick on that traverse,' Huw said. 'Couldn't feel my fingers very well.'

For me, getting from the end of the traverse to the belay a few feet away was a long stretch and a frantic, strenuous struggle above a big drop.

In the end I managed. With that climb over the chill started to eat at our resolve to do another route and finally gobbled it all up, so we squelched a way ever so carefully down a mucky wet gully and back to the little roadside refreshment shack near the lake for a warming cuppa. The climb, the descent and the tea were all that much more enjoyable with the elements against us.

My first easy climb in Wales using pitons (the metal pegs which are hammered into cracks) was memorable too; it was as high as a four-storey building and overhung steeply for the first fifteen feet, relenting for a few more feet to a little less than vertical before bulging and then overhanging again.

'Keep your head to one side if a peg pulls out,' my companion, Gordon Stainforth advised. 'When your weight is on them they come out with a hell of a force if they go.'

One piton, which had been taking all my weight seconds before (you hang from them as if you are dangling in a parachute harness), I was able to tug from the crack. It had moved out a little while I was clipped to it; I had seen it move, and I was twenty feet above the ground. My, oh my! An uncomfortable scarey sensation flowed like liquid through my stomach.

'Look at the ground. Savour it!' Gordon, safe at the top, told me, as he moved about taking photographs.

'Pay more attention to the rope, Gordon.'

'Stop wittering.'

It was a fine experience, once it was over. Perhaps I was fortunate that my legs introduced a greater element of the unknown, of exploration, because I could not always imitate the movements of others.

No two climbs are the same and one relatively easy one sticks in my mind because of its character: it is called the White Edge, in Mewslade Bay in South Wales. This steep 200-foot pillar rears sharply up from a beach, more like a mini Dolomite peak than a British sea stack. I remember it because it looks so impressive but when you get half-way up it turns out to be a splintered horror of loose limestone which almost attains verticality at the top. If you could glue everything in place it would be all right, but those who had climbed it described it as 'a rotting pile', 'a tottering heap' and ''orrible'.

'It *is* loose!' Dave Parsons said as he led, and, 'The block I'm standing on is loose so watch out below!'

When I followed him rain came on as I neared the final steep section, and limestone becomes slippery when wet. It was awful in a way, yet when I looked back I was glad to have climbed it, because it looked so good.

The practice on rock went on but more and more I began to see success in terms of climbing mountain after mountain and never risking the whole mountain future just to get up one short bit of rock.

'I'm taking Lilac to Chamonix this summer,' Des announced one day. 'Want to go?'

'Yes please.'

'Right.'

'Dave Parsons and some of the other South Wales Club people will be there in July too.'

To my usual equipment I added a pair of items not used for fifteen years: crutches. Frequently the long, hot walks to and from mountains were more responsible than actual climbing for skin being rubbed from my stumps. With the assistance of crutches I hoped to move more quickly and with less harm to the stumps on trails in the heat of the day. To my way of thinking they would be the right tools for the job if they increased range and stability and at the same time reduced stump injury. Only misplaced pride could influence me against taking them.

Another advantage of crutches was that if an artificial leg broke I could still move over rough ground on one leg and crutches. I had sometimes bound the legs with nylon string and insulation tape for added strength, and apart from a few cracks here and there, and a loose foot once, they had stood up to very harsh treatment. (They are not special legs in any way, I should point out.) Crutches would provide added safety because they would allow me to rescue myself independently in certain circumstances. If there was a target it was to try another grade 3 route (how tame that ambition seems in retrospect!), and the one that appealed most was the Arête des Cosmiques (see 'Arête' in Glossary) on the Aiguille du Midi in the French Alps; but foremost in my mind was testing the crutches.

At the tail end of July we left, Des, his friend Alan and I, for Chamonix, a famous mountain town of about 8,000 people which meets the needs of tourists, walkers, skiers and climbers, through hotels, restaurants, cafés, bars, and souvenir and equipment shops.

We tracked down a ten-strong brotherhood from the South Wales Mountaineering Club, camped near the town. Four of them led by Dave Parsons had already agreed they would head for the Cosmiques hut; that suited me because from there the Arête des Cosmiques could be climbed. Des and Alan had no plans, so we tagged along, up in a cable-car, then a half-hour mist and snow trudge to the wooden hut, perched on a little brown rock island in the snow. The guardian and his wife served soup, drinks and meals to the twenty or so people who turned up, while their Alsatian dog wore goggles in the bright sunlight and chased snowballs for anyone who would throw them from the porch. He could never find them when they landed, of course!

Dave Parsons' group had their own plans and we went our separate ways. A sluggish pair trailed behind me amidst the strange, sharp early morning sounds of a cold place, to the foot of the Arête des Cosmiques of the Aiguille du Midi; the Midi is distinguished as the highest of the Chamonix Aiguilles, reaching about 12,500 feet (3,842 m).

'I don't feel like doing it. Got a stinking headache,' Des said, and Alan's only comment was in the same vein: 'I don't mind if we don't.'

But this was a day made for climbing so I tramped on hoping they would follow, and they did.

The easy bit of the arête is at the bottom so it was not long before we had only 600 feet to go on a ridge of pinnacles separated by deep cleavages, up, down, up, down, up. Des and Alan still followed, conscripts, but more willing than before. We could expect short problems of up to Very Difficult or Severe. Considering the ascent normally needed only three hours or so it was ideal for early in the holiday.

23

We had reached the feeling better stage and went on, until after a step around a corner the mountain plunged into its first cleavage where the rock overhung. That was the way we had to go, down under the overhanging rock, sixty-five feet by abseil (sliding down a rope). But first there was a delay while climbers ahead slid down. There were so many people we had to hang around for over half an hour. This was not the way to climb; seeking quiet places took on an even greater priority from that day. Not long after came another abseil of fifty feet down a steep, polished ice gully, a narrowing ridge, and then the mountain steepened suddenly into a blunt buttress, blocking the way. A near vertical wall faced us at the buttress's base. There was one vertical crack though, and that weakness alone would be enough by the look of it. Des led, I went next, fifteen feet up the crack, to shuffle horizontally left for several feet on a ten-inch-wide ledge to a tight vertical chimney of only nine or ten feet. Poor Alan suddenly turned pale and looked awfully sick, and fell without injury a few feet to the bottom of the wall. The sudden illness was a mystery.

He rested for a few minutes and then Des and I gave him a nice tight rope and up he came. I lessened his load by taking the abseil rope and went ahead while he rested limply. Morning had run out and heat left the ensuing gully snow soft. There was no enjoyment in climbing the untrustworthy porridge, which collapsed at every step.

An advantage came of having waited for a little while: the other climbers had gone ahead. Alan soon seemed back to normal and in any case we could see there was not far to go. After the last enjoyable couple of pitches on dry slabs we approached the luxury which waited: we could go down to the valley by cable-car from the summit.

Alan felt better but was too tired to have enjoyed himself and a grumpy Des moaned about having to pull people up on the rope. In contrast, I was delighted with the day; I appreciated the experience even though it was rather frayed at the edges. We had taken more than twice as long as we should have, and I had not managed as well as I might have, but to do a grade 3 route on the second day was far harder and more rewarding than my companions could appreciate.

For the greater part of the next day we washed, ate, drank and lounged around, until Des and Alan started to walk to Montenvers and I took the train; this privilege was granted me without too many hints that it was a shameful thing to do, on condition I carried up a bottle of wine. Montenvers, where the railway ends its steep and winding way up the mountainside, overlooks the famous Mer de Glace, the sea-of-ice glacier which at the time presented a grubby face; a fresh snow fall would have prettied it. Des and Alan arrived at dusk

looking like they had been up Everest, having missed the trail at some
point.

The following day was not planned as anything special (but turned
out as a special day in an undramatic yet important way). To see the
Montenvers area for the first time and to try out the crutches was
enough for me, and no one else had any plans. At first light we took a
rising wooded footpath; Alan had to turn back after an hour and a half
with a nasty blister on his heel. For me there was no turning back
because those crutches gave me wings! For the first time since losing my
legs I felt as if I could run. In reality, on level or downhill stretches the
pace was no better than a fast walk, but what a joy that was! No longer
did I have to take every step with care on the rough path, for with two
sturdy outriggers it was possible to make long strides or short, to pick
and choose where my boots landed, to drop lightly on movable stones
and pass by so quickly that it did not matter if they rolled over. Now I
had become a four-legged animal, there was no need to concentrate on
keeping in balance all the time or to use back and stomach muscles to
correct a lean this way or that. A slight stumble of one leg or crutch was
of no consequence because there were always three other legs around to
keep me under control. Immediately, and delightfully, it was apparent
that approaching mountains would be not only less tiring but safer
because I was steadier. The walk from John o'Groats to Land's End
toughened the stumps a good deal but still they were vulnerable in the
heat. Hiking from a valley for five or six hours to a high alpine hut
could be a terrible slog when the sun was up; now, with the new-found
freedom, the magic carpet, those walks could become another part of
the fun. Crutches could even help on snow sometimes, I felt sure. Snow
had always been my worst foe when the sun turned it soft, and to battle
along in mid-day heat, sinking up to the knees or further, made me hate
snow. But sometimes bad snow had to be tolerated. In an attempt to
keep the stumps cool and less sweaty at one time I used to wear long
socks and fill them up with snow when the sun grew hot. The theory
was that by keeping the metal legs cold the stumps would stay cooler.
While sitting on my rucksack and scooping handfuls of snow into the
socks you can imagine I was the object of many a questioning glance,
and people who came my way chose a wider than necessary detour to
get past! If the method had any effect it was slight, and I had soggy
socks all the time. Now with crutches adapted like ski poles the snow
problems could be reduced. There was another advantage which I did
not realise at the time: crutches took so much of the effort out of
balancing that the 'nausea barrier' had to be broken through less often.

The wretched random rubble of a glacial moraine gave a lot of

25

trouble and I floundered there almost as badly as I always had, but everywhere else easy movement and the freedom to gaze all around were mine. I saw the forests and pastures as never before; the need to watch every step like a head-down man looking for mushrooms was gone. We were out for twelve hours that day, and though the balls of my thumbs looked red as ripe tomatoes through taking the weight, I was overjoyed to have discovered the best way to get about on the lower mountain slopes. The trails seemed suddenly to have become prettier and to have shrunk to a third of their former length, so without even trying to reach a summit a great feeling of satisfaction was mine. And I started to think more seriously about longer ascents on bigger mountains. That was how much difference the crutches made.

Soon after, with Des and Alan, I climbed the easy Tête Blanche at a bit over 11,000 feet (3,429 m) and had an enjoyable jaunt with Harry Curtis from the South Wales Club on the Index. The short south-east ridge of this mountain is a safe grade 3 climb on sound rock. I followed Harry up a hard groove to a congenial slab, then to a brown arête decorated with yellow lichen, and on to a knife-edge section and a wall, and in one and a half hours we were there, at 8,500 feet (2,595 m). A long and impressive abseil down to scrambly rocks and a loose, clattering scree couloir put me once more in a place where the crutches were a tremendous boon.

Two days later, with Des, a two-hour walk from a cable-car station under an angry evening sky. The cairned track disappeared and reappeared capriciously in moraine gravel, boulders and ice. At somewhere around the 8,500 foot contour (2,500 m) we settled down for the night under a boulder. Dark night came insistently, to be torn apart by brilliant flashes and hollow crashes of a ferocious lightning storm. Like miserable trogolodytes we watched from under our rock as rain streamed down and blew in and found other ways to get at us through gaps and cracks. Even so, the boulder gave a feeling of security in the midst of a hostile environment; comfort is relative.

'Mummy! Mummy!' Des shouted every so often while we huddled in big polythene bags and laughed a little nervously and polished off a small bottle of rum, while the thunder and lightning drifted away to frighten people elsewhere. We lay in darkness in a contrasting silence broken only by the crisp-packet crackle of polythene bags, and the drip and trickle left behind by the storm.

Cheerless morning crept towards us very slowly, with grey sky and wetness, and we reluctantly accepted it to be folly for me to do any but the easiest of routes. A feeling of 'let's do anything rather than nothing' just triumphed over the option of going down. The only suitable candidate was the Aiguille de l'M (called M for its profile when seen from Chamonix), about 9,300 feet (2,844 m) high.

A slow start over glacier ice and a slog up a foul couloir of loose stones took us to the col we had reached on the day when first the crutches were tried out. A final twenty minutes of climbing to the summit on good and easy rock left no feeling of satisfaction with our efforts, but as we descended the rotten couloir the weather threw rain and then hail in our faces to remind us why we were cautious. People above dislodged stones and it became like a children's game, make yourself as small as you can, while stones clunked and jumped by.

Des walked down to Chamonix and I went to get the cable-car; the mental approach of the pre-crutch days was still there.

Time had run out. The young woman who ran the camp site hoped we would, 'Ev a god treep 'om,' which we translated eventually, and off we went. Stopping at Boulogne for a meal in a café with a resident terrier, Alan ordered steak tartare and the waiter flatly refused to serve it, saying in good English, 'It is no good for you.' He seemed to know what he was talking about for the food turned out to be awful. We didn't eat much but the dog kept coming up to beg. It seemed an unfitting end to the holiday, for now I was not just picking a poor or single item from the mountain menu as I had so often in the past. From now on there would be a feast of mountains.

3

Plans for Peru; Huascaran N. Summit
21,830 feet

Mooching about in the Lake District beneath a crag to pick a route I slipped on a stone and twisted one leg. A purple swelling, half a hen's egg, rose up immediately on one stump and a large area was bruised.

'Your stump's like a giant plum,' Judy said. 'Moby Plum.'

After all the time spent climbing without much in the way of injury it seemed incongruous to be hurt on a path. Walking was very painful and the crutches came to my aid. The stump swelled so much I could not get the artificial leg back on, but with one leg and crutches it was possible to get about. So I had learned something more, that if a leg failed mechanically or if a stump was injured crutches really would enable me to move over rough country. Practice bore out theory, and greater independence was a proven fact. So how about those bigger peaks?

All at once in me was a real yearning to go to the Andes. The Andes. The Andes. The name conjures up a feeling of excitement, of greatness, of seriousness, of adventure, of challenge, of peaks around 20,000 feet. But where, in the huge Andes?

Little bits of information, whether correct or not, coupled with impressions and assumptions, nudged me this way, then that. A couple of visits to the Alpine Club in London to browse through books and journals led further towards the Peruvian Andes and gradually I homed in on one region: the pretty Cordillera Blanca.

Invitations to go on other people's expeditions do not pour in when you lack the lower parts of your legs so it soon became clear that if I wanted to go there I would have to do the organising myself, and in all probability lead the expedition as well.

It must be emphasised that if it were not for the greater independence which resulted from using crutches, I would not seriously have considered going. After experiments in different types of terrain it was obvious that spikes on the ends would be an advantage sometimes, and at first I opted for wooden ones covered in sheet metal as the lightest, and they worked well on earth and snow, but were not effective against the hardness of ice. In the end metal spikes were the answer.

To get an expedition going several hurdles had to be cleared, not the least of these being the fact that I did not know anyone else who wanted to go. An expedition of one. It was hard to decide where to start, except that it was clear other expedition members had to be found. I had less time than most to seek out a team; usually it takes a year or more to organise a venture of this nature, but because of the shingles I had shelved the plans for a while and when they were taken down from the shelf again we had less than seven months to go.

Early on I contacted Julie and Terry Tullis, climbing instructors who also ran a climbing equipment shop. They said they would go and suggested that a globetrotting friend of theirs, Dennis Kemp, might like to go too. He soon wrote from New Zealand to say yes. As well as having built up wide experience in the Alps, Himalayas, USA and Antipodes, he had climbed in Peru. His appearance was that of an ageing hippy, and he was a lot tougher than first impressions might suggest. Another member, Harry Curtis, was invited as much for his good nature as for anything else. He wrote back saying he was excited by the prospect and was getting himself fit 'doing three push-ups a day and jogging the hundred yards to the pub.' Then someone who was prepared to help with the organisation of the expedition, and put in some funds too, turned up. His name was Mike Welham and he worked as a diver. Mike's experience included alpine climbing and an expedition to Arctic Norway in winter. Most of the work of an expedition goes by unseen and this was where Mike's help with the organisation was extremely valuable. His wife, Jackie, enthusiastically joined in the work too, and few expedition organisers can have been as fortunate as I in coming across so much assistance. One of Mike Welham's friends, Mike O'Shea, was taken on more to look after base camp than as a climber; he was so keen to go he even gave up his draughtsman's job and became self-employed so he could have time off. So when Terry and Julie finally sold their shop and committed themselves to the venture, we had seven members: the two Mikes, Harry, Julie, Terry, Dennis and me.

Raising sponsorship was hard work. Write to this one, write to that one, everyone suggested helpfully, but the problem of approaching the apparently most likely sources was that lots of other people thought the same way. The result of fifty letters to various large commercial and industrial organisations, appeals through newspapers, radio and television, was many expressions of good will but hardly anything to reduce expenses.

I applied for a Winston Churchill Travelling Fellowship and got to

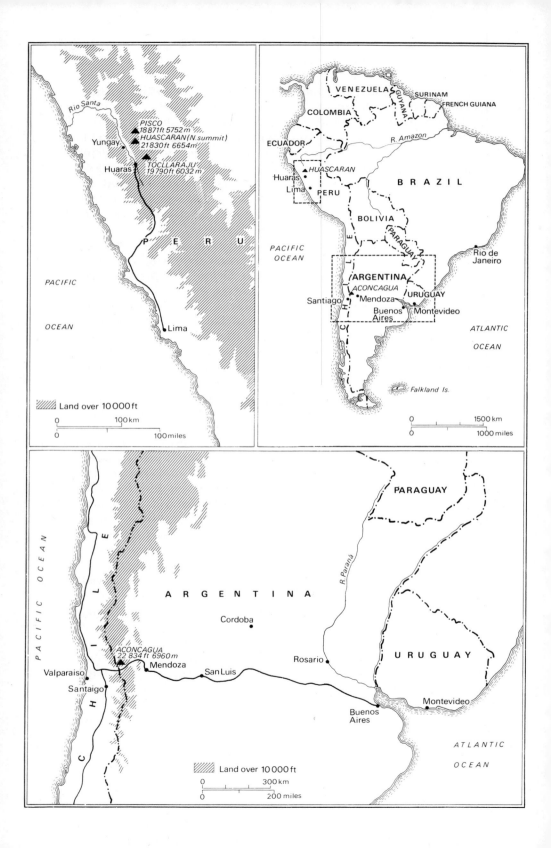

Land over 10 000 ft

0   100 km

0   100 miles

Rio Santa

Yungay

PISCO
18871ft 5752 m
HUASCARAN (N. summit)
21830 ft 6654 m
Huaras
TOCLLARAJU
19790 ft 6032 m

P   E   R   U

PACIFIC

OCEAN

Lima

VENEZUELA

GUYANA

SURINAM

FRENCH GUIANA

COLOMBIA

ECUADOR

R. Amazon

B   R   A   Z   I   L

HUASCARAN

Huaras

Lima

PERU

BOLIVIA

PARAGUAY

PACIFIC

OCEAN

Rio de
Janeiro

ARGENTINA

ACONCAGUA

URUGUAY

Santiago

Mendoza

Buenos
Aires

Montevideo

ATLANTIC

OCEAN

Falkland Is.

0   1500 km

0   1000 miles

PARAGUAY

PACIFIC OCEAN

C   H   I   L   E

A   R   G   E   N   T   I   N   A

Cordoba

R. Paraná

U   R   U   G   U   A   Y

ACONCAGUA
22 834 ft 6960 m
Mendoza

Rosario

Valparaiso

San Luis

Santaigo

Montevideo

Buenos
Aires

ATLANTIC

OCEAN

Land over 10 000 ft

0   300 km

0   200 miles

the stage of being short-listed for an interview. In the year before, 1976, over 3,000 applications were received and just over a hundred awards made, so I did not overestimate my chances. However, shortly after the interview by a very distinguished panel I was awarded a generous grant of £1,400. Considering that mountaineering can be a risky activity, I felt their decision to back me was very enlightened.

Jackie sent off two dozen more letters seeking sponsorship, like casting two dozen hooks at once into the sea. Until then the bait had been taken by very few fish, and they were small ones. This time we caught forty pounds and some offers of free food and medical items.

Then we were offered film at trade price, a welcome gesture as we had several photographers in the party, and good news began to come in from several quarters. Terry and Julie, having been in the climbing equipment business, had the task of procuring equipment, and despite their reluctance about approaching suppliers whom they regarded as friends, the response was good. Polar jackets and tents were the most valuable items, and they obtained many less expensive but equally essential gifts. Soon after, Hangers, the firm who make my legs, put up £500 through their parent body, Intermed, and another Intermed company supplied some very good aluminium trunks for baggage. That £500 was the biggest single donation apart from the Churchill Fellowship.

A host of details required attention: injections, travel arrangements, visas, equipment, currency, elusive sponsors still to be found. With expedition members living in Wolverhampton, Norwich, North Wales, Kent and London, communication was not always easy, particularly as two people were not on the telephone. But slowly, detail by detail, things came together.

Denny Moorhouse, founder and managing director of Clogwyn climbing equipment manufacturers, readily promised us a lot of equipment, and some weeks later he showed an interest in going himself. I said yes, and that made us eight.

Up to a few weeks prior to departure, air fares were still the biggest problem. In the end, through Twickenham Travel, we were booked on flights with Viasa, the Venezuelan airline. Paperwork went on and on, as important as physical effort if we were to succeed.

All eight expedition members were invited to the official opening of the Calvert Trust Adventure Centre for Disabled People in April 1978. The expedition team all seemed very favourably impressed with the place. We knew the expedition would attract a certain amount of publicity so we decided early on to use that publicity to promote the Calvert Trust.

We gathered from our separate directions on a wet Sunday in early

July at Heathrow's Terminal 3. All the people and all the equipment arrived in good time. Ten rucksacks, three kitbags, four metal trunks and one cardboard box containing a pair of legs were stacked outside. Soon, Senor Gonzales-Mata, London Sales Manager of Viasa, personally supervised the acceptance of our baggage into the system.

A small and rather forlorn group bade us farewell when the flight was called: Mike O'Shea's daughter, Jackie Welham and Judy.

The DC10 trundled fast, faster, very fast, roaring, lifted its nose and jumped into the sky at 2.20 p.m. It stopped briefly at Lisbon, and delivered us to Caracas, Venezuela, that evening. An overnight stop was required, and Twickenham Travel had arranged hotel accommodation. We wanted to leave our equipment at the airport but Viasa's storage space was full; they were in the process of building more, we gathered. A conversation with a local architect who started talking to us while he awaited his wife's arrival led to an introduction to Venezuela's Minister for Youth, who happened to be at the airport. A few words from him and some previously unco-operative customs men became co-operative, and locked away our heaviest baggage for the night.

A day was enough; we wanted to be on our way. The customs men had other ideas, however, for they had moved all our equipment to another airport a few miles away and had no intention of releasing it in time for our flight to Lima. A form they had issued and stamped, confirming that the equipment was in transit, carried no weight with them at all. Consequently, we had to leave two people behind in Caracas to retrieve our equipment; Mike Welham was one of them because he could be noisy and pushy, and Harry was the other because he was intelligent and could also get on the pushy side when roused; young men from Liverpool are not famous for shyness.

The rest of us flew with our rucksacks to Lima airport, where a representative of Lima Tours saw us without a problem through customs and escorted us in one of their buses to our hotel. Mike and Harry turned up there at about 7 p.m. the next day having suffered a tiring battle with customs officials. A female employee of Viasa proved to be our saviour; she got them a driver and vehicle to travel to the other airport and ferry the baggage, and she bullied the customs skunks relentlessly. Mike and Harry had lived through a complicated series of ups and downs of fortune, eventually repossessing our equipment. If they did nothing else they had earned their places on the expedition. With that and the work he and Jackie had put in Mike had earned his place three times over.

The following morning Denny and Dennis went ahead by bus to find accommodation in Huaras, the mountain town which was to be the civilisation centre of our activities. There was no rush for the rest of us to go because we wanted to talk to Senor Morales Arnao, the Andean expert of the official government sport body.

'Would you like to meet Walter Bonatti?' he asked when we met.

WOULD WE LIKE TO MEET WALTER BONATTI?

For those who do not know, the Italian Walter Bonatti is one of the most remarkable hard climbers whose triumphs include a solo first ascent of the south-west pillar of the Dru and an ascent of the north face of the Matterhorn in winter. Through reading one of his books, *On the Heights*, Harry started climbing; Harry was our truest disciple. We trooped in reverent manner to his hotel and spent half an hour talking to the small, grey-haired, alert and charming man who commanded so much of our respect. The audience was a significant and delightful start to our adventure. With customs problems behind us, we had all our equipment and ourselves in Peru; hopes nourished over a long period might flower now.

Senor Morales Arnao went out of his way to be helpful. Amongst other things he arranged for a truck to run our equipment to the bus station early the next day, and gave us letters of introduction and a map.

While the bus was being loaded we had a moment to enjoy the Mike Welham Street Theatre, for he had discovered that his *very* expensive new camera was not functioning for the second time in two days; he was our chief photographer, on his own recommendation. Crimson-faced and swearing, he threatened to smash the camera against a wall.

'This is all going down in my book!' he shouted, referring to a document which he hoped to write but never did, as far as I know. The book was an often-used threat and he had a habit of jotting down notes about anything or anyone, including us, which displeased him.

'I see Chaucer's at it again,' Mike O'Shea remarked as his namesake scribbled away furiously.

The bus, with every seat filled by a local or a foreign visitor, droned out of early morning Lima, past plush hotels and big statues and monuments, past single-storey hovels half hidden behind bamboo fences, past buildings with crumbling faces. Over all there was a greyness which came partly from thick fog, the 'garua' sitting on the city for months each year. The city has a population of almost three million people, many of whom live in slums, or in shanty towns hung on dry dust hills or planted on dismal flat land.

By no means everyone is poor; in some parts of Lima the grand Spanish-style houses and squares are well kept. In ten minutes you could leave a slum and be drinking tea in a bit of old England, out of time, out of place, in the Lima Cricket Club, or eating in an expensive restaurant in the Miraflores district. Towards the city's outskirts the road verges deteriorated into dust and rubbish tips, and the smell of rotting matter took over.

In simple terms we had to head north and a bit westwards on a road hugging the desert coast, with the sea on our left. The steep plunge of 200 or 300 hundred feet down red sand to the sea was a constant danger; some time later twenty-six people were killed forty miles along that road from Lima when a bus collided with another vehicle and went over the edge. At about the half-way point a hundred miles up the coast we turned right to zig-zag roughly north-east through rapidly rising country, and then left to go a bit west of north again. Houses and shacks thinned out as we went further up the desert road, until there were no dwellings and hardly a speck of growth to break up the sandy monotony.

We slipped gradually into the sort of Peru that was to fascinate us all for the next six weeks. Flashing by like a quick taster of a way of life we would get a little closer to, went cacti of highly individual species, barefoot children, women with babies in colourful blankets slung on their backs, bright home-woven clothing, dark skins of smiling Indian faces, small scavenging dogs, roadside cafés, and drinks stalls, dirt roads and donkeys, and hairy little pigs wandering free and quite tame. Nearly everyone wore a hat of straw or a trilby or a bowler, against the sun.

We had followed our right-hand turn and the road was soon a real mountain twister, taking its time to get up to the high country. Now almost always on one side or the other was a gigantic drop but the driver hammered on. In Peru, driving seemed to involve faith as much as it required petrol; some taxis had on their dashboards little shrines in which bulbs lit up each time the brakes were applied.

Ladies spinning wool while they walked along, cows, pigs, goats, horses, lambs, potato and maize crops and thatched adobe houses sped by the bus windows, and as we topped a hill a surge of excitement ran through the gringos, for there ahead were the fantastic sharp peaks with their gleaming white coverings of snow. Between us and the mountains light browny yellow, almost golden, plains intervened and the sky above was bright blue and clear. It was unbelievably beautiful.

A screech of brakes blasted the mood away and the bus jerked to a stop.

'What's happened?'

Slowly the facts came together from bits and pieces of accounts which travelled down the bus to us near the back. A boy on a bicycle pulled out, overtaking a slow lorry on the lonely road. He had been coming downhill towards us, fast. He hit the bus. We peer out of the windows to the left. There's a bike lying there with a crazily buckled front wheel, and a small group of people has gathered near it. Where is he? At first most of us did not spot him. Then we did. A lad of about fourteen, tears on his cheeks and one limp forearm cradled protectively in the other, is the centre of attention. He stands there with his arm hurting and his bike busted, and now someone is shouting at him and most likely telling him what a fool he is. He knows that already, or doesn't want to know, so why try to tell the poor young man? Now is not the time; he's hurt, and his prized bike is a distorted mess. People leave the bus to even the scene out a bit; he may have made a mistake but we all feel sympathy for him. We take him in the bus to his home further along the road. A tearful scene with his family outside their adobe home ends when a woman, probably his mother, comes with him on the bus to the hospital in Huaras. So it was that we made our first acquaintance with that hospital.

I saw the woman with him later. His fingers on one hand were splinted and he looked all right.

Huaras. We had arrived. There around us was the town, population 50,000 people, 10,000 feet (3,050 m) high. Only a slight shortage of breath told us we were that far above sea level.

Denny and Dennis had found us a dormitory in the Hotel Barcelona, and a couple of tricycle baggage transporters were quickly bargained for to carry our equipment there. On the fifth floor of the square concrete hotel we dumped our rucksacks on some of the mattresses and hurried upstairs to the flat roof just above. Being the tallest building around, the hotel made a fine viewpoint; the countryside rolled away and away in humps to a superb array of peaks dominating the skyline.

How can Huaras be captured in words? Any attempt must be inadequate but, first, think of straight concreted streets, some of them recently built after earthquake and alluvion damage; an alluvion is a rapidly moving mixture of rock, sand, mud and water spilled by collapse of a lake's morainal dam, or by massive ice avalanches falling into a lake and displacing the water.

Earthquake hazard influences the height of buildings, which mostly have no more than two or three floors. Away from the main streets most are single-storey, while larger structures of reinforced concrete have been put up in the centre. Roofs are made of red tiles or corrugated iron. Some of the living creatures that crowd into the town centre I have already mentioned: barefoot children, women carrying babies in blankets, donkeys, little pigs and street traders. Shoeshine boys and

35

newspaper boys wander everywhere, and ice-cream or drinks vendors pedal their three-wheeled barrows slowly around. In all of the several markets, squatting women sell vegetables, eggs, and fruit spread out for display on blankets, and there are stalls, too, for meat, ironmongery, clothes, wool and herbs. Higher up the scale are bookshops, shoeshops, chemists, dress shops, like anywhere else. So it is a spectrum, from the lady squatted beside a single cake sold slice by slice, through small tattered stalls, through big and well-kept and well-stocked stalls, through small shops, to some large ones. Eating out is characterised by a similar spectrum of style and price. You can buy a slice of that cake or some bread from a barrowboy or a stallholder, then there are scruffy cafés and better ones, and a few good restaurants. Wide-eyed adults and children stare in through restaurant windows like they were watching TV. Grubby stalls, grubby feet, grubby children, grubby streets. Bank-notes are tatty, begging by children is commonplace, buses are crammed full, fares are cheap, the police are armed, there are lots of rickety, ramshackle cars and gaily painted trucks coming and going. The air is more of activity than bustle, with people going about their business but not rushing. The hills and mountains stand all around but not too close; Huaras does not feel closed in. And usually the sky is clear and bright blue. As you leave the centre you come across adobe huts and shacks on rough and dusty stone roads, amongst cacti and glossy eucalyptus and other trees. Patchwork farming, corn and other crops and grazing for cows and pigs, creeps into the edges of town. By day the parp, parp, parp of horns on the tricycles of ice-cream vendors, and tinny South American music from cassette and record stalls, and the traffic noise, are constant. At night the streetlighting is good because the surrounding mountains give the town hydro-electricity.

We soon made the acquaintance of Pepe, the young man who with his family looked after the Hotel Barcelona and its guests. Dark, smooth haired, demonstrative in a Spanish way, friendly, shrewd-eyed, Pepe had the never-still nature of a small bird. It was to him that we turned if anything needed arranging.

'Ees possible,' and, 'Ees no problem,' were his usual responses. First, he fixed up a storage space for our food and equipment, and then when we wanted to transport it to our first base camp he got his truck out and drove us up an exceptional track bulldozed out of steep mountain flanks.

Denny and Dennis had ridden up the day before, to spend a headachy and nauseous night at 14,500 feet (c. 4,400 m), and this was the fate of some of the new arrivals, who wandered around like sick ghosts next day. One reason for selecting a camp with a road quite close was that anyone who had trouble acclimatising could descend for a while, and this is just what Denny and Mike Welham did, at different times. Trees, grass and flowers flourished in the steep-sided valley all around the tents and a small stream conveniently supplied fresh water.

While the rest of us lazed around for a day, waiting for acclimatisation to put a bit more life in our steps, Dennis scouted ahead up the valley. At fifty-six years of age he was our senior member by far, a most experienced expeditioner and somewhat intolerant of our inexperience.

All at once one of my legs began to rattle loudly with each movement. My heart sank; this was even before the climbing had started! Julie and Harry were about to descend on foot to Huaras to replace two defective paraffin stoves, and they volunteered to run a spare leg delivery service at the same time by collecting the reserve limb from storage at Pepe's. A feeling of guilt crept over me as I watched them hurry down the hill and out of sight because as soon as they disappeared the rattling stopped. They arrived back in darkness the next evening, having had a difficult time because Harry had twisted a knee. To ease the pain on the way up that afternoon he had taken to bathing the poorly joint in streams, and in order to do this he had to slip his climbing breeches down to his ankles. As they passed close to a village Julie decided nothing was to be lost by trying to hire a donkey and she succeeded in persuading a teenage girl with such an animal to come to a stream and pick up Harry. The intention was that Harry would be transported a considerable way up the hill, but Harry had chosen that moment to cool his knee. The girl arrived to find him kneeling in a stream with his trousers down, and she may have noticed a leg lying on the bank, too. Whether she did or not, the scene can have done nothing to convince her that gringos are civilised or sensible, so she turned her donkey around immediately and went straight back to the village! Harry shouldered my leg and soldiered on to arrive at camp just after dark. My rattling noise had not returned, its cause remains unknown, and the replacement limb was not required after all.

Amongst other things, acclimatisation to the altitude we were at resulted in a sixty per cent increase in red corpuscles. After a couple of days at base camp three people emerged as getting on best with the altitude: Julie, Dennis and me. Dennis set off and took a tent up to about 16,000 feet and returned to base camp, and then Julie, Terry and I set out carrying quite heavy loads. Terry intended going part way to help with the weight.

The hiking was easy on grassy slopes made prettier by lupins and a yellow flower looking like a cross between a big daisy and a marigold, but possessing little or no stem; it seemed to hug the ground to survive.

After a rise of 600 feet we escaped leftwards from the confines of the valley up easy grey slabs, and Terry turned back as planned. Julie and I took on board the things he had carried for us.

The weather had been deteriorating and, after two hours on the go, hail started to patter down through coiling mist. This was followed by a clap of thunder which shook the ground.

We took shelter in a cave beneath a boulder, and considered bivouacking, but an improvement in the weather allowed us to go on to a tent left by Dennis. He had left a note, suggesting a peak we should try. The right skyline ridge, though nearly vertical in places, did not look too hard, and the summit was only 1,000 feet above us, so it was a suitable choice for an acclimatisation climb.

Next day brought steep walking for a short way, then a scramble over boulders to the foot of the ridge.

I led a short pitch up a steep step, and was amazed at how I puffed on the relatively easy rock. Fresh snow during the night had made it harder, but to an extent you could not grade technically; here and there it was slippery, and you could not say much more than that. We alternated the lead, with Julie doing the hardest bits first: a short, vertical crack and a rather unstable snow slope to the summit, reached two and a half hours after leaving the tent.

Within just over a week of arriving in Peru the expedition was successful, though not wildly so. This 16,800 feet (5,120 m) mountain was modest by Andean standards. It had been a cautious and gentle introduction. We were overjoyed.

Descent to the tent took only an hour and a half so we were back in the early afternoon. Dennis, Terry and Harry arrived soon after, flushed under heavy loads. Terry and Harry looked awful, just how we must have looked the day before. We all sat and stared at the mountains, prettier for their fresh coats of snow but at the same time dangerous in consequence, and it was amicably agreed that it was not the time to attempt other peaks in the area. The loads were taken down again. The slabs had iced over and were none too easy in a couple of places.

The night of the following day was spent by several of us in a hut below our base camp. We cooked a meal and shared it with the guardian of a nearby dam. Language was a problem because our Spanish was thin and the guardian had no English. One of the few things Terry could say in Spanish was 'a dog with fleas', which was best left unsaid as the guardian had a dog and gave Terry a dirty look when the phrase was used. Then Terry got into a real tangle trying to extract the Spanish for 'aristocrat'. Things like doors, windows and tables we could get by pointing, but try explaining 'aristocrat' in sign language. Egg; that was another word we needed, so I demonstrated with an orange which, after due clucking noises, was laid on the floor. We pointed at the orange and asked its name.

'Orange,' the guardian said in Spanish, and gave me a look which seemed to say, 'Stupid gringo. Everyone knows oranges grow on trees.'

Eating good food and drinking rum and honey by candlelight was only the first of many celebrations we would enjoy.

We slept on the floor that night. In the faint dawn light Harry was woken by a movement and found a rat nuzzling his arm, so for half an hour he played smash the rat with a ski stick whenever the persistent little creature returned. The rat did not lose, but retired when good light came.

The next two days were spent returning to Huaras, bathing in a natural spring bath, eating, drinking, wandering about the town, writing postcards, talking to anyone and everyone who liked to chat to gringos, dancing in a disco and having an interview with a reporter who wanted to know if I had been carried up. Some of the newspaper reports were hilariously inaccurate: they had us up the wrong mountain, with a mother called Julia Turbiens (Julie Tullis) and I had broken two legs on the way.

We shopped for food in the colourful local markets, where tiny potatoes came in so many bright hues you could have strung them like beads for a pretty necklace. Because the next camp could be approached from a reasonably close track up which a truck could be driven, we were able to take fresh fruit and vegetables. With the food bought, it was off for thirty miles (fifty kilometres) along the beautiful Rio Santa valley, a deep river cleft of rich green and yellow plenty growing on red earth, topped higher up the sides by the more mellow colours of drier country. Our truck took us to Yungay, the tragic scene of the worst alluvion in history. In 1970 earthquake tremors set off the alluvion which became airborne and smothered the town, killing an estimated 17,000 people. The total of deaths in Huaras at the same time was put at 16,000.

Pepe had arranged the transport and came with us as far as Yungay, a new town rebuilt a few miles from the former site, and he took us to one of his favourite restaurants. The waitress, Patti, was as much an attraction as the excellent cuisine, and our amorous Peruvian friend chose to stay in Yungay. We continued by truck up a bulldozed track. Eucalyptus trees, bulbous cacti, yellowing grain crops and adobe houses blended and pleased the eye. Exchanging waves with colourfully dressed people, particularly with the children, was like giving gifts equally; they appreciated having notice taken and shouted 'Gringo' in a friendly way as we went past. Just now and then the mood changed and they threw stones at us, though we did not know why.

Delays occurred in a couple of places where bulldozers cleared rocks and earth which had tumbled on to the track; on the running board was a man whose job it was to leap off every so often and trundle boulders aside. The road wiggled back and forth, back and forth, an embankment on one side and the usual frightening drop on the other. Around sharp bends and across little wooden bridges we hurried. In a straight line it was only ten miles (sixteen km) but the road was forced to twist and turn all the way. We climbed for an hour and more, up through a gorge whose steep walls were staggering to see.

'Heads!' someone cried every so often as we drove under low branches of gnarled and twisted papery-barked trees into the broad Llanganuco valley, and past two of the most beautiful copper sulphate blue-green lakes you could imagine.

After unloading our gear a mile or more above the lakes we transported it on our backs to a pretty, flat-bottomed, grassy valley. There we set our base camp on the edge of trees beside a river washing quickly over white stones.

Next morning was cold and we huddled in our sleeping bags, waiting for the sun to let us have its warmth. At 8.45 a.m. the rays touched us and suddenly it was a different, warm world.

Everyone was asked if they wanted to attempt the next mountain, Pisco, and of seven of us Terry and Mike Welham opted just to carry loads part way, which was a great help. Mike O'Shea stayed behind in the vital post of camp guard.

By crossing the river on a rough wooden bridge of three thin logs, we could begin to rise up nice walking country. Starting from base camp at 12,500 feet (3,800 m) we tramped in silent single file on a self-imposed treadmill: Denny, Mike Welham, Harry, Julie, Terry and me. Dennis, as usual, was somewhere above, having come up two days earlier to scout.

At first only the white tip of Pisco's head was visible, but gradually our target unfolded and grew. About 2,000 feet above base camp, Camp 1 was set up on a broad plain.

'If I had brought my equipment I could have stayed here and gone higher tomorrow,' Mike Welham moaned, and went down to fetch it.

The next stage for the remaining four of us was a sharp gradient up a stony moraine. From the top of the moraine we faced a steep descent of forty feet on dry, loose dust and grit into a mass of precariously perched boulders and rubble, half a mile wide. It was our misfortune to follow a line of cairns which went too far to the right.

'This is a cow,' Julie said as we clambered about in the burning heat, rucksacks pressing down like they were full of rocks.

We got there in the end, to a tent Dennis had left at about 16,000 feet. Though we had met him as he descended he seemed mostly to float ahead as a phantom, rarely if ever glimpsed. His work in the planning stages had not amounted to much, but he had picked out precisely how he could best help the expedition in his own way and he served us well in his solo role. Denny and Harry turned back to the camp we had just left to bring up a tent and more supplies next day.

Next day, for Julie and me it was a leisurely time, carrying the tent and equipment a few hundred feet higher in two journeys. We pitched the tent by a little blue-green lake at the snout of a big glacier, up which we would have to climb. Washing and basking in the sun, we waited for the others. An extra day would give Mike Welham time to make up his mind and come with us if he wanted.

They arrived in the early afternoon, Harry, Dennis, Denny and Mike Welham, a slow-march crocodile which at sea level would have looked comical, but we were at over 16,000 feet (4,900 m).

That evening I went a short way up the glacier snout to see which would be the best way for the next day, and found the steep ice to be stepped conveniently.

Pisco's top was nearly 3,000 feet higher. To reach a summit close to 19,000 feet high would indeed be success, but luck did not come our way for during the night snow fell quite heavily. That would mean deep, fresh powder snow higher up and powder was one of my worst enemies, a pet hate. But still, at 4 a.m. I quit the tent to rouse the others.

Mugs of tea, and away at 5.20 a.m. in faint moonlight, up steep ice. Some of us wore head torches, some managed without. With no more than a hundred yards of the glacier slope behind us one of my crampons came off. We stopped while I put it back on, heaving on the straps hard enough to stop the circulation in a normal foot. Twenty more yards and the damned thing jumped off again. It was difficult to understand how a crampon could escape from a rigid foot, but there it lay in the snow. A previous set of crampons had given no trouble in years. The third time a crampon dropped off a few minutes later, Denny suggested managing without. That made it harder, but was better than fiddling about with straps all day.

We tramped on for an hour in our brightening crystal world, watching out more closely for crevasses but still taking the time to look around as the sun turned the high peaks pink, then gilded them splendidly.

There was a big crevasse in the way, one with the far lip higher than the near one, a blue-green grotto of a hundred feet depth. From a few feet width at the surface it widened to ten feet half-way down, and then the walls came slowly together. Fall down there, and the likelihood was that the victim would hang free and have trouble getting out, or be wedged in the narrowing bottom, injured by the hard ice walls. In the past I might not have got across but the crutches allowed a kind of double pole vault and the gaping hole was left behind. We weaved a way through hummocks of snow, giving a wide berth to more lurking crevasses, nothing unless you fell in, awful if you did.

Crossing a white plateau we took on an ice slope with a few inches of hard snow cover. It would have been easier with crampons, but Denny cut some good steps, quite close together, and now and then Julie shoved the shaft of her ice axe under my boot if she thought it might slip. At forty degrees at the steepest the slope was not really hard but high up to the right was an ice cliff draped with gigantic icicles; if any of them broke off several hundred pounds of clear ice would torpedo our way. We might just as well be walloped by a telegraph pole. There was an additional hazard: at the bottom of the slope in the line a sliding body would take was a broad snow chute which would channel everything, everyone, over the top of a huge ice cliff.

Mike Welham began to lag behind, but kept going. The slope lessened and the snow got more powdery; we sank to our ankles, then to our knees, and Denny and Dennis found their alternated work as trailbreakers growing harder. At the worst we were up to mid-thigh as we ploughed along in a line. The altitude had an effect and though there was little or no conversation a curse burst out from one or other of us every so often. The route was technically easy but powder snow at 18,000 feet is no joke. That's a feature of big mountains: a hard slog may be technically easy but exhausting all the same. Already I was planning that if we did not get there this time we would try again next day when the sun had chased some of the fluff from the snow.

Particularly in view of the recent snowfall, there was some danger of avalanche. To have eliminated the hazard completely would have meant staying off the mountain; the small risk just had to be accepted if we wanted to climb. Experience can help, but you can still get killed. We had to like the mountains enough to put up with the risk.

The wind picked up, whipping snow into our faces, and we pulled across face masks stitched to our fibre-pile jackets. Inside the masks, breath roared in and out.

'Much harder than when I did it before,' Dennis said. 'Much harder.'

The weather remained good, as it did much of the time in the Cordillera Blanca. We toiled up a massive snow mound to the relief of a steadily easing gradient. Denny and Dennis continued to break trail, then stood aside for Julie and me; we were close to the summit and they were letting us get there first. The order in which we arrived was of no concern to me, but it was thoughtful of them. Julie and I were on the summit at eleven o'clock, then Denny and Dennis, with Harry approaching soon after, swearing at himself to keep going, and then dropping to his knees every forty paces. He drove himself on competitively.

'Every time I looked up there was some rat on crutches still going so I had to do it,' he said of the easy but long final stretch. He lay down on the snow and hit it repeatedly with his ice axe, all the time shouting, 'I hate you! You're going to melt! I hate you! You're going to melt!' Climbing was never dull with Harry around.

Like a man with lead legs, Mike got there eventually. He was on fairly safe ground so was not roped to anyone. After that day he went quieter.

Feasting on Christmas pudding and oranges, we stayed on the summit for three-quarters of an hour or so. With the ascent of the first peak nine days earlier we had no reason to go home feeling we had made fools of ourselves; and now, at 5,760 metres, or 130 feet short of 19,000 feet, we had even less reason to be ashamed. The expedition was a success and the faith of a great many people had been rewarded.

When we packed up camp next day, with Dennis leading we found a better way through the moraine mess. As we passed the flat area where we had put up our first camp above base, two porters looking after someone else's camp called us over for some tea, which was taken gratefully. Their names were Manuel and Pedro; some of us were to meet Manuel again and share some important days with him.

Within three weeks of arriving in Peru, and in two weeks of climbing, we had done what we came to do. And we had over three weeks left. From the start I had planned that the team would split up once we had achieved our rather vague objective because it seemed wrong that people should be held back by me all the time on what might be their only visit to Peru. Not only that, if we had to stay together for the full expedition period I would have been more fussy about the composition of the team. For three or four weeks our little idiosyncracies were not serious as long as we were achieving our objective, but over a longer period they might have created problems. There were bound to be a few differences of opinion and complaints, but disagreements all stayed within reasonable bounds, and everyone made a predominantly positive contribution. I was more than a little fortunate in having a team which functioned so well.

Over two days we rested in Huaras, ate, cleaned ourselves in the warm natural spring water at the Hotel Monterrey near the town, and danced and drank in the local disco. We sampled the local fire-water, a brandy called pisco as it happens; it is said the mountain got that name because after a French ascent in 1951 the porters consumed two litres of the stuff.

During this period we shaped our plans, or our plans shaped themselves, partly based on who got on well with whom, partly on how people had been managing at high altitude, partly on how ambitious each individual was, and partly on many other threads of this and that. To start with, Dennis met a Swiss climber and they were keen to climb together, so they headed off to their chosen peak. As Mike O'Shea was more of a walker than a climber he was quite content to be left out of further climbing plans. Chaucer was his friend so they stuck together and went touring. Harry, Julie and I liked climbing together, but Terry did not want to because he worried about Julie. Denny did not think the weather would be good enough for the route we had in mind so he went off sightseeing. 'The route we had in mind.' Not *we*, really, but Julie. Unlike most expeditions we had not selected definite objectives before arriving in Peru because my performance at high altitude was an unknown; we had to plan as we went along. One thing we had decided before leaving England, though, was that the real big ones of the Andes, 20,000 feet and more, were too much for me. The others might do one or two like that, but not me, so Peru's highest mountain, Huascaran (pronounced Wasca-ran) was out because it was about 22,000 feet high. However, Julie changed all that.

'Why don't we do Huascaran?' she asked.

'Too big,' I said.

'But you're getting on very well. Let's do Huascaran. Harry, you'd like to wouldn't you?'

'Yes.'

'Come on, Norman,' Julie coaxed. 'Please.'

I knew someone who was not going to take no for my answer when I met her, but I wanted a while to think first. Trying Huascaran could be biting off more than I could chew even though things had gone far better than they might have on two preceding ascents. Now Julie had brought Huascaran, formerly filed away in the mind under 'Forget It', back into circulation, and it had to be reconsidered. We heard that the higher of the mountain's twin summits, the south, was out of condition, but the north was all right.

Early next day I was up and looking out of a dormitory window of the Hotel Barcelona. From the dormitory we could see Huascaran, or rather, on that day we couldn't see Huascaran but could see the gigantic, fluffy stormcloud mass that wrapped itself around the mountain. Aha! An excuse for not going. Excuse, yes, but bad weather could not be ranked as a real reason. The sun was lighting up the cloud, turning it reddish. I watched for a while and then the realisation came that my mind was made up already. I could not resist this one. The spell was cast. And if we were going we might as well go right away.

Julie and Harry were delighted, but not Denny, who thought we were mad to go when the weather was, to say the least, inclement. But the bad weather was higher up, and it would take us a couple of days to reach it. If we did not leave Huaras until the weather on Huascaran was favourable we would waste part of the fine period. It was a simple view, not something founded on any special knowledge of meteorology, and it had a great bearing on subsequent events.

We bumped into Manuel on the street. Yes, he had been to Huascaran before. Yes, it would be wise to take a porter to help carry lower down, and to look after base camp; we could hardly have expected him to say otherwise. Yes, he was free and could go tomorrow. He jumped at the chance. Back at the hotel Pepe refereed as a deal was struck: Manuel would receive 1,000 soles a day and his food. At 300 soles to the pound it would not cost us a fortune and by local standards Manuel Fabian Oropeza, married, aged thirty-two, would be earning well.

Two days had passed since our return from Pisco, so we had not wasted much time in relaxing after one climb and getting ready for the next. We selected and packed our equipment, bought fresh food and ate a lot, and waited for the next day.

'Pepe, can you get us a pickup to Musho tomorrow, please?'

'Ees no problem, my friends.'

We climbed into the back of the pickup belonging to Pepe, who had found five girls to share the cab with him. Terry was coming along for the first part of the walk to base camp.

Pepe roared his vehicle up the road which followed the river valley northwards and a little to the west until five miles (8 km) short of Yungay we came into the little village of Mancos. Within three minutes he had bargained for another truck for the last leg of the journey on wheels to Musho. Quite a few vehicles stood around in most villages and you just went up and asked how much, beat the driver down a bit because it was expected, and there you were. Equipment was soon transferred and away we went up a road which was hardly horrifying at all. Rough, bumpy, dusty, yes, but not much of a horror. Straight ahead lay our destination, less than 180 feet short of 22,000 feet above sea level. Already the unwanted weather had slipped away and we could see it all gleaming.

The tree-lined village of Musho, where lived the poor local farmers, was about 9,900 feet (3,000 m) high. There the truck driver pulled up in front of a little café and we unloaded. Harry paid for the truck hire; he was keeper-of-the-purse for communal expenses like that and he handled the job very well. The top left pocket of his jacket was known as 'the bank'. There always seemed to be someone who was behind with his contribution, but Harry kept it all straight with great patience. Meanwhile, Manuel was bargaining with someone in the café for two donkeys; the café seemed to be the centre for such deals. Within minutes two donkeys and a tiny girl, about ten years old, appeared, and Manuel loaded the beasts. With four rucksacks and two kitbags as well as two tents we had more than was necessary, but we had allowed for the fact that the weather could keep us waiting at base camp or the next one, and we could get extra food to those camps with little trouble. In other words, extra time could be bought with food. I had played the waiting game with many a mountain, and won sometimes more through patience than great effort. It's not that I am by nature especially patient, but I can wait when there is no other way.

The two donkeys may have been in excellent health but to us they looked like the sort of creature for which old ladies set up sanctuaries in this country. The laden beasts, looking ready to buckle at the knees at any moment, moved slowly forward, sounding like wrestlers who had been at the beans.

For half an hour Terry was with us under a boiling sun, then he shook Harry and me by the hand, kissed his wife, and turned back down the trail with a quiet, 'G'luck.'

At one point on the trail a large group of very well-dressed Austrian climbers looked aghast at Harry's untidy appearance, which included trailing bootlaces and a face smeared white, clownlike, with ointment because of sunburn. They looked even more aghast when Julie appeared in view. A woman! 'We do not climb with women!' one of them had announced. Imagine their reaction when around a corner appeared the third member of this small band, with his crutches quietly clicking at each movement.

'That's our leader,' Harry said.

'But where is your expedition?' they asked me.

'This is my expedition,' I said, and they stared in amazement at our tiny group.

The biggest part of an afternoon disappeared in a nice walk between stone-walled fields, over open grazing land, up through a kind of giant honeysuckle forest, and finally amongst twisted trees to a flat area with a cascading stream nearby. We had gained about 3,500 feet. Already in place were two tents belonging to a large American expedition whose members were higher up the mountain. Two porters and a doctor sat around. The latter was conducting research into cerebral oedema, a fairly common sickness at high altitude.

'What are the symptoms?' Harry asked him.

'One of them is simply swearing.'

'Bloody 'ell,' said Harry. 'Is that so?'

Tents up, brew on, food, another brew, more food. Lovely sunset. We nearly started very early next morning. I woke Julie.

'Wha's up?' she asked.

'Time to go.'

'Go where?'

'Up this mountain. What's it called?'

'Huascaran.'

She looked at her watch, one which lit up.

'It's one o'clock.'

'Oh.'

I saw the dawn come but couldn't really pick just when; it was so slowed down by waiting. We had a fifty-foot rock step to start, then steep walking up a moraine. Taking a gamble, we carried everything to an advance base camp only 1,500 feet higher, rather than taking less and going on to a higher camp. Personally, I was glad of another day for us all to acclimatise instead of rushing at it, and I favoured increasing our chances of success from a higher base even though it meant we did not make full use of a good weather day.

Fifteen thousand feet. Several crestfallen Americans passed by in small groups on the way down. Two were descending because of breathing problems, three had not reached the summit because of high winds, and another four failed for the same reason. Quite a few people climbed Huascaran in any year, and quite a few failed. Three died on the route while we were in Peru. So were we biting off more than we could chew? Perhaps not; we would take it nibble by nibble.

When the time came we all put on crampons and roped up to begin threading a way up a huge glacier, between high ice blocks here, up ten feet of steep ice there, along a narrow ice bridge between deep, open crevasses, stepping over gaps, mostly up, occasionally down, on slopes of all angles. Anything steeper than seventy degrees was only a matter of feet high. Once a way had been found through the worst jumbled area of ice, in about half an hour, it was uphill snow all the way, for hours. Manuel went better than any of us, dumped the load he had been carrying at the next camp, and went back down to base camp with another porter descending from that high camp. Packing, snailing up the glacier and pitching the tent again took about seven hours that day. It may not seem long, but we felt it was enough at that altitude, 17,500 feet.

At high altitude the need for liquid increases; serious dehydration is a risk. So we guzzled tea, soup, meat extract, hot chocolate and orange drinks, all made from melted snow. Porridge, a rice meal cooked in a pressure cooker at base camp and reheated, fruity Christmas pudding, egg powder and some very good dehydrated meals made up our solid food.

We seemed to have picked the busy season. Sharing the level snow patch were three Americans and about nine Austrians. Some of the Austrians had reached the summit that day and the Americans were aiming for it the next day. One of them, Eric Perlmann, a twenty-eight-year-old, freckle-faced, red-haired adventure journalist traded some of our matches for a length of strong rubber cord, which solved my crampon binding problems.

The sunset was the best of many in the Andes. The breast-shaped sugar bun that was our target blushed salmon pink while golden clouds surrounded a sun as red as a ripe Peruvian tomato. Gradually, wide blackberry juice stains spread through as the clouds turned to pale custard.

Sunday morning came and the fine weather held. The Americans had a problem: three porters they had engaged to carry skis part way were late, or had not set out at all. The longer they delayed the less chance they had of making it, and even if they set out as early as possible they would not arrive back before dark, after a long day. Though we did not need them we said we would take the porters off their hands, which was twenty per cent co-operative international gesture and eighty per cent laziness, and Eric, Rick and Bruce set off. We could afford to go later as we intended establishing yet another camp higher up; most did, some didn't. It was just one of many equations to be balanced: carry more weight and go slower or carry less and go fast. Our way was safer, and perhaps less certain of success; we aimed to have something in reserve at all times on this one. This one?

'What's this mountain called, Harry?'

'You forgotten again?'

'Yes.'

'Huascaran.'

For some reason the name would not stick in my mind; this mountain did not seem like one of mine somehow, and that bothered me a little. I wondered if I might finish up hating its very name.

The porters straggled up, unladen, late, and most of the morning had gone before we got away. Perhaps it was silly to take them on but we were glad that we had for they took weight from our backs. There was no rush. We knew four hours or so would be enough, for the next stage, a rise of 2,500 feet. The porters soon pulled a short way ahead; living in a high village conferred an obvious advantage and I envied them. Snow slopes of only forty degrees were a hard pull at that altitude and then came a snow step of thirty feet which was at about eighty degrees. At that altitude even short stretches of steep climbing really take it out of you. That particular step had a yellow fixed rope hanging down. Harry went first, relying a lot on the rope lower down and less and less as he gained height in case it gave way. A bulbous lip at the top soon hid him from view.

'It's attached to an aluminium stake,' he shouted. 'Bit wonky but it seems all right. OK Norm.'

Scrunch, scrunch, scrunch, crampons bit in like a sprinter's spikes, and pointed forward too in imitation of a boar's tusks, except that the tips were aimed downwards. A gloved left hand took the rope, an ice hammer borrowed from Eric dug in high up on the other side. A crampon kick followed a hammer chop, each in turn making sharpened metal claw into hard snow. The ice hammer pecked, like a hard beak, more a humming-bird's than a thrush's but not nearly so thin. A higher grasp of the rope, crampons dug in again, a higher whack with the hammer, and so it went on. Half-way up was a ledge as wide as a chair seat. Hanging on to the rope I waited for my panting to subside before resuming the movements which won a foot at a time to join Harry. Julie came up; no problem.

We found ourselves on a narrow horizontal ice spine with the wall we had climbed falling away on the left and a big crevasse on the right. It was not hard but 'For God's sake be careful' country. And careful we were as we balanced across for forty feet.

Soon we were heaving ourselves up another fixed rope of a hundred feet, and another, on steep and very tiring slopes of snow. We belayed quite frequently in other places and then the hardest ground for that day was left behind. The porters dumped their loads, Harry dipped into 'the bank' and paid them, and they descended. Downhill and without loads they would be back at base camp quite soon.

The sun's heat hit not only from above but also by reflection from the snowfield we were on. We were about 19,000 feet up and heavily laden; the altitude punished Harry most.

'You'd better go on. I'm going to take hours,' he said.

The gradient was not too bad and, though there were a few crevasses around, the area held no special dangers. However, Julie and I preferred us to stick together. Every few minutes as we ploughed through the soft crystals Harry flopped down for a rest, then forced himself up to march

49

on, grunting and swearing at his pack, the snow or the ski stick he carried. Blame did not lie with them, of course, but under stress Harry had a habit of grumbling at himself or some innocent, inanimate object close at hand. He never blamed anyone else unfairly, a trait which helped make him a very good climbing companion. It was probably his well-tuned power of self-criticism which made him such a pleasant man; he sought no scapegoat when the blame was his.

A massive ice avalanche had crushed down a slope which we had to traverse, leaving in its wake ice chunks, some as big as cars, over a width of 300 yards. The biggest chunks were avoidable so the way was not so bad as it might have been, but the ice cliff which had spawned the avalanche looked ready to send down others, large and small. One day it would send down ton upon ton of grinding, charging, concrete-hard ice.

'We had to give up on Huascaran because three or four large avalanches wiped out the route just above Camp I,' a friend wrote to me the next year.

Having crossed quickly beneath the hanging menace, Julie was moving best and went ahead up a stiff snow ramp. At the foot of the ramp was a flat area surrounded on three of its four sides by high mounds of snow.

'Julie, this would do as a camp,' I called when I got there.

'Don't like it,' she shouted back. 'I'll look ahead a bit.'

Harry soon puffed up.

'Camp here, Harry?'

'Yes. Not going any further.'

'Julie, we think here's all right. It's high enough.'

'Think I can see a tent further up,' she insisted. 'Come and have a look, Norman.'

'Not going any further,' Harry croaked again. He slumped to his knees and rolled over to lie with his rucksack on the snow. I felt like he did. I dropped my pack and started up the ramp to join Julie. With Harry and two rucksacks at the bottom of the ramp I could appeal to her better nature.

In front there was a very large crevasse.

'See up there. Looks like the edge of a tent,' she said. It *could* have been a green tent. We were not sure.

'Don't fancy crossing this crevassed area after the sun's been on it, and with heavy packs. And it doesn't look so sheltered up there as in the hollow below.'

'Suppose not.'

'We may cross the crevasses and find it better to come back here

50

again. We won't know until tomorrow whether it's the right decision but I'm prepared to accept the consequences of that.'

'All right.'

The minority joined the majority. No argument. I came to feel increasingly that I was fortunate to be with Julie and Harry. We were three individuals, different from each other in many ways, but at the same time very similar because what mattered now was that we were three vulnerable human bodies 20,000 feet up on a mountain. Differing philosophies, faiths, political beliefs, incomes, professions, cultural back-grounds, were irrelevant now; all that mattered to us was taking place in a tiny segment of the world of mountaineering, and we were depen-dent on each other. Shelter, food and drink were foremost in our minds, along with some thoughts about how the next day might go. The tent was soon up, and snow was heaped on a pan to melt over the stove. I was obnoxiously cheerful, the others were quieter; I'd have to watch it or I'd get on their nerves.

The three Americans passed by at dusk having made a successful ascent and a fast descent mostly on skis.

We had taken much trouble lashing my crampons on and we did not want to go through the same performance early next day, so I left them on and parked my legs, trousers, socks, boots, crampons, bindings and gaiters in a polythene bag under the flysheet. Then we zipped up the tent and got into our sleeping bags; night time temperatures above the snowline could drop to minus 20°C.

It nearly always seemed something needed doing, some little job, a piece of equipment to be checked, adjusted, sometimes just fiddled with for the reassurance this brought; there was food to be sorted, clothing to be chosen, a hundred and one tasks to increase our safety and our chances of success, not only in reality when the time came but also in our minds. Though sleep might occupy eight or nine hours and climbing only seven hours or so in a day, in the remaining hours there was surprisingly little time to take things easy. Now and then, when we had ceased ferreting about, we would be still in our sleeping bags, in warm flickering light from a candle carefully placed in a pan, and we would talk. This night we had time and it was revealed that my partners, both teachers by the way, had been expelled from school. Julie's final crimes were falling off a rocking horse and breaking her wrist, and pushing a button up her nose. The latter sin was considered to be grave because a doctor had to be called in to retrieve the button. She had felt herself to be a victim of extreme injustice; after all, it was *her* wrist, *her* nose, *her* button. Harry's offence was more obviously defiant, the deliberate plan of a fertile young mind: he threw a lot of paints at a teacher and when a senior girl was deputed to supervise him he cleared up the mess and threw it all over the girl. Harry was rapidly expelled from school and put in another where his brother was a pupil; that was where he had intended going all along.

Doziness came over us in pleasant, deepening waves.

'Tomorrow, if the weather's right, we'll be on top of ... what's its name?' I said.

'Huascaran,' they reminded me.

The wind worsened in the night and I went out to fix extra guylines on the tent. Julie woke as I got back in.

'Wind sounds bad, Norm.'

'Yes.'

'Hope it drops tomorrow.'

'Expect it will.'

There was no point in saying anything different to someone who had just woken up, who was 20,000 feet above sea level, and who knew that at that altitude bad weather could be very serious even if you were only trying to retreat.

Six o'clock in cold morning daylight. I had been awake and lying still on my back for a while. At first the hammering wind had made getting up seem pointless. Now it had fallen a bit so I took a look outside.

'How is it?' came from one or other of my companions, with just the tops of heads and faces peeping from their sleeping bags and looking like shy tortoises.

'It's all right. We should go.'

The words sunk in and as if someone had thrown the switches on two robots they suddenly got into action. All at once the tent felt very cramped with three moving bodies in it. Thick breeches and fibre-pile jackets were donned hastily in the cold. We had slept in thermal underwear. I left breeches, legs and boots till later because they had crampons on; when I did come to put them on a lot of time and effort was saved doing it all in one go. So I did have some advantages.

Breakfast went down because we knew it should. The porridge seemed more like a medicine we had to take than a meal we wanted to eat, but the tea was enjoyed. Ah, liquid.

Harry had trouble putting on his gaiters.

'Take mine instead,' I offered. 'I don't really need them.' I wore them to reduce the likelihood of a crampon point catching in a sock but I could manage without, so it was no real sacrifice.

'No, it's all right thanks, Norm,' he said, continuing the struggle with his own. I thought no more about it; later I would wish I had.

The wind had almost died away. Balaclavas, mitts, windproofs on. Rucksacks hoisted. Glacier cream and lip salve smeared on. Rope on. We were ready and it had taken nearly two hours; much of that time had elapsed while we melted snow.

Leaving the tent and all but essentials behind, we crawled out into the sharp bite of the cold. Julie led off up the snow ramp we had been up the day before. A right turn at the top took us along a crest above the huge crevasse we had seen. Trying to find a way around either end would have involved going into very badly crevassed areas. So, instead, we had to descend a steep slope of forty feet, drop straight down seven feet of vertical hard snow directly on to a little platform, and step or jump from there across the horrible hole. The top of the vertical bit was in fact one lip of the crevasse, that much higher than its partner. It was only a few feet, a wide stretching step, to the other side. One by one we made the step, each time hoping that the snow on the far side would not collapse. Julie, me, Harry. Nothing went wrong. Getting back was going to be a bigger problem.

Crossing that crevasse put us in a long, wide snow trough. Turning left, we walked the length of the trough, parallel with the crevasse, then took a level ridge with gaping holes running its hundred foot length on either side. Another giant crevasse barred the way; no, it was spanned by a snow bridge. We would have preferred a more substantial one but there was no choice. We crossed.

The tent we thought we had seen several hours earlier turned out to be a triangular ice face. Ours was the best spot to camp, after all.

At first the slope remained at a few degrees above or below thirty-five. Julie kept up a steady pace but every so often I was brought to a halt as the rope pulled tight behind; Harry was having trouble with the altitude.

'The pace on Pisco was all right,' he said.

After an hour of stop, start, stop, start I remarked to Julie, 'We're not going to make it at this rate. I'll be slow on the descent so I must get up there reasonably early in the afternoon. We're stopping too often, for too long, and going too slowly in between. The longer we take the softer the snow is so the longer we take, and so on.'

Going slower than the pace which feels right can be very tiring, like doing slow press-ups. We had to face it: one or all of us would have to turn back. We could try again tomorrow I thought, not liking the idea. Nothing more was said for a while because I hoped Harry would feel better. Half a minute after we had restarted following a rest the rope went tight, dragging me to a halt again. I tried, only partly successfully, to suppress pointless anger by reminding myself that Harry was a friend

53

who was prepared to attempt a big mountain with me, and he had always been patient with me.

'My crampon's come off,' he shouted from a kneeling position. Then he called, 'I think you'd better go on without me.'

It was natural enough to feel disappointment for him because he had put in as much work as anyone to get us that far, but I must admit that the predominant feeling was one of relief.

'What a shame,' Julie said, as Harry untied from the rope. 'But I think he ought to go down.'

We had spotted two men descending from Huascaran's south summit after a bivouac. They would have to cross the worst crevasses so Harry could join them to get back to the tent.

The two of us started uphill again, swinging along at a good pace. I lost track of time but probably an hour had passed before I noticed how frequently we were stopping to rest.

'You'd better take the lead,' Julie said. 'You're going so well.'

In good snow, leading was only marginally harder. The firm south-west slope of the north summit was getting steeper. Eric's ice hammer and an ice axe were a great help and the rhythm came just right. For *very* short stretches of a few feet at a time the angle may have gone over fifty degrees but that was not common. Climbing as I usually do, in a rather hunched-up position, I could look back under one arm and see there was not too much slack in the rope, and also judge when Julie was likely to stop.

'Just a minute,' she called a couple of times, but I tried to anticipate her halts so she would not have to. It was better that she should not; better that the rat ahead should stop first.

Another hour elapsed. Julie had been standing catching her breath for a while when she said, 'I think I may not make it. My leg's hurting.'

She would not have mentioned it unless it was really troubling her.

A lot of time had been wasted already and it really would have been sticking our necks out to hit the summit in the late afternoon. I couldn't skip back down nearly as fast as other people. The weather was good but the thought of moving in the dark amongst the crevasses, in a strong wind and with tiredness upon us, seemed too big a risk to take.

An idea crept into my head: if I soloed on quickly that would give us a reasonable chance of one person reaching the top and the expedition would be an enormous success. But I could not leave Julie on her own, especially with a bad leg. We were finished for this day, and I was not optimistic about the weather for the next.

Below us, far, far below, a lone figure climbed slowly up. It looked like Harry. It was Harry! He would not reach where we were for a long time but he was on the way up again and here was a solution: Julie could join Harry.

'Be good for the Calvert Trust if I get up this one,' I said, avoiding a direct proposal that I should solo.

'Oh yes. Superb.'

I never had to worry about climbing being futile because mountaineering often had beneficial effects on my work. Always there seemed an added sense of purpose which could not be divorced even if I had wanted it so. But was that really me being swayed by a non-mountaineering reason? To some extent, yes; but I wanted this one for me too. The ambition dragon was back again, big and fiery. And with only 800 feet to go I did not want to let down all those people who had helped put us that high. Every reason pushed me up. There might be a small risk from crevasses but the angle of the snow was going to ease before long. Solo was the only way. Unless we turned back. I would have to put it directly; try it and see what she says.

'One of us has got to get there, Julie.'

'Yes.'

'Better unrope then. I'll solo.'

'Yes.'

It would not have come as any surprise if she had said no. When you earn your living through climbing instruction your work might well be affected if you did nothing to discourage a double leg amputee from soloing a big mountain, particularly if he got hurt or killed. People would not understand if anything went wrong; a few might, but most would condemn. What they would fail to understand is that those who have climbed with me, or helped me in other ways to go climbing, have led me along a path to the finest experiences of a lifetime. The mountains have already given more joy than a man could expect in ten lifetimes. Sometimes I am troubled by what may be said of companions who may one day survive on a mountain when I do not. In some ways, more than those who would try to overprotect, they have given me life; if they are in at my death they should not be censured. They deserve no blame, only praise for their understanding, for not backing away when they could so easily have done that. Perhaps I might live longer if I did not climb, but that is arguable, and life must be measured more by quality than by length alone. Certainly, a long hollow life has no appeal to me.

Julie coiled the rope.

'See you on the top,' I said tritely; who the hell stops to make up a good speech at a time like that anyway?

Almost immediately I was faced with a wall of hard snow, eight or nine feet high. A mere garden wall, when you think about it, but running along the bottom was a body-width crevasse. Stepping across and climbing up made me sweat a bit.

My beloved crutches, joined by a cord which let them dangle from my shoulders when not in use (so repeated stops to strap them on my rucksack or take them off were avoided), got in the way of my crampons on some steep sections and had to be kicked out of the way; but I knew the crutches had to be there and anger would be wasted, and I kept reminding myself that this was so. And it worked; useless, tiring anger was avoided.

I have already said that Huascaran's north summit resembled a white breast, and it even had a snow cone nipple at the top. It was a deceiver, though, for behind the nipple the mountain still rose for quite a long way; I had been warned that this was the case. The gradient eased, eased, eased back to thirty degrees, then less, getting more pleasant all the time, and I topped the false summit, slightly on its right side. Behind the phoney nipple summit, which looked so like the real one from lower down, the mountain stretched back and back for a distance I could not judge. Now steepness was not a problem, though it was slightly, tiringly uphill all the way; distance and soft snow were all that stood between me and the summit. I wondered how many people had turned back through disappointment and fatigue at that point. My body wanted to go up, but at the same time did not. It was such hard work, such an awful, awful slog, like climbing in a suit of armour.

Though distance was difficult to estimate, shortly after passing the false summit I thought forty minutes would see me up this soft, lumpy mattress laid thick on the mountain. Many times I stopped to catch breath; I did not want to stop, but had to. Before long I was down to a hundred paces between unwilling halts for gasps of thin air. On a slightly steeper slope only fifty paces separated the stops, then it was back to eighty or a hundred. At each stop I would wait a few seconds before saying to myself, 'Stopped isn't going,' and it was strange how much that sea level silly sentence helped me keep moving up there. Another helped even more: I kept approaching mounds which I hoped would be the summit but they never were and each time I avoided disappointment by saying, 'It is what it is.' What I meant was that these things were essential, for I needed the mounds one after another as a steady stairway to the final one, so there was no sense getting angry and wasting energy. They were there to be accepted as elements of a game I had chosen to play and wanted very much to play. Over mound after mound I went, looking for a summit which seemed to be running away and hiding. But I knew it could not hide for ever, and gradually I leaned less and less on my sentences as a different strength which required no willpower took over; almost nothing could stop me now, even if I had to crawl, and a feverish elation began to fuel me for the finish. Shouts and giggles and laughs came from my mouth like it was someone else making them.

'Hey! Hey! Hey! You're going to do it! You're going to do it! You're going to do it!'

Now we were on a big mountain and not a British rock climb the fact that part of my legs were artificial was creeping more and more into the background. I had found where fulfilment lay.

I shouted loudly, happily, mad with joy, and turned to look back at the ground which had been covered. And there, twenty minutes or so away, was the tiny figure of Julie, still going.

'Hey! Hey! Hey! *We're* going to make it!'

She was too far away to hear.

Five more minutes pushing on and I turned again to see how she was getting along. There was another figure close behind Julie. Harry! The more distant figure fell down in the snow, got up a minute later, slumped again within another minute and lay there. He rose again, managing no more than fifteen or twenty paces between halts.

'Hey! We're *all* going to do it! Two of us at least and probably three!'

Where was the nausea barrier? Dismissed because of the crutches. Formerly I had been ill purely through trying too hard; I had vomited long and often through effort alone. That was all over now.

Every muscle was tired but eager. And then I spotted it, the fairly level area of slightly ruffled snow that was the top. A rush of emotion came over me, a weepy feeling that is not uncommon in such circumstances, and my eyes were wet out of sheer euphoria. I didn't mind; Bonatti cried a lot, anyway, when things went well.

Could it be done in fifty paces, in one go? No. After fifty it was still a long way away. Another forty and a pause was inevitable. But now it was within reach. The summit had one last steepish bit, a mere twenty-five degrees but exhausting all the same. Then I was there. In front the mountain plunged away.

'You've done it,' I said to myself.

I had indeed! It was 2.15 p.m. so it had taken six hours. Twenty-one thousand, eight hundred and thirty feet (6,654 m). Over four miles up. Nineteen years of effort had led here by stages and it was fantastic! Ten years of rock climbing, John o' Groats to Land's End, eight summers in the Alps, finding out all the while, the toil of expedition organisation, and now this. Through my blood surged that wonderful sensation which no words can properly describe – sweet as love, warm as friendship, and overwhelming. All the effort was repaid.

Julie arrived fifteen minutes later, bright-eyed with the thrill of success.

'Well, we've done it Julie.'

'Yep!'

The people who made the first ascent could not have been happier than us. It was a moving moment, particularly as Harry was still on the way up too, half an hour behind Julie. Eventually his head and shoulders approached the final steepish bit.

'It's here Harry. We're standing on it,' we called.

The head and shoulders dropped instantly from sight as Harry crumpled in the snow, down for a count of sixty. He was up again, to stumble-step nearer before buckling knees let him down again. Flop. He dragged himself up once more, managing twenty paces before going down. But he was on the summit this time. His determination had received a just reward, and I had learned a lot about Harry: next time he stopped on an ascent I would be more inclined to spend some time encouraging him to go on.

To discover something you burn to do, and to do it, is one of life's greatest rewards, and a privilege which does not come often. The discovery can be as elusive as the success; we had been lucky on both counts.

'Seems daft though,' I said.

'What?'

'Our most important ascent is the only one we said we wouldn't do.'

We nibbled at chocolate and took photographs, some of them with Harry's camera, which, along with the film, was stolen later. Of our seven cameras three more went wrong and Mike Welham, the main expedition photographer, made only one ascent. So the pictures were rather disappointing.

There was little time for Harry to rest before we started back, but he moved downhill with no trouble. About half-way back to the false summit we met the first of five Austrians (whom we had seen on the march) who toiled to the top the same day. Now gravity was in our favour their laborious movements looked strange by contrast.

Where the snow was steep we belayed; a slip was more likely on the way down. At one place where I went down first I hammered an aluminium tube, the lower piece of a crutch, into the snow, and wound the rope around it a couple of turns as a belay. Julie descended towards me. She came near and then level with me on my left, when something frightening happened in an instant. Suddenly she cried out and her body sank in the snow.

'I'm in a crevasse!'

Left Judy Croucher.

Below left Practice on ice in North Wales.

Below right The author abseiling in Glen Nevis, Scotland.

Above The Matterhorn's Hörnli ridge runs up to the right of the sunlit east face.

Below An ice pick and ski round attached to a crutch greatly assist the author on snow routes.

Right Dave Parsons (top) and the author on the White Edge.

Facing page One of the author's early rock climbs, Little Chamonix, Lake District (photograph by the author of an unknown climber).

Above Figures approach Pisco.

Facing page The author beneath Pisco.

Left and below On the glacier Huascaran.

Centre Left to right – Denny Moorhouse, Julie Tullis, Dennis Kemp.

Right Julie Tullis stands at about 20,000 ft before Huascaran's north summit.

Below Harry Curtis at a fixed rope on Huascaran.

Above The author on the east summit of Ameghino.

Below Snow penitentes which had to be climbed on the east summit of
Ameghino.

I held on to the rope and prayed the crutch tube would not pull out. She dropped up to the top of her thighs into the snow-covered hole and went no further.

'I've got you.'

It is impossible to say whether she might have fallen far. Perhaps she would have, perhaps she would not. Such minor falls without serious consequences are not uncommon. Some crevasses widen as you go deeper and it can be a real problem to get someone out, but we didn't go poking around to see what shape this one was, I can assure you.

'That's all I need,' was Julie's only comment after she had climbed out, and then she carried on with the job. Her leg was hurting still, so she took a pain-killer.

This was just the sort of incident which the press might exaggerate so I kept quiet about it for weeks when we got home. But it was a significant event because we had learned that the crutches could double as belay stakes as well as tent pegs in snow. If I took them to pieces we had four items of hardware which could increase our security.

My stumps started to get very sore after ten hours out and I had to push myself quite hard. Now we were in the most dangerous part of the day, with sun-softened snow bridges and tiredness against us. Another hour, and we approached the big crevasses in near darkness. Three of the Austrians were just ahead, having overtaken us an hour before because of my slowness in descent. Crossing a snow bridge to join them, we found that one of them was preparing to bivouac because he felt unwell.

'Our tent is nearer than yours,' we explained. 'You are welcome to come in.'

The other two Austrians favoured the idea and persuaded him to join us, and they crossed the last big crevasse ahead of us without preparing any belays. We could not treat it that way. An ice axe and a crutch were arranged as belays and Harry stepped across from rather soft snow to the other, higher side where he hooked in his ice axe and got himself tight up against the seven foot wall. He stood on a small bulge of ice with Lord knows what sort of hole below and behind him. We heard bits of dislodged hard snow clump clumping down the crevasse and suddenly Harry let out a sharp squeal of fright and said, 'Oh, God! Oh, God!' Whether he felt he was toppling back into the black hole or thought his feet were going to give way I do not know, but for a couple of seconds he whimpered, a very frightened man; most of us get like that now and then. Reaching rapidly over the top lip of the wall he got his ice axe deeply and comfortingly into the hard snow, and pulled up, while his crampons ran up the wall. A relieved man stood at the top and moved back many feet to set up a belay. Me next.

'Keep your belay on too, Julie,' I said. 'Please.'

After a quick step across I whammed my hammer into the wall. Now I knew something of what Harry had felt. I didn't like it. Though not hard there was an indefinite, unreliable character to the problem. What I stood on could have broken off, and the top of the wall arched gradually in a soft and untrustworthy snow hump to join the slope above, rather than providing a distinct and firm junction. I moved up far enough to hammer my ice axe into the slope, and pulled up. A mere three feet of height was gained but the danger of falling into the crevasse was over. Julie followed with no bother.

The poorly Austrian had not waited. That was fortunate in a way because we had been out twelve hours and were ready to flop down and get the stove going; it would have been very cramped in the tiny refuge.

The gas stove's hissing purr and faint blue light said welcome home. This was a wonderfully secure and warm shelter to us now. Harry had assumed the role of fetcher of snow for melting, without anyone asking. Jobs were done, with no more than an occasional suggestion by one or other of us that they needed doing. And when the food or drink was ready the light aluminium plates or plastic mugs were handed out almost reverently, with utmost care; food and drink were comfort, fuel, and life in the end.

'Let's have something else,' one of us would say, and another pan of snow would be stuck on the burner. The white cone would sink slowly and shrink, we'd pile more snow on, that would go down, and we would make up our minds what to have next. We spooned down tasty oxtail soup, and sipped tangy hot orange, meaty Oxo and good old tea, and had some more tea and orange.

Harry had trouble getting his boots off but managed in the end. He felt his feet for a while and was quiet. Then he said, 'Frostbite.'

We both turned towards him.

'I think my toes are a bit frostbitten,' he said, and Julie softly said, 'Oh, Harry.'

'My own fault,' he murmured. 'Should have put my gaiters on. The snow got between the inner and the outer boot.'

Everyone but me on the expedition wore a pair of double boots, a soft leather inner like a plush red slipper that laced high up the ankle, and an outer like any big brown mountain boot.

On Harry's toes white patches and angry red blisters had formed. He wrapped his feet in his sleeping bag. Julie's leg was sore, and my stumps were a bit hurt, but she and I had not paid dearly for what we had had. What it would cost Harry in the end we could only guess. In a period of six months I heard of three climbers who lost their feet through frostbite. So it was a rather subdued trio that settled down for another night at 20,000 feet. Our down sleeping bags smelled familiar and gave us some reassurance.

During the night the wind started. Harry slept almost without a break, but many, many times Julie and I woke up, took a few sips of cold orange juice and lay there listening to the devil wind blasting at our tent. The fabric flapped fiercely with a noise like someone hammering an iron roof.

At eight o'clock we still cuddled our sleeping bags and downed hot tea, while the tent shook just as badly as during the night. At nine o'clock it was as unrelenting as ever.

'I think we'd better go anyway,' I said. 'We should be sheltered lower down. Don't want to get caught up here in a storm.'

We had all been approaching the same conclusion. The contents of three rucksacks do not take long to pack, and when this had been done we crawled out to get the tent down. After kneeling and sitting on the writhing brown monster to prevent it flying away once it was down, we finished up with a lumpy bundle.

The sun shone in an almost cloudless sky, yet after quitting our hollow we entered an even worse wind, which picked up white crystals and blasted them at us; it was choking to breathe. Face-masks on our fibre-pile jackets solved the problem. Thin clouds of snow were drawn up and chased hither and thither, now in a curve, now a whirling vortex, as the wind left a clue to its path, marking its way as in a fog. It buffeted unevenly from different directions. Julie moved up a slope on to a sharp horizontal snow ridge, with crevasses on either side. The bully wind blew even worse and Julie dropped to one knee, head down, her body rocked by violent gusts. She moved forward a short way on one knee and both hands, stopped on both knees, moved a little further and halted once more. We had to watch it here because of the crevasses. If the wind had been from a constant direction we could have crossed the ridge on the sheltered side, but it kept changing and pushing us all ways. I crawled for a short way behind Julie.

One thing was certain: a day later, and we would not have reached the summit.

Descent into a downhill snow trough brought some relief from the wind, and I felt a little more relaxed. However, a sudden cry from behind soon changed that: Harry was sliding down the snow towards a crevasse. Face down and feet first, he gathered speed very rapidly, and almost immediately stopped himself with his ice axe.

The wind still pushed us around as we crossed the big avalanche track.

'That fixed rope's gone,' Julie said as we reached the first steep snow slope. 'But we don't really need it. Just have to go down carefully.'

It was worth belaying, which we did. The next fixed rope had been removed as well, but that did not matter too much either. We would really miss having a fixed rope on the near vertical section, though. We approached the top of that step. A glimpse of yellow, yes, it was still there, and it helped us down in turn. In that small height loss the shelter turned the wind to a mere whisper; even the thin white fringes of blown snow swirling from the heights could not convey the force of the monster still roaming up there. The sun's warmth forced us to take off our windproofs right away.

Only the glacier trudge to go.

'Sod!' Harry said to a rucksack shoulder strap which had worked loose. He had been uncomplaining about his feet but grunted a lot as he walked. 'You'll have to go on. I'll be ages.'

For a while the rope was not essential so Julie and I moved ahead, but with no intention of leaving him; we knew him better now and expected that he would not lag far behind. This was so and in a few minutes he joined us again, muttering quietly to himself. We stuck together and weaved in and out of ice humps, between crevasses, over ice bridges and around small pools. There rarely seemed to be a right way, a best way; it was just a matter of picking a route every few minutes out of many options. Time and time again two, three, four or five possible ways lay before us.

Julie was a constant optimist, always seeing a 'right' way, whether it was there or not.

'To the left a bit I think, Harry,' Julie would say.

'*Where?*'

In his voice now was a faint edge, a barely perceptible trace of sharpness, but he was well-controlled. Everyone was a bit edgy because as the afternoon wore on it began to look as if night's rapid approach would catch us out on the glacier. Harry's feet, Julie's leg and my stumps were all giving pain, our packs were heavy, and we were tired. I have climbed with people who in those circumstances would have been at each other's throats, but we had no rows. Temperamentally, these were two of the best climbing companions I have come across.

And we lolloped down the glacier we had no way of knowing that there was a scarey bit to come. We had been just that little bit too slow to escape from the glacier before night. In failing light we tried to find a way between high ice towers and perched blocks, and watched the darkness creeping up from the valley to get us. Up steep slopes, down steep slopes, across gaps, through gullies, we pressed on. By torchlight we could not see far enough ahead to pick a way which did not soon become a dead end. Half the dark holes turned out to be non-holes while some real holes thinly covered by ice and snow were difficult to recognise. We came upon a huge crevasse, twenty feet across. A retreat and detour were called for. I began to wonder if we should start to face the prospect of a bivouac.

'I think we should bivouac,' Julie said, beating me by ten seconds. Harry was in agreement. We back-tracked to an ice block with a level top as big as a dining table and removed our rucksacks. Sleeping bags and spare clothing were coming out when suddenly we all jumped. *Bang!* The block shook as the ice beneath cracked through the enormous pressure it was under. Hell's bells! We scattered.

Next we settled on an ice sofa; an insulating closed-cell foam mat on the seat, another on the backrest, made it comfortable enough. With extra clothing on, good sleeping bags, and the tent laid over us and tucked in, we were warm as kittens in hay.

In good weather a night out 15,000 feet up was not serious in the Andes, though by temperate sea level standards it was as if we had gone from summer to winter in an hour.

What was serious, though, was that we were near the end of the glacier tongue, where it cracked and broke up continually. Around and under us the ice was moving, mostly at an infinitesimally slow speed, but every so often big blocks reached a point at which their equilibrium was disturbed and they tumbled over with a fearsome noise. Tremendous pressures forced cracking and movement, and the resultant sounds, like slamming doors, pinging bedsprings and creaking floorboards could have been caused by human beings in a block of flats.

'The people are in downstairs,' Julie remarked as she handed out our rations: chocolate, sardines and peanuts. I had the stove hissing beneath a pan of snow, to make a drop of tea for our parched bodies.

'This is one of the hardest mountain trips I've ever been on,' Harry commented in a resigned way.

The glacier emitted from its bowels a groan, a bang or a high-pitched crack once or twice a minute. We lay back, silently promising to lead better lives if we came through a night in this awful place. The unsought and unwelcome was with us and would not go away for hours. However, it was not as bad as it might have been because the weather was dry and not too cold. In fact I was so warm I had to remove some clothing; it is one advantage of being an amputee, that body heat is retained better, and one day that could mean the difference between survival or death.

For a long time I watched the flit of brilliant shooting stars sowing sparkling trails across the sky, and made a wish on each one: wish morning would come. The others fell asleep long before I finally nodded off.

I awoke suddenly. Something was wrong! At first I could not register what it was until I noticed in the faint light that though Julie was beside me Harry had gone! Then I saw him; he had slipped down an ice slope while asleep. He was still asleep a few feet below us, with his feet just inches from a crevasse. I called out some sleepy stupid words.

'Harry, Harry, should you be down there?'

He woke and, still in his sleeping bag, wriggled back up to us.

Who woke first in the morning I don't know, but it was not until long after light had reached us. With daylight on our side it took only fifteen minutes before we had our boots on the crunchy little stones of the moraine. Had we tried the night before we might have made it in twenty minutes or an hour, or we might have wandered around much longer in a dangerous area.

'Congratulations, Norm,' Harry said. 'I didn't want to say it before, but we've finished it now.'

As we approached base Manuel rushed easily up.

'Cumbre?' he asked. ('Summit?').

'Si, Manuel.'

The mountain was left behind, the snows and intricate ice patterns constantly changing shape through sun-melt and wind-blow and gravity's downhill tug. It remained for others to enjoy, if they were lucky. We left nothing there, and took away nothing but happiness; and now the cloud of gloom which had hung over us and dulled that happiness was dispersed. Our hearts were free of anxiety and we began to feel the lightness which came with the realisation of a dream. Even our concern about Harry's feet was reduced, and I don't think any of us expected him to suffer permanent damage.

Now base camp had a different atmosphere. The excitement of the way up was replaced by the contentment of success, and the place seemed different because we were changed in mood. We ate and drank and mid-day drew near. They had been a hard few days and a rest was inviting.

'How about waiting so we can get you a donkey or a horse, Harry?'
I suggested. 'You could ride at least part way.'

'No. We couldn't get one until tomorrow. I want to go down and see
a doctor today.' His mind was made up firmly.

Julie bandaged his feet and very gently rolled one sock on. She had
the second one almost on when she said in a voice full of concern, 'Oh,
Harry.' Two words, quietly spoken, but they rang out.

What now? I thought.

'Harry, there's a big lump on your heel. We'll have to get the sock off
again and see what it is.'

Poor Harry. The sock, so carefully put on, was peeled off with great
gentleness.

'Well?' I asked. 'What is it?'

Julie examined the heel, and frowned, then looked in the sock. She
turned to me and said, 'Knickers.'

'Pardon?'

'Knickers. A pair of mine.'

Apparently, not wishing Manuel to stumble across her underwear,
she had hidden various items in her socks and other places.

'Those are not *my* socks,' Harry burst out defensively.

We laughed and laughed and laughed. The elation of our small
triumph was beginning to sweep over us even more.

'Fantastic expedition!' Harry said. 'And what happened was my own
fault. I *think* it's mostly blisters anyway. Will this be worth a *foot*note in
your book, Norm?'

'It may be worth pointing out that you can expect trouble if you will
go around with those old-fashioned legs.' His laughter crawled out with
the deep hump, hump, hump of a distant pump.

Soon after, our casualty shambled out of sight through the trees in
short, wincing steps. Within a few hours he was back in the Hotel
Barcelona.

At eight the next morning the donkey arrived in the charge of a
sixteen year old called Nelson. In response to his curiosity about my
crutches, I showed him one of my legs on the way down. We had been
descending for two hours when a slender man in ragged pants and shirt
appeared through the bushes. In one hand he carried an enamel dish
with a lid, in the other a bottle. It turned out he was Nelson's father,
and the family were working on a small field on a steep hill opposite the
trail. They had seen us coming and dad had run over with Nelson's
breakfast of boiled potatoes, which the latter tucked into right away.
Before long dad had been told about my legs and he came up to where
I sat on the trailside bank; with a finger pointed at himself he made a

gesture with the other hand which meant, 'Can I touch?' Si. He felt the metal in the region of the knees, grinned, took a hasty step leftwards to where Julie sat, and felt her knees too!

As far as we could discover the only transport leaving Musho village to go down the valley was a pickup, rumoured to be heading for Mancos at two o'clock. Julie went on a successful beer hunt, and we sat in the shade with a bottle each and said things like, 'Boy, what a climb!' and 'I wouldn't have dreamed of doing Huascaran!' and 'What a great time we've had!' Children streamed out of a school and a hundred curious brown eyes surrounded us. A score of dark hands reached out to touch my legs when Nelson explained about the gringos who had been up mighty Huascaran. For twenty minutes all, whether five or fifteen years old, stood and stared and smiled and chattered around us. We told them her name was Pedro and mine Maria, that a scar on her arm had been made by a lion which Pedro had killed with her bare hands. It wasn't the beer, well, hardly at all, it was just joy and relief made us talk that way. We did wonder what happened when they went back to school, fifty children insisting to the teacher they had met a woman called Pedro who had killed a lion, and a man with metal legs had climbed Huascaran and his name was Maria.

With the return of the children to school the village resumed a quiet afternoon air; most adults would have been out working in the collectively owned fields and looking after their animals. Compared with the poor of Lima, village life conferred upon them great richness and security. The pickup driver turned up and readily gave us a lift. After an hour's dusty drive, there was Terry walking up the road. He was taken on board and he seemed even more pleased than we were that the ascent had been made. From the Datsun we transferred to another pickup with several members of a family in it. The papers had already put the story of our ascent around so as soon as they realised who we were they traded a twenty-five mile lift for some autographs.

Terry had been thoughtful enough to bring towels and soap, and we stopped off at the baths to soak away a week's grime. My stumps found such relief in the warm water; it was almost worth doing another climb just to repeat such pleasure. Most important of all, they were not rubbed raw in a single patch. That was unusual, and was the result of training, of taking the climb by reasonable stages, and of using the crutches.

The Hotel Barcelona, 6,000 miles from England, felt like home. Harry was limping but thought his feet would be all right; the blisters seemed to be the main problem. Terry, Julie and I went with him to Huaras hospital. Rest, the doctor said, so he and I stayed at the Hotel Barcelona.

Everyone else went touring various parts of Peru. We were due to meet one week later in Lima.

'I think I'll fly home for treatment, to be on the safe side,' Harry said. 'Get close to some nurses, the little darlings.'

Two seats to Lima were soon booked on a colectivo, which is a cheap communal taxi. For about £5 each five passengers travelled 200 miles (330 km).

'If ever you come here again this is your home,' Pepe said.

We rode to Lima and somewhere along the way Harry's camera and the film taken on Huascaran went missing. After a couple of beers and a bit of thinking we came to the conclusion that the colectivo driver might know where they were so we headed for his office. He could keep the camera, all we wanted was the film, we intended saying, but once we had the film we had it in mind to cause him a certain amount of physical discomfort. So on a pair of sore feet and a pair of artificial legs we took purposeful steps towards a showdown; it was all very Gary Cooper and High Noonish. Harry grunted with pain and muttered, 'Four foot six of Peruvian crap! I'll blow 'em all over.' We turned right off a main street into the side street we sought. Harry wanted me to take his wallet and watch, for safekeeping. No, we're in this together, Harry. A hundred yards to go. Fifty. Twenty. The office was closed.

As we swore our way back up the street the thought did cross my mind that the short colectivo driver had a fair amount of muscle under his shirt, and there never seemed to be less than eight other drivers hanging around the office. We tried to comfort ourselves with the notion that it was better to have climbed Huascaran and lost the film than to have nice pictures but have been denied the ascent. There was little comfort in the argument that night though; it mattered a lot at the time but, as these things do, it faded in our minds with the passing of months. It was not so bad as it might have been, anyway, because a picture of Julie and some views from the top taken on my camera came out reasonably well, as did some which Julie took of me with the same machine. But we had not a single shot of Harry on the summit.

We decided against reporting the camera's loss to the police in case the colectivo driver was innocent after all. Eric Perlmann's ice hammer had gone missing as well as the camera, and when we came to book into a cheap hotel for the night we had to enter through a lion's cage door, and spend the night in a room with windows barred like a prison cell to keep thieves out (or us in if the place caught fire). Our tarnished impression of Lima was polished up a bit the next day when we rang

Don Montague of the South American Explorers Club. He invited us along right away, our equipment was soon in storage there, and Lima Tours responded very quickly to arrange an immediate flight home for Harry. A representative picked him up in a huge, black, hearse-like car, and that was the last I saw of him for a long time.

Meanwhile, Dennis climbed two more peaks, Chopikalki and Ishinca, before being laid low by the Peruvian runs. Terry and Julie visited Cuzco: Mike and Mike and Denny travelled to tourist spots. I had time to take it easy and reflect. After sending off fifty postcards to sponsors and others who had helped, I visited a disco where one leg, after surviving two weeks' training in Italy, and the expedition, finally gave up and broke under the strain of some very energetic dancing.

Seven of us gathered together and boarded a Viasa plane for London in mid-August. As we descended the steps from the aircraft at our destination a dozen photographers and reporters waited.

'Tell them you were first on Huascaran,' Julie said.

'I wasn't going to. They'll exaggerate it all as usual.'

'It will help the Calvert Trust and Harry would want you to.' It was like the sort of thing you say when someone has died.

A large number of people had helped us, so the story was not one to be hoarded. Terry, Dennis, Mike, Mike and Denny, all of whom had contributed a great deal to the success, melted away in the crowd. Julie and I faced the cameras but it all felt incomplete because Harry was not there.

Harry. What happened to Harry? Well, in the end he suffered the loss of just two toenails, removed because of an infection underneath. It was a tremendous relief to learn that success had not cost him more, and we were amused at his account of his visit to hospital. Picture him, an untidy man who has no need of the fripperies of fashion to prop up his confidence, scruffy after two days of flying and considerable delays, and tired through pain. Of all the hospitals Harry could pick in London he chose one which sees a large number of vagrants and alcoholics. On a hot day in August he wandered into the casualty department and announced, 'I've got frostbite!' As you might imagine, there was a certain amount of scepticism on the part of the nursing staff.

A radio broadcast centred partly around the expedition brought in several thousand pounds for the Calvert Trust, so from that point of view, too, the trip was a success.

We had to go back home and 'settle down'. Many people expected, suggested and advised the same thing: settling down. Damned settling down. Awful settling down. Horrible settling down. Maybe they were right, but I could not believe it. The settling down could only be temporary; there would be other mountains, other adventures. I had found a slice of life as good as any I had ever tasted, I had the recipe and I wanted to make it again. Settle down? I would sooner die.

4

Hard Work, Scotland and Switzerland

I can offer a partial explanation as to why I climb. Though I am rather lazy about any work which does not interest me, it was evident in my teens at grammar school that I was capable to great effort when I chose. Being keen to 'get on', whatever that meant, I blindly studied hard at all subjects. In examinations I was always in the top three overall for my year, and while in the end my academic achievements were not outstanding, I came top each year in the whole school for 'effort marks'. Under this system teachers subjectively rated each pupil according to how hard they thought he was trying, and I was rammed down the throats of peers as the goody who was 'an example to you all.' I redeemed myself in their eyes by turning down the role of head boy and being demoted from prefect twice for 'crimes' I had not committed (throwing a snowball indoors and talking in class). I did not protest my innocence too strongly because, as is common under these circumstances, there were other undiscovered misdemeanours, really bad things, like not wearing a school cap and breaking a window. But my point is that I did put great effort into what I was doing; unfortunately what was lacking was enthusiasm.

Concerning sport I was more enthusiastic, and I put a lot of effort into cross-country running, rugby, gymnastics and gliding. Despite the fact that after my first kamikaze-style attempt at landing a glider my instructor said, 'Son, if you make another landing like that you'll be sitting on your arse in the grass in the middle of a pile of firewood,' I did improve, and his report said, 'Worked hard.' Though I ran in the school cross-country team and captained the gymnastics team, my efforts in sport were not rewarded with shining success; no matter how hard I tried, I did not seem to have what it took physically to excel. The one exception was when I started climbing, and everything fell into place. If I tried hard, I succeeded. Lack of enthusiasm for the subjects, and a poor memory, held me back academically, and in most sports enthusiasm and effort did not seem enough on their own, but for climbing I was both physically and temperamentally suited. Climbers come in all shapes and sizes and the sport does not demand a certain ideal physique.

For a while it seemed that climbing would satisfy my desire for a challenge, but my next big effort went into rehabilitation after losing my legs. When, within a few weeks, I was fitted with two pylons (like peg legs) and given a pair of crutches, I fought hard to walk further each day and to manage more and more stairs. My surgeon played a game of motivation with me, saying he was treating a seventy-year-old lady who had two pylons, and if I walked 500 yards she had covered 1,000, if I climbed fifty stairs she had managed a hundred. But as soon as I started tree climbing, we heard no more of the mythical lady. Within two months of being fitted with a pair of artificial legs I found myself a job in a chemistry laboratory, and one of the chief reasons for selecting that employment was that it involved living away from home. I was forced to look after myself and to walk quite a long way to work with the help of a pair of walking sticks, long for those early days, that is. (Ironically, it had been a desire to travel and to 'look after myself' which led to me sleeping out in a wood and losing my legs.)

Learning to ride a bicycle and a motor scooter, doing a little gliding, skating (badly), hitch-hiking around the Continent for ten days and going climbing in Cornwall were all done energetically for the challenge. Even when I joined in the dance of the day, the twist, I went at it with such energy that some of the rivets popped out of my legs.

Branching further out, I went to a teacher training college in London to increase my independence. The work I finally settled in for four-and-a-half-years, as a social worker at St Martin-in-the-Fields church in London, was satisfying as much because it was challenging as worthwhile. I worked mostly amongst drug addicts and young people who hung around certain London haunts like Covent Garden, Soho, Trafalgar Square and Piccadilly Circus, and derelict buildings. A lot of walking was required and quite often the work meant being in these places at night. We put emphasis on tracing missing teenagers, who were often very vulnerable in the atmosphere of prostitution, muggings, wanton violence, venereal diseases, mental illnesses, begging, drug pushing and theft. We surely dealt at the dirtiest end of the spectrum.

Promoting outdoor pursuits for disabled people was another challenging mission which came my way more by chance than by intention. And, since climbing was crucial to my being a credible spokesman, this campaign gave an added and respectable incentive to enjoy the mountains. In any case, the challenge, adventure, excitement and emotional rewards I sought were found in greater depth in climbing than in any other sport I had experienced, and in greater depth the more effort was put in. When I resumed climbing after the loss of my legs, in essence nothing had changed; trying hard brought rewards, and enthusiasm produced the necessary effort.

Naturally enough, work allowed too little time to enjoy the special life of the mountains, for my days were filled with varied and interesting work. As time went by I wrote two editions of a guide on outdoor pursuits for disabled people and I gave talks on my climbing experiences and on outdoor pursuits for disabled people; a considerable amount of time was consumed on writing articles and booklets on these and allied subjects. Though formerly I had not been one for sitting on committees, from 1970 onwards I selectively accepted membership of several which did produce good results. I had a great many other casual voluntary commitments, so was very busy, and earning a living was not easy to accomplish simultaneously. Over the years it was a question of managing with temporary or part-time work as a clerk with the Post Office or Civil Service, as an evening telephone canvasser with an accommodation agency, as a BBC consultant, as an adviser to a fund-raising organisation, as a correspondent with an outdoors newspaper, as a lecturer, as a writer, and as a washer-up in a hotel. It was an insecure way of life but there was no realistic alternative but to take whatever work was going or adopt a more 'responsible' lifestyle; ironically, that 'responsible' way of living would have entailed less climbing, less voluntary work with disabled people and, in my view, an abandonment of what I was supposed to do in life.

From all this you might assume me to be a man dedicated without any reservation to the service of disabled people, but this was not so: it is only honest to admit that I did not always enjoy such a heavy involvement with disability, disability, disability. I grew tired of hearing patronising talk of how wonderful a disabled person was because he or she sailed or fished (there's no reason why most should not). And I was weary, too, of hearing some disabled people adopting the negative line that no one cared – that was taking rather a lot for granted. I was driven as much by a pragmatic sense of what I ought to do, as by a feeling that I wanted to do it; I felt I should do all I could to help on positive aspects such as access, mobility, sporting and leisure provision and, above all, integration.

It became evident I would be asked to be even more committed to voluntary work when the United Nations designated 1981 as the International Year of Disabled People. More demands were inevitable and the first came well in advance in the form of an invitation to join a national committee co-ordinating the efforts of 'The Year'. Oh, how I struggled to make up my mind whether to take on yet more work; in the end I joined the committee. Before long I became vice-chairman, but it was still quite a good committee.

Throughout this and many preceding years Judy maintained a saintly indifference to things material. We managed in a cheap rented bedsitter, did not run a car, and spent little on clothes or meals out. Much of the time my earnings were about one-third of the national average. We were not complaining, for life was interesting and reward-ing, and by the standards of two-thirds of the world we were well off. We believed that many people were too concerned with material poss-essions and too mean to have adventures.

In January 1979, without my realising, another important element was about to slot itself in: ice climbing. It all started in Scotland, with two instructors from the Loch Eil Outward Bound Centre near Fort William. First with Alan Kimber, I tested out some crampon bindings which kept the spikes in position with wire cable. It's not for me to say how they work for other people, but in my case they were like Cinder-ella's slipper on the foot of the rightful owner. That was a big problem solved for ever. Next we tried out an ice axe pick clamped to a crutch to see if it would stop me in a fall on ice or hard snow. I slid down head first, feet first, on my front and on my back, and found that it worked quite well as a brake. The extra second which it took to apply, by comparison with an ice axe, meant there were some limitations to the method, but the pick and the bindings increased my safety on the mountains.

Alan suggested Achintee Gully, a narrow icy gash up a steep moun-tainside. One rope length of snow gave way to forty-five degree ice. I led a bit, swinging two short axes in turn to dig into the here clear and brittle, there translucent white and firm ice. An ice bulge at seventy degrees was Alan's task; I was glad not to be leading, but soon it was obvious that in some ways ice would give me less trouble than rock because ice always allowed options. The hands and feet could be placed more or less where desired, in moves which were as short or as long as I wished, so if I wanted I could make a dozen reasonably smooth moves where someone else might gain the same height in six or seven moves. This made ice climbing a good deal less strenuous than rock climbing, for me, and I suspected that if ever the urge came to tackle some more serious mountain routes the way should lie mostly on ice and snow. Until then I had tackled only short ice sections, believing the longer and steeper stuff to be beyond my abilities.

From a vague guide-book description we expected 400 feet or there-abouts of climbing, but after a break for a sandwich the peering up ahead started and simultaneously we arrived at the conclusion that this winter there was much further to go than the book estimate. 130 feet of rope ran out as Alan climbed pure ice. We hurried on for another rope length, another, and the afternoon wore on. One more rope length, and we escaped from the shadowy top of the gully on crisp snow, and into winter sunshine. We were back at the road just before dark.

'Eleven hundred feet. Grade 3 at the top,' Alan said. 'Not bad for your first Scottish snow and ice climb.' (There are five grades in Scottish snow and ice climbing.)

The next one was even better. With Allan Roberts I walked one grey morning on three-inch white sheet ice, up Glen Nevis towards 600 frozen feet of white and gentlest turquoise, the Steall waterfall. The ice mass descended in several humpy steps, spilling like melted sugar poured and instantly turned solid in the cold. It bulged and humped and hung in thick beards and shrouds and portcullises, vertical walls, columnar organ-pipe icicles, bulbous scollops and shining, slippery slopes.

'Good grade 3,' Allan said, as he set off, chip, chip, chip, half an inch in with ice axes and crampons. Occasionally we could move rightwards to the waterfall's edge, where trees were put to work as secure belays. We needed them, for it was steep as the sides of an 'A' in places.

Three hundred feet up. A lost axe or a crampon off and the waterfall might just as well expand to five times its size; we were dependent on our equipment, and no mistake. Allan led, then I, then he took over again. Chunks of ice levered out by his axes bounced past all the way to the bottom. Two-thirds of the way up he started to yodel and sing, and we climbed on great arches of pure ice curved clear of the rock wall, with water thrashing beneath. Already it was melting, a playground disappearing to find its way down Glen Nevis and to the sea.

The finish was up easy snow, the descent safe and easy, down more snow.

It was bound to happen: ice climbing and the splendid experiences in the Andes were themes which reinforced each other and set me dreaming about the Himalayas. In 1979 I started planning an expedition to Nepal for the spring of 1981. Four people were invited and all accepted the invitation, and I started on the work of organisation. After some months we had promises to cover fifty per cent of the costs in one form of sponsorship or another, permission to do the climb had been granted, and work on other aspects was going ahead satisfactorily. But then the blows came. Firstly, a newspaper which had offered to cover about twenty per cent of our costs was threatened with closure because of union problems, so we lost their support; then because of budgeting problems an airline withdrew the largest part of the assistance provisionally offered, resulting in a further loss of fifteen per cent or more; and then three of the four prospective expedition members said they could not come up with their share of costs. They all made a living through climbing in one way or another and were hard hit by the recession of the time. These setbacks came fast one upon the other; in a period of about three weeks, over half of the promised money and three out of four members disappeared, and 1981 was only a few weeks away.

I came to understand more and more that organisational setbacks were just part of expeditions, as much a part as soft snow or loose rock or porters going on strike. Eventual success could come only to those who overcame these obstacles before starting on the real climbing. The preparatory stages sorted out who was sufficiently committed to the venture; this was how you qualified for a try at the big prize, in this tiresome form of eliminating heat. You had to take knocks, but as long as you knew that, it was possible to plod on; those who did not expect the knocks might stagger at their impact, and perhaps not recover. As in many sports, the winner must overcome the extraneous difficulties which have repulsed those of equal sporting ability but less commitment.

Perhaps the setbacks were a blessing in disguise, for I soon decided against trying to shore-up the planned expedition. One reason for this was that I was already extremely busy, and organising an expedition in a hurry did not have any appeal; another was that as 1981 was the International Year of Disabled People and success would help the campaign, it might be as well to increase the chances of success and go on two expeditions. The latter reason sounds rather virtuous, but the former was really the one which mattered, and even if it had not been the International Year I needed no urging to go on two expeditions in one year! Flexibility is an important element of problem-solving and by changing the objectives I wiped out most of the problems and greatly increased the chances of having a successful year. The choice of peaks was out of my hands this time; I had to accept what was available and go on any expeditions which would have me. In twenty hectic days I found myself places on two.

Before the expeditions, September 1980 brought three quiet and unambitious weeks based at Arolla in Switzerland. I went alone, largely because I felt the need to fend for myself completely. In an emergency it could be an advantage to have had the right mental preparation, in case a companion was ill or injured, for it might be necessary to go for help alone. I made an ascent of L'Eveque, described in the guide-book as 'steep and elegant', with an English climber I met there. We dawdled, and enjoyed the day. Then I undertook two safe and easy solo climbs of peaks of 11,000 feet (La Luette and Pointe Kurz). Unsensational as it may seem, that predominently solo holiday was as much a part of my mountaineering life as any of the more dramatic climbs. It involved no more nor any less hazards than harder routes done with companions, because the routes were carefully chosen, and I could find within myself no sound argument against soloing easier and safer routes under the right circumstances. It required experience to pick the right circumstances, of course, and I would be opposed, particularly, to soloing by relative novices. My nature is gregarious and for that reason I would rarely, if ever, solo mountains by choice. The important words here are 'by choice', because I was heading towards a set of circumstances in which choice would be very limited and my solo preparation would make a lot of difference.

5

A Broken Leg in Argentina

It was time to grab some living again; it waited there to be taken, I only had to go out and get it. There was ambrosia for the asking, trees to be plucked of their magic fruit, call it what you will, if you knew how to find them. In my case climbing was the way to reach the ambrosia and the fruit. If life became drab that would be my own fault, for I had found my path and the initiative lay with me. I felt privileged to have found the way, which was now to take me to the Andes of Argentina as a member of an American expedition. Our objective was Aconcagua, 22,834 feet, the highest point of South America's Andean spine, by the Polish glacier route, which is quite hard. I had telephoned one of the organisers and been in touch by letter, and being accepted had been a relatively trouble-free process but last minute hitches, or apparent hitches, were almost inevitable.

The Argentinian authorities laid down certain medical requirements which included having an electro-cardiogram and running a kilometre at high altitude. If they insisted on the latter I would be making a wasted journey to South America. There are reliable reports of a very experienced climber being refused permission (by a non-mountaineer) to attempt Aconcagua because it was thought his trousers were too thin. Another tells of an Englishman who was given a psychological examination in Spanish, a language he did not speak; it is hardly surprising that he was turned down.

At Miami airport I met five of the team with whom I would share a month, unless I were refused permission. We flew off immediately to Mendoza, Argentina, to join the leader and deputy leader, Bruce Klepinger and Dr Peter Cummings respectively.

Argentina. Plenty of open space. Scrub patches around us, vineyards, orchards, farms and ranches, with pampas a long way to the east. Ten times the area of the British Isles. By appearances, a fairly affluent country compared with Peru, though I was told there were quite a few poor people there and unemployment was fairly high. Inflation, inflation, worrying everyone.

Mendoza. Almost one million population. Spanish and French influence in the architecture. Tree-lined, wide, straight streets. Frequent and inexpensive buses running like good blood through the city's veins, reducing the relative underprivilege of the poorer classes. Busy with traffic, bad parking problems in the centre. A clean place where people take a pride in their dress; European and American fashions. A high proportion eating out at pavement restaurants after 8 p.m. Orderly.

Concerning the medical requirements there was news of great significance. We sat in a hotel lounge for a briefing.

'The regulations have been scrapped. Everyone can climb,' Bruce announced.

There was no explanation from those who formerly enforced the regulations, but we speculated that they had reached the conclusion there was no point in applying the rules because Aconcagua still killed a lot of people.

'I thought I might have to start shouting in Spanish on your behalf,' Pete said to me. As well as being deputy leader he was expedition doctor.

Things got moving. Equipment was sorted and packed, and the local press came to interview us. I kept out of their way to avoid attracting attention from the authorities. In two hired trucks we drove a hundred miles and passed without incident through a military checkpoint, where our passports were retained until our return from the mountain. Aconcagua, being close to the border with Chile, is in a sensitive military zone. Four Americans whom I met had made the mistake of checking in at the wrong army post, and at 1 a.m. were taken at gunpoint from their tents by soldiers who came from the post at which they should have checked in. It was all sorted out in the end, but cocked weapons left the Americans in no doubt that the formalities were to be treated seriously.

Unloading the trucks a little further on at the end of a dirt road, we pitched camp for the night in Punta de Vaca, a valley entrance at 7,500 feet (2,285 m), close to tall poplar. Now it really felt that the adventure could begin; there had been a greater possibility than I had admitted to anyone that I might have been refused permission to climb.

The first day on foot to base camp was hot; someone recorded it to be 31°C (88°F) in the shade at 4 p.m. Under packs of forty to fifty pounds (eighteen to twenty-three kilograms) the fairly gentle gradient was enough. Two valleys, the Rio de Vacas and then the Rio Relincho, would allow us gradually to cover thirty miles up something over 6,000 feet (c. 2,000 m) in three days. We walked with our water supply, a big river, on our right, up the steep-sided canyon, through shrubs and yellow flowers and grass and thistles, all the time close to smooth, washed, buttocky boulders. At the end of day one, approaching a high valley plain known as Pama de las Lenas at about 9,500 feet (2,900 m), one of our party who had been ahead dashed back through the scrub towards me. Born in Germany, brought up in Australia, resident now in the USA, Mike Skreiner was one of our comedians.

'Hey, limey, there's an army officer up ahead with a dozen men. They're staying in a hut up here.'

The army. Blast. Would they try to stop someone on crutches? I might get away with saying I was only going to base camp. Or was Mike joking?

'I'll carry your pack,' he offered. 'You can manage better without the crutches then. They've got a big wood fire going so just carry a few sticks.'

Collapsing the crutches, I put them in my rucksack, which Mike shouldered. With a few sticks under one arm I followed him a hundred yards, past a large green tent to a stone hut. No, Mike was not joking.

Outside the hut I first made the acquaintance of Lieutenant José Alberto Guglielmone and his men; it would not be the last time I met them. The green uniformed soldiers were busy handing out bread and cheese to everyone, a kind gesture followed by the even more friendly gift of large chunks of delicious freshly cooked meat, then prunes. The lieutenant handed around whisky, and the soldiers plied us continually with mate (rhymes with paté), a strong local tea drunk through a metal straw.

Under the orders of the lieutenant, the soldiers had cheese and ham rolls and warm, sweetened milk ready for us in the morning. We were fairly sure the lieutenant would not make any attempt to persuade me not to climb, but to avoid any possibility of controversy I headed out of their encampment first and put some bushes and boulders between us before resorting to crutches again.

Two-inch lizards basked in the sunshine, to dart off at our approach. A condor wheeled and soared 3,000 feet above, taking advantage of the up-draughts from a cliff to our left. A low flank of that cliff forced us to scramble along the steep left rock bank of the river, and soon after we had to climb ten feet of a seventy-five degree slab on tiny toeholds to insecure earth, then unstable scree. Bruce stayed with me, helpful, attentive and reassuring, and practical at the same time.

'Take care now,' he said in one spot 200 feet above the river. 'If you slide you'll go over the edge into the river.' The vertical part of the earth

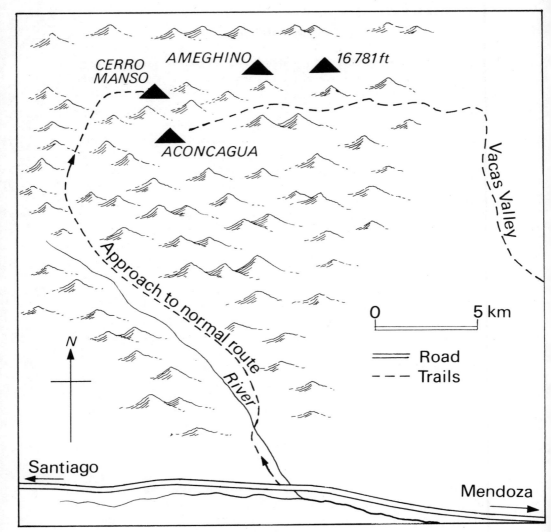

Aconcagua Region

bank dropped fifty feet straight into the river, which was thirty feet wide, and fast and deep. With metal legs on I had no chance of swimming or floating.

Two hundred feet of loose traversing later he pointed out: 'Still have to be careful. You'd drop fifty feet on to the shingle bank.' A hundred feet of that and we were safe.

'Thanks, Bruce.'

'No problem.'

Pete had broken an ankle the previous year, so was familiar first-hand as well as through his patients with trying to get around on crutches.

'I've seen what you can do Norm, and I keep thinking tonight you're gonna take your boots off and show us a real pair of legs and say the joke's on us.'

With such a compliment fresh on my mind I felt spurred to catch up with the leaders of our column, so charged after them, missed a rock with a crutch, and ended up ignominiously in the river! Fortunately at that point it was shallow and slow.

Steep, loose earth and stone banks just above the river were neither particularly dangerous nor to be taken for granted. Towards late afternoon the terrain turned more sandy and gently angled, in a broad valley bottom.

Tents, some equipment and food were travelling up separately on the backs of mules driven by two gauchos. We met up each evening but, being able to ford deeper and faster water than us, they often followed a different route. At eight o'clock that evening we had our first sight of Aconcagua's tip peeping down a steep V-shaped valley. Everyone was very tired, and though we camped in sight of our goal and this raised our spirits, we could see too little to get very excited.

The third day's march on a loose stone bank above the river was scarey for me, less so for the others because they could manage better. Expedition marches like this would be quite dangerous for me, it was clear, with river crossings and loose banks. The bank dropped fifteen feet in a sudden, firm rock step at one point, so rucksacks were ferried down hand to hand; but elsewhere it was just a case of walking or scrambling on loose banks in the sun.

A short jump from one big boulder to another in the middle of twenty feet of fast river was nothing to the others, a time for a tiny bit of courage on my part. Bruce sat on the far rock ready to grab me. It was soon done.

'Thanks again for your help, Bruce.'

'No problem.'

He had accepted me, as had Pete. As far as I could assess, the degree to which the eight others accepted me was proportionate to the extent of their climbing experience, with the least experienced, though friendly enough on the surface, being the most uneasy.

After one steep pull up a sandy vegetated slope for 500 feet, we got a proper look at Aconcagua, and what a beauty she looked, as did her sister peak, Ameghino, standing to the right.

The land turned to grey and red desert, sandy, dusty, parched. Valley walls rose in dry scree slopes to typical weather-sculpted desert rock towers. Of a few hardy plants surviving, the most common was a spiky green species growing like giant macaroons a yard across. A gently sloping plateau of red earth and stones took us almost to base camp; we then turned right into a boulder field, and that was it. In a wilderness of cracked rocks we found sufficient clear, dusty space to stand the tents. Though in fine mountain country this was a desolate place.

Henry Bergner had trailed into camp last, just behind our only lawyer, Tony Battelle, and both looked ill from the altitude, which was about 13,800 feet. Tony ate nothing that night, and Henry managed only a morsel of tuna.

We turned in around dark, two to a tent except Bruce, who was on his own. I was fortunate to finish up sharing with Tom Vaughan, an even-tempered doctor with a wife and three children in California. At the age of forty-three he reckoned he had better get some of his high altitude ambitions behind him before it was too late, so had borrowed the money from his bank to go to Argentina. I wanted him more than anyone else on the expedition (except me) to succeed.

Just about everyone was asleep when someone clattered downhill through the rocks into camp. It was a lone Argentinian who had been in a party of four on the Polish Glacier route. One had fallen and been badly injured, he told Bruce. My knowledge of Spanish is not good, but I believe Bruce asked if there was anything we could do and the reply was negative, and did we have a cigarette? No one did, and the man continued down in near darkness.

A day of odd jobs and rest followed. At 8.30 p.m. Pete and Tom diagnosed pulmonary oedema (fluid in the lungs) in Henry, and he was put on emergency oxygen immediately.

Next day at dawn, with over thirty hours of rest behind us, we were eager to get moving, so with thirty-five pound packs all of us bar Pete and Henry set out to carry gear 3,000 feet up. The plan was to dump it there, return, and make two more carries on subsequent days from base camp.

'We're going to go at what may seem like a ridiculously slow speed, but you all know why,' Bruce said. Yes. Altitude. It had stopped Henry already.

We were no more than twenty minutes about base when I heard a faint crack that made my heart sink; as my left leg lifted at the next step it felt strange and confirmed what was wrong. My left leg was broken. And I had no spare.

Bruce was just ahead.

'Bruce, I've got to stop. My leg's broken.'

Sitting on the stones, I lowered my trousers as the others gathered round. Just by the knee a steel strengthening bar had snapped. Further walking would only damage the limb more.

'Metal fatigue,' Jan Balut said. It was his subject and he knew. Jan was fifty-six years old, a metal fatigue expert with Boeing Aircraft Corporation. He had settled in the USA after making an escape from Poland in the early fifties.

Someone suggested trying the mountain with the leg splinted and without a pack on my back.

'No. I'd only be a passenger then. It would slow everyone.'

Our two engineers, Jan and Mike, began a short discussion on whether the leg could be splinted or otherwise repaired. They thought not, and as their conversation approached this conclusion I felt increasingly dejected, and said, 'I think it's finished for me.'

'How will you get down?' was the anxious question of John Pratt, an English physics lecturer who was prone to worrying.

'No sweat,' Mike said. 'There's always the mules.'

Two or three people stooped and patted me on the back in genuine and touching sympathy, and said things like, 'What a bitch,' and, 'Aw, hell, Norm.'

'Well, you can't win them all,' I said, at a loss for anything else to say. 'Anyway, you lot had better get going.'

Pete came to meet me and took my pack down. I followed on crutches.

'Tough luck, Norm.'

'I'm going to do *something* though,' I said, partly to conceal the disappointment I did not want to talk about, and partly because I did think it might be possible to get up a small peak on one leg.

Pete decided to take Henry to a lower altitude to assist his recovery; he was not getting worse but he was not getting better, either.

'At one point last night I thought he might die,' Pete told me.

They left base camp at 1 p.m., walking extremely slowly, and I was left alone in my disappointment. If only I had brought a spare pair of legs! But the reliability of the limbs over many years had led to complacency beyond reason; intermittent breakages were to be expected, taking into account the severe treatment to which the legs were subjected.

Disappointment. Following shortly on the relief of finding the medical requirements scrapped, this was a particularly savage blow. Yet disappointment is something which anyone operating near his or her limits must face and come to terms with. By sticking to the Alps I could expect to get up most mountains eventually if I chose routes which were not too hard and if I was prepared to wait out the weather. But the Andes and Himalayas are different, and failure is a large inherent risk on the high peaks.

What to do? Various vague plans for one-legged ascents sprang to mind but I could see no reasonable options; the stony peaks all around would lack water. Vainly, I hoped those who had climbed higher might have spotted something for me to do. When the group descended that afternoon they looked tired.

'D'you think there's any reasonable alternative around here for me Bruce?'

'No, don't think so, Norm.'

It looked as if I would be sitting alone in the desolate base camp for a couple of weeks or more before trekking out on one leg, or taking a mule.

A few crumbs of comfort for the future came from Jan, when I asked him if I should give up expeditions because of the possibility of leg breakages.

'No. Just replace the broken bit with a new one, don't let them get too old and fatigued, and take a spare pair.'

Pete arrived quite early the next morning, got the stove going and admonished everyone in an authoritarian manner for not being up. Being deputy leader and expedition doctor he had a lot of responsibility, which he took seriously. Early on he showed himself to be hard-working and efficient. I would apply the same description, efficient, hardworking and physically and mentally tough, to Bruce, but he was more paternal than authoritarian. Henry's condition had improved so Pete planned to make the carry to Camp 1 and return to base camp, then descend around 1,000 feet to Henry. It occurred to me that it would be preferable for Pete to be with the main party if Henry was well enough to be left, so without giving it much thought I volunteered to look after Henry. Pete jumped at the offer, saying he would descend with me to check Henry out after the loads had been carried.

At the same base camp were four members of a Canadian expedition bound for Everest in 1982. Though described as the 'Canadians' three of them were in fact English expatriates. They were short of a plastic funnel for filling their stove and also lacked Valium tablets; I possessed both commodities and did not want either, so traded them for half a bottle of cognac and a khaki kit-bag which had burst when one of their mules fell from the trail. The latter item could be converted into some knee pads if I found it necessary to crawl, and a mini skirt so I could slide on my bottom.

The sun was within a few degrees of overhead when Pete descended, eager and well ahead of the others, to base camp. Together we went down easy dust, earth and small stones to the tent where Henry waited. Pete examined him, pronounced him much improved, said, 'I owe you a million dollars, Norm,' and returned to base camp. As he left I was aware that his departure reduced to little or nothing my chances of making an ascent because Henry would require care for several days. He had quite bad headaches, coughed a lot, was bringing up a little blood, and had more fluid in his left lung than his right, though this was reducing. My responsibilities were to cook and fetch water, make sure he took his drugs, and see that he did not do too much.

At 6 p.m. Lieutenant Guglielmone and a soldier arrived on mules. When I explained our circumstances he kindly offered us a ride down. Henry did not want to go, and I did not try to persuade him because his sense of balance was poor, two mules between four would mean two to a mule or a lot of walking for someone, and it would take at least seven hours, much of it in darkness, to reach the military camp. If Henry had not been getting better descent would have been advisable, but his condition was improving, and in any case the lieutenant had come up to look for and help one or more Argentinians; it could be a matter of life or death for them, whereas our emergency was over. The lieutenant gave us bread and some cooked guanaco meat (from an animal related to the llama; it was with great regret that I learned later that guanaco are not as common as I had thought) and departed uphill. Within a few hours he passed by again, taking two Argentinians down. What had happened to their companion we would not learn for several days.

I was four nights and three days with Henry. At times he joked.

'Anybody can climb a mountain but it takes a real man to get pulmonary oedema,' and, 'Why do climbers rope together? To stop the sane ones going home.'

At times he was depressed.

'Worst thing about this is when you go home and everybody says, "Hey, show us your slides!" and, "Three thousand bucks I've wasted on this trip," and, "It's all screwed up."'

He ate well all the time, and drank plenty, and mostly seemed content lying back being looked after. If he was morose or apathetic it was easy to make allowances because he was not well, and because of his disappointment.

One mountain was framed by the tent doorway and in between trying to improve my Spanish with the aid of a book, or being housemaid to Henry, there was plenty of time to study that peak and wonder if the patient would recover so I could attempt it. I judged it to be almost certainly possible to get within 800 feet of the summit, but the final cliffs or steep ice would quite likely be too much for anyone on one leg. The river stood in the way and each day I spent two hours searching up and down the bank for a way across. The explorations were fruitless, and the roar and hiss of the river were inescapable, day and night.

By the third day Henry was greatly improved, taking long walks, and getting restless.

'I'm getting antsy. Approaching the limit.'

So on 5 February 1981, nearly two weeks after landing in Argentina, it looked as if another little adventure might come my way, and I started to make preparations. The ripped kit-bag made two knee pads for crawling, and a mini skirt. The stove and most food had to be left with Henry, so the choice of provisions was very limited: a small tin of tuna and another of corned beef, some stale bread, and nuts, mostly peanuts and walnuts.

During the night I was unsure whether I could make myself go. If I had not climbed alone in the Alps the previous summer I would not have considered the prospect at all.

Shortly before 8 a.m. I woke, and packed: sleeping bag, insulating mat, bivouac bag, torch, jacket, waterproof jacket and trousers, mittens, crawling pads, two water bottles, spikes and an ice axe pick for my crutches, small first-aid kit, knife, camera, film, a mug for soaking the hard bread, and food.

'Henry, I'll either be back in a couple of hours because I can't get across the river or I'll be gone several days.'

'Have a nice time,' he mumbled from his sleeping bag.

I had already pointed out where I was going; he could see almost the whole route from the tent. Heading westwards and uphill towards base camp, I kept close to the ravine cut by the river. In half an hour there was below me a spot where the river divided between four shingle banks. Sliding a hundred feet down the stony bank I had a closer look, and felt reasonably confident that if I could just bring myself to make a few jumps with the crutches I would be across the twenty feet of noisy white water. After a short hop on to the first bank I had to put my left stump on a rock submerged two or three inches beneath the water, and make another jump, thrusting with the right leg and crutches to roll forward on to the next bank. From there it was easy and by 9.15 a.m. I was across on the far bank, a loose earth and stone slope of no more than thirty degrees. I began to realise what I was taking on when it took fifteen minutes to crawl a mere hundred feet.

Gently sloping ground permitted the use of crutches again. Perhaps five per cent of the dusty earth was covered by the giant green spiky macaroons, so when it was necessary to resume crawling I could go between them. For three hours, crawling alternated with crutching; I gained height mostly through arm strength, in little jumps on the crutches. This soon brought on a very unpleasant ache in my wrists, and sore palms, and a sharp muscle pain developed in the left shoulder. So, soon it was a relief to crawl, even though this was extremely slow.

At the time I did not know that the mountain towards whose east summit I was headed was called Ameghino, but I had a vague recollection from a map that its height was 5,116 m or 16,800 feet; this was correct. The route to the summit of a mountain whose name I did not know was influenced by the availability of water. There was a more direct route, it seemed, but it was devoid of water. At that altitude, where the body dehydrates rapidly, I could not risk three or more days without finding water, because I had no stove to melt snow, and lacked sufficient containers to carry all that would be required. It was a relief and pleasure, therefore, to discover there was a stream where I had estimated there would be one.

Below a very steep scree slope of 400 feet I picked out what I called my three o'clock boulder and reached it by 2.45 p.m., after an hour and a half on my knees. I felt good, and crawled on with head down. Shortly afterwards I passed close by the first snow penitentes, an unusual formation of snow like shark fins sticking out of the sea of scree, or like six-foot axe blades, or arrowheads, or dagger blades. They varied in shape and size, up to six feet or so, but all were brilliant white and thin, and clustered close. How snow could stand up in sunshine in blades so thin – perhaps a foot thick at the base, tapering fairly evenly to the top – was a mystery to me.

By 5 p.m. I had had enough for that day. On thirty-degree scree I settled down for the night on a body-sized level platform beneath a big, stable boulder. The precious tin of corned beef was opened, and half was consumed with bread made soft and soggy with water. The other half was saved for the next day, wrapped in an empty soup packet brought specially for the purpose. Every spare morsel of food had to be saved for the diet was not only dull but frugal.

Perhaps by then I had reached a little more than 13,500 feet, having gained not much over 1,000 feet in a day. It was indeed slow going, but I fooled myself into believing I might be as high as 14,000 feet.

The next day was much the same as the day before, except that as well as crutching and crawling there was rock climbing too. I followed a brown rib, at sixty degrees to start, and rapidly easing back to thirty. It would have been bad enough with both legs on because of the looseness, which meant not only were most holds likely to break away but also what holds there were had a layer of grit and small stones covering them. Cleaning the stones away and testing each hold was very time consuming, and the padded left stump was cumbersome because it would not fit on anything small. However, I gained seventy feet more quickly than I would have on the very steep scree to the left and right. Though at the most I could not have fallen more than forty feet from the rib, climbing minus one leg gave a deep sense of vulnerability.

Soon the rib was too broken to be of use so it was back to the scree, where each knee gained only eight or nine inches at a step and more often than not slipped back half that distance. Sometimes I crawled on all fours, sometimes I was on my knees in an upright position, digging in the spiked crutches. At 11 a.m. I took a gully crammed with snow penitentes; using a boot and a crutch spike on the right, on the strange snow formations, and the left knee on the gully's gritty left wall, I moved more rapidly than anywhere else. After 200 feet the gully petered out. Scree again.

Lunch was bread and nuts. Then the scree got worse. Some of it was too steep for me to gain any ground at all; at each movement of a knee I slid back further than I had climbed. By aiming upwards and to the left I went downwards, but gained the bottom of some slabby rocks. These, too, were hard to climb because of loose stones and grit, but they gave me another twenty-five feet. On sore knees I struggled up more scree, scree, scree, barely rising at all; it must have taken an hour to get my body a hundred feet higher. When I chose to stop for the night at 6 p.m. I was close to 15,000 feet high, but based on the over-optimistic estimate of the previous day I thought 16,000 to be nearer the mark.

In a few minutes I had arranged some stones around a level space to prevent me rolling off. That's night's treat was the remainder of the corned beef. The hard bread had to be chipped with my knife from the round loaf, but was eatable after a couple of minutes soaking.

At 9 p.m., far away to the south-east a thunderstorm lit up the clouds almost every second, turning them into giant, translucent, internally illuminated mushrooms. The storm was too distant for thunder to be heard, but I awoke intermittently over hours and it was still going on. The weather had been kind to me so far.

Having over-estimated my altitude, I began the third day believing this might soon see me on the summit. Once more it took ages to clear the debris to climb on loose rock, and I had to lose a hundred feet to avoid a rock spur which was beyond my capabilities while on one leg. An unpleasant slope of fractured, sharp edged boulders went on for 300 feet and led to more loose rock climbing, then to a scree traverse and another scree slope as long as the boulder slope that went before. By mid-afternoon it was clear the summit would not be mine that day, if at all.

How I looked forward each day to ceasing the fight and sliding into my sleeping bag, and eating. I want to stop, my mind said most of the day. Keep going, another part said. Why? You will know why, if you succeed; you have found out why in the past. That's true.

By now I was drawing close to the snow and ice field which might be the key to getting through the final steep cliffs, but from a few hundred feet away it looked too steep and dangerous. Beneath an overhang of 300 or 400 feet of cliff I chose a spot for the night, but before turning in explored along the cliff base to the right; it ended in a chasm and offered no way up.

Being at the bottom of the cliff allowed a more accurate assessment of altitude; at around 16,000 feet I was only as high as I had believed myself to be on the previous night.

Though freezing temperatures made the streams quiet every night, I was never cold. The hours of darkness passed in fitful sleep punctuated by vivid dreams and brief awakenings. That night I had eaten tuna mixed with wet breadcrumbs, but I thought and dreamed of meat and two veg, meat and three veg, pork, lamb, beef, chicken, mutton and gravy. The vividness of high altitude dreams usually stayed with me when I descended to sea level, diminishing in intensity over a week or two. At times, whether at high altitude or at home afterwards, it was impossible to distinguish the dreams from reality. This was the case when I dozily got out of my sleeping bag and sat on the edge of the flat platform to relieve myself down the icy gully to the left. It seemed real, in a dreamy way, but I could not be sure whether I was awake or dreaming. I remember wondering if I was dreaming, and realised that indeed I had been when I woke up properly to find myself at home, where I had returned two days earlier from Argentina; what had appeared to be the platform was the bed, the icy gully was moonlit floor, and I was sitting on the edge of the bed and piddling on the floor!

Nuts and soggy bread started the next day, as soon as the sun struck me at 8 a.m. It may have been reluctance to face failure which made me unwilling to start, and I sat quietly until 9.30 a.m. Yet I was fortunate, for I was free of any fear. Though three days away from anyone else, there was nothing here to be frightened about, certainly not by comparison with many a climb I've done with companions.

Crossing between snow penitentes and up a slope for an hour, to the bottom of the way I hoped to go, I left most of my equipment beneath a rock wall. Food, waterproof clothing, camera, water bottle, jacket, mittens and crutches were chosen to go up.

The way I hoped to go. At close quarters the impression of the previous day returned, that this was too serious. The mixed snow and ice slope reached sixty or sixty-five degrees in places and was composed of hard, unstable snow penitentes weighing up to 400 pounds (180 kg) each.

An alternative route up an ice-crammed gully to the right looked more attractive, so, traversing the lower part of thirty-five degree ice, I headed that way. The transparent gully ice went up in steps, six feet up, four feet flat, five feet up, three feet flat, and so on. A higher section looked dangerous and added to that there was frequent stonefall. Uneasiness increased, and determination waned, after thirty minutes. One o'clock approached and, feeling very low, I turned back.

Sliding down the scree towards my equipment at the bottom of the snow and ice which had at first appeared to be the way, I found myself saying, 'Thy will be done,' over and over again. I think I did this merely for comfort but as the words came out I looked again at the snow and ice I had originally thought might be the way, and I knew I should try it.

It is impossible to think of any other configuration of snow and ice reaching sixty or sixty-five degrees which might be climbed on one leg and one knee. The shark fins lay in rows across the slope, and a lot were only five or six feet high. Some of the highest must have reached fourteen feet or so. Where it was impossible to climb between the fins because they were closely packed I had to get over them. This was done by knocking the top from one with the crutches to form a little platform the size of a narrow tea tray, on to which I dragged myself to stand or kneel and reach across to knock off the top of the next up the slope. The crutches were long enough for the job but I had a limited stride through having only one leg. Sometimes it was too far, so I had to slither down from one snow penitente and haul myself up the next. Movements had to be made with great care to avoid toppling several hundred pounds of ice on to myself.

The ice went on for 500 feet and at 3 p.m. it had all been climbed. I was on a wide stone ridge like a huge whaleback, leading me to the left. There could be no more than 300 feet to rise to the summit. On the broad back of the rounded ridge stood vertical rock towers of between 200 and 300 feet and I knew I could not climb them on one leg. To the left, the whaleback fell away in vertical cliffs, so that way was barred also. With the left side and the crest blocked, everything depended now on whether the ridge would let me through on its right flank, or whether that too fell away in impossible cliffs.

Though the ridge was angled gently I lacked the strength to use the crutches, so was forced on to all fours again. To the right of the towers I crawled slowly, and the slope unfolded gradually. At first I was fairly optimistic that the slope would let me through to the right of the towers and then all the way to the summit. I skirted the first big tower and could see the slope continuing a hundred feet ahead, and the further I crawled along beside succeeding towers the more the slope opened out, revealing itself to be gradual, and it became evident there was nothing in the way. The stone slope went right to the summit.

At 3.35 p.m. I crawled on to the east summit of Ameghino at 16,800 feet. I could not have been more pleased with an ascent of Aconcagua itself. Ahead I looked down the cliffs all the way to our lone tent, though I could only just pick it out. I waved in case Henry happened to be looking through a telephoto lens.

By 6.10 p.m. I had picked up the belongings left below the field of penitentes. What had been hard on the way up was easy on the way down, and I slid on my bottom down the scree with my one boot dug in ahead like a plough, and spiked crutches forward and ready as brakes. A couple of times I had to arrest the rapid descent for fear of tobogganing on a mass of sliding scree over a cliff, but mostly it was exhilarating and fast. The khaki mini skirt helped prevent ripped clothing to some extent, though the legs of my waterproof trousers took a battering.

It took only two and a half hours to get from the summit to the height I had been at a day and a half earlier; by 8 p.m. I was bivouacked where I wanted to be. The last of the tuna was delicious and a crescent moon came up over my peak. Excitement drove away sleep throughout almost all the night, and it didn't matter a bit.

The scree slide next day lasted until mid-day and it took an hour to find somewhere to cross the river. The last crawl up an earth bank was over in twenty minutes, and I crutched to our tent. Within half an hour the weather turned bad.

Henry had left a note saying he had gone up to base camp or higher, so I was alone for the fifth day. I did not mind, and started in on the food. He had left a stove, and first I cooked cream of asparagus soup, because it required the least time to cook. Vegetable soup and bread was the next choice, followed by hot chocolate. I must confess to feeling very pleased at having prompted Pete into pronouncing that Henry should not drink any alcohol, for otherwise there would have been none left; half an inch of cognac remained, and I settled back with a drink, to savour the contentment of a climber who has made it. I had had my mountain; I had proved to myself that if a leg broke I could rescue myself.

Three inches of snow fell during the night. Though I would have preferred a rest day, it seemed right to go up to see where Henry was.

Simultaneously, I started to heat up some soup and to stitch my badly torn waterproof trousers. In twenty minutes I had burnt cream of chicken soup and the ugliest trousers in Argentina.

I was almost at base camp when along came Lieutenant José Guglielmone and half a dozen men, on mules. He was going up to base camp and offered to take a note from me for Bruce, and leave it at the camp if no one was there. It transpired that Henry had gone higher looking for the others, so I descended with the lieutenant. He shared a mule, giving up his own well-behaved animal to me; if he had not offered the ride down I would have had to have started down immediately.

At first the ride was easy, down firm red desert, but it was a different matter when we were on boot-width tracks traversing forty-five degree dirt slopes 500 feet above the thrashing river. The big mules (as large as horses and not to be confused with little donkeys) plodded up steep scree, across steep scree, down steep, sliding scree on a trail I had hardly noticed on the way up. I noticed now; perched high on the animal, with only the right foot in a stirrup, I was scared. The animals waded, feeling all the while for a firm footing, hesitating, belly deep in the fast river, and walked precipitous slopes just inches from the edge of high river banks. I was aware that with a metal leg on I had no hope of floating or swimming, even with a water wing blown up inside – a method I had tried once. When the mules coped with steep dirt and boulders I had to work at balancing to stay on, and succeeded, except once; using only the right stirrup, eventually I tipped the saddle in that direction as we turned a corner on a steep zig-zag track. For several seconds my brain was not clear as a dull pain registered, and I realised only slowly that I had fallen off and landed right on the stump of my leg. My mule stood absolutely still beside me. For the rest of the ride I was scared quite often, and suffered an awful pain in the stump which had taken the knock.

In the early evening we reached the army refuge, where large portions of meat, salad and mate were consumed and I was made very welcome. Clearly Lieutenant José had assumed I would stay until the others descended from Aconcagua, and I was pleased to fall in with his plans.

'This is your home,' he told me. 'If there is anything you want you say me.'

For four nights home was a stone-walled, iron-roofed refuge ten feet by ten feet, in which five of us and José's Alsatian dog, Neger, slept on the floor. These were the quarters of the officers and NCOs; the men had a tent.

Twenty-four years old, dapper Jose wanted to improve his English, something he did with great persistence, and in only four days his conversation was much better. In return I learned a little Spanish, was fed generously on meat, tomato salad, cheese, onions, bread and apricots, and was plied with mate, sweetened milk and wine.

'You are the adopted son of the Argentinian army,' they said to me. 'We will shave off your beard and put you in a green uniform.' (Beards are not permitted in the army.) Unbeknown to me, of course, they were soon to be our enemies, but there was no hint of forthcoming trouble in early 1981.

Three of the 'Canadians' arrived first. They had reached Aconcagua's summit on the same day as I had climbed my mountain, 9 February. On the way they had come across the body of the Argentinian who had fallen, sustaining head injuries. Not far from his body was the wreckage of a search helicopter which had crashed while attempting his rescue, with the death of the pilot and serious injury to the co-pilot. The 'Canadians' had moved the body down 1,000 feet to a flat area from which it could be lifted off by helicopter. On the descent one of the 'Canadians', Dave Reed, had been snowblind for a while and walked through a cornice, but got himself out of the predicament. Everyone but Henry and Tony had made the summit. Tony just seemed to have run out of steam, having failed to eat or drink much after seeing the helicopter wreckage. He, Henry and Pete had been at Camp 3, ready to make a try (Pete's second) for the summit, when an avalanche ran over their tent at 1 a.m. There were no casualties but after three hours digging themselves out and re-siting the tent they were in no shape to go up.

Bruce and Pete had been strong in a physical and mental sense and worked hard to see that their companions got to the summit. John Pratt had been affected on the descent by cerebral oedema (fluid on the brain). He fell quite often and at base camp sat wild-eyed on a rock saying, 'I am proud to have won the race to Camp one,' before falling over sideways. His sense of balance was gone, temporarily. Physically he had been strong and fast, until the descent. Because of the cerebral oedema poor John had undergone a dream experience which sounds amusing superficially: he thought he had found a cure for scurvy and believed he wandered the world trying without success to convince people that he had an answer to the disease. He suffered terrible nightmares about it and cried a lot in consequence at night. The 'Canadians' described him as 'a gibbering idiot' but felt the improvement would not last as he came lower.

The team arrived in ones and twos on the day after the 'Canadians', and were fed generously by the soldiers.

The time came for me to descend from the army camp. José presented me with the wooden cup from which we had drunk many a mate, and a set of bolas, the three weights strung together and thrown to catch animals by entangling their legs. Not long before we quit camp I was informed that an unladen mule had fallen from the trail lower down the day before, and was dead. However, this ten-mile section was not nearly so horrifying as the twenty which had gone before. We headed for a roadside bar, where several of us congregated to thank José for his kindness.

A truck took us back to Mendoza where we had a rest day and a huge meal in celebration. I had to get home on one leg, but as my luggage could be carried in a rucksack on my back this was no great hardship. Within three days we had scattered to Barbados, Peru, Chile, Canada, the USA and England, taking with us our disappointment or our joy, according to what we had done. I was full of joy.

6

Kashmir

When distant mountains called again I joined an expedition not as a candidate for reaching the summit, but as one of several working towards putting even one climber on that summit. The mountain in question, Nun (23,410 feet, 7135 m), had had several ascents but only one success and three failures by the east ridge. Even the successful Japanese team who achieved the ascent put only two of fourteen members on the top. So, when I joined the team to climb Nun's east ridge in 1981 I was under no illusions; I could help by attracting a certain amount of sponsorship, I could carry loads and assist in other ways, but the success of the expedition would have to be placed before any personal ambitions.

'You're here to make the expedition financially viable,' Steve Berry, the leader, had said. 'It's not a "Get Norman Croucher to the Top" expedition.'

That was fair comment and, though I more than paid my way, I did feel somewhat like a hitch-hiker at the time. When it came down to who had any prior claims to the summit I was last in the queue, because I joined late and thus evaded much of the preparatory work. I would contribute, I hoped, to a successful team effort; and the experience of a Himalayan expedition was something to build on.

'If you want to get up Nun you should try the west ridge,' was the advice of Pete Cummings, the doctor on the Argentina expedition. 'Not the east.'

'I agree. But this is the only expedition I could get on so I'll have to be content with the experience.'

The reason behind Steve Berry's choice of the east ridge was interesting: in 1946 his father had attempted the route. After a very long march to reach the mountain he was plagued by trouble with stoves, and was forced to retreat when his army leave of six weeks expired. Even so he succeeded in climbing an adjacent peak, White Needle, about 21,500 feet (6,553 m), which in face of all the difficulties was a satisfactory

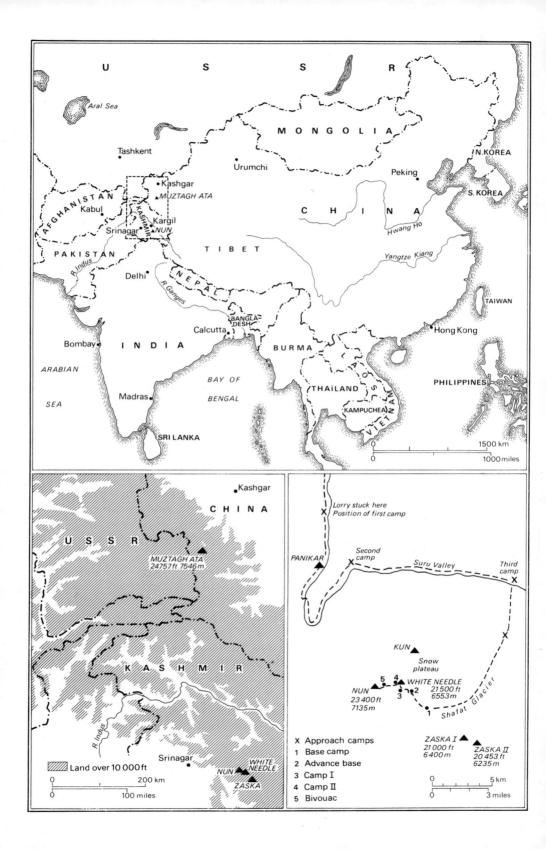

Top map labels:

U . S . S . R

Aral Sea

MONGOLIA

Tashkent

Urumchi

Peking

N. KOREA

S. KOREA

Kashgar

MUZTAGH ATA

AFGHANISTAN

Kabul

KASHMIR

Kargil

NUN

Srinagar

C H I N A

Hwang Ho

PAKISTAN

TIBET

R. Indus

Delhi

NEPAL

Yangtze Kiang

R. Ganges

BANGLA-
DESH

TAIWAN

Calcutta

BURMA

Hong Kong

Bombay

I N D I A

ARABIAN

SEA

Madras

BAY OF

BENGAL

THAILAND

LAOS

PHILIPPINES

VIETNAM

KAMPUCHEA

SRI LANKA

1500 km

0

0

1000 miles

Lower-left map:

Kashgar

C H I N A

U S S R

MUZTAGH ATA
24757 ft 7546 m

K A S H M I R

R. Indus

Srinagar

WHITE
NEEDLE

NUN

ZASKA

Land over 10 000 ft

0   200 km

0   100 miles

Lower-right map:

Lorry stuck here
Position of first camp

X

PANIKAR

X

Second
camp

Suru Valley

Third
camp

X

X

KUN

Snow
plateau

5

4

WHITE NEEDLE
21 500 ft
6553 m

NUN
23 400 ft
7135 m

3

2

1

Shafat Glacier

ZASKA I
21 000 ft
6400 m

ZASKA II
20 453 ft
6235 m

X Approach camps
1 Base camp
2 Advance base
3 Camp I
4 Camp II
5 Bivouac

0   5 km

0   3 miles

outcome. From the beginning I wondered if White Needle might be a reasonable target for my Himalayan initiation. So, though the main objective would have to come first, and it was not certain that there would be an opportunity to attempt White Needle, I asked Steve to obtain permission for us to climb this peak too. It was not strictly true, therefore, that I was going just to help on an expedition; a chance, however small, to attempt White Needle was a big temptation. If I had seen a good photograph of the mountain the attraction would have been even greater. ·

'Will my new legs be ready before the twelfth of May?' I asked Brian Campbell, my limbfitter.

'Hope so,' he said, with mock indifference.

They were ready the day before, so I was able to join my first Himalayan expedition with reasonable confidence that the stronger legs would not let me down. I took another pair as well; Argentina had taught me that was wise.

From my point of view the venture commenced on a bad note, for on the departure date I was suffering from bronchitis, an ailment which has troubled me with decreasing frequency since my early twenties. (I was asthmatic as a child.) I took the risk of travelling, fully realising that I might get worse in consequence.

Because of the International Year of Disabled People Air India had given us two free tickets and sufficient excess baggage concession to take all the expedition equipment free of charge, and they treated us especially nicely on the flight. I remember equally well their free champagne, and their courtesy. There were five of us on board, and two more had gone to Delhi a week earlier to handle the paper work.

In the early morning hours next day we touched down in Delhi. In a stupor from travel and bronchitis, at first I walked off without my spare legs, which had been stowed in a forward cabin. That afternoon we went to take a train northwards to Jammu. We moved by taxi through the crowded streets to New Delhi station. In temperatures up to 41°C (106°F), and with a fever and bronchial burning sensation in my chest, I saw little and remember even less. There is just a vague recollection of being in the land of pyjama-trousered men in the streets, the hungry dogs of India, searching, always searching for a morsel, thin, thin people with skinny, skinny arms, the incongruous conjunction of big bellies created by malnutrition, beggar cries of 'Sahib! Sahib!', dingy cafés with walls covered in old posters (many of religious topics), and lit at night by paraffin lamps.

Every foreign expedition in India is obliged to have with it a liaison officer, who may be very helpful in overcoming language problems, amongst other things; the one allotted us by the Indian Mountaineering Foundation, Neelam Kumar, joined us at New Delhi station. On the train we found two wooden benches where we sat crushed four to a side, with equipment piled all round, for the fourteen-hour journey. Everywhere beside the track, in shanty towns or in the open, adults and children squatted by cooking fires. To a coddled European comes a wonder at where the excess of people find a continuing supply of wood fuel, food, and whether, amongst such an inevitable volume of human excrement, there is any clean water. Shelter is part of the equation of existence too, but less critical in warm climes, and thin, grimy, dusty, sweaty rags sufficed for clothing. On the flat plains we passed good brick houses and straw-roofed mud huts, tents, lean-tos, jerry-can houses, hovels of sticks and mud with polythene roofs, and tarpaulins strung between trees, as we clattered along all the hot night.

The transfer from train to bus at Jammu in the early morning was accompanied by protracted argument and haggling about taking our equipment on the bus roof. A crowd of onlookers gathered for the entertainment, and joined in, until money changed hands and the driver smiled again.

Meanwhile, an almost totally blind and ragged woman who might have been thirty or may have been fifty, I couldn't tell, attempted for three minutes to beg from one of our rucksacks which stood upright on the ground. I was unmoved, a sign of how unwell I felt; or was the thick skin of indifference, which you must have in India, growing already?

Through the bus windows we had a view of cacti twenty feet high, vultures, wild peacocks, hovels, and people in foreign dress. With blaring horn the bus chased fast along a good road at first, but it grew worse in the mountains, where muddy rockslides had torn away as much as half the road width in collapses over drops of hundreds of feet. The road itself is a remarkable piece of construction, clinging to cliffs in gorges of enormous proportions, and its upkeep is a tremendous and never-ending task as successive winters attack. At many points slogans exhort careful driving: 'The Icy Hand of Death Grips Speed Kings,' said one, and elsewhere in India we saw, 'Sleeping While Driving Strictly Prohibited,' and, 'Darling, Don't Nag While I Am Driving,'! A certain number of serious accidents are inevitable on such a hazardous and busy road; two days after we had travelled the route an army lorry ran off into a ravine and twenty-four people were killed, and eleven seriously injured.

It took twelve hours to get to Srinagar and we would have liked to have rested immediately, but first we had to argue at length with the local taxi drivers, while the police enthusiastically wielded batons to drive away touts for hotels, houseboats and various commodities. We stayed two days in Srinagar, a city in Kashmir, which is in the far north of India. Here we bought rations and made travel arrangements. I felt ill, and guilty at not being able to pull my weight, but some antibiotics began to bring improvement.

From Srinagar airport the next stage was only half an hour by Boeing 737. Forty items of baggage accompanied us to Leh.

This town, at an altitude of 11,500 feet (3,505 m), population 8,500 people, has been influenced strongly by Tibetan culture and Buddhism, and is attractive as a result. An eight-storey palace standing 200 feet up on a rock spur overlooks all, and several hundred feet above that is a monastery. Buildings are of a distinctive Tibetan architecture which helps them blend with the dry, hilly landscape, and prayer flags brighten the place. There are sufficient trees, introduced quite recently I would assume, to give the air of an oasis in the middle of Ladakh's moonscape scenery. Between the Second World War and 1974 the area was closed to foreign intrusion, thus arresting the march of modernisation, but recent tourism has resulted in rapid change. Smiling faces and colourful clothing give a far more welcoming atmosphere than in some other regions of Kashmir, and visiting Leh, however briefly, was a highlight of the expedition; we planned to be there less than a day. The essential gentleness of Buddhism was pervasive, though partially submerged by the infiltration of other cultures, other values, and the attitudes of the rigid Muslim religion.

When accompanied by a lot of baggage, travellers may find movement around India to be far from straightforward, because they are at the mercy of those who provide the vehicles. At first it appeared that the only means by which to complete the next leg of our journey from Leh to Kargil, 127 miles (203 km) away, would be to hire four jeeps with drivers at a very high cost, but then we found a truck driver prepared to do the job much more cheaply. Next the jeep drivers informed us the truck driver had changed his mind 'because of union problems', and he in turn later told us this was not so and he still intended taking us. We believed ourselves the victor until at 8 p.m. two khaki-uniformed policemen presented themselves at our hotel to tell us we could not travel by truck for this was contrary to the law. The next stage saw Richard, Neelam and me accompanying the police officers to discuss matters at the home of the local police superintendent. This gentleman proclaimed that as the verbal contract with the truck driver had come to light he had to insist that we were forbidden to travel by truck. Eventually, after lengthy argument, we managed to extract permission for our equipment to be conveyed by truck and for us to travel in two jeeps instead of four, and those charged at the official rate rather than the high price demanded originally. The affair was settled reasonably amicably, and the night had a genteel ending when the policemen came back to the hotel for tea.

After a 3.30 a.m. start at loading, departure was achieved by 4.20 a.m. Past paddy fields in a hundred glinting mirror steps of the sky, and monasteries, Tibetan faces and the distinctive clothing which went with them, donkeys, horses, cattle, sheep, prayer flags, sparse poplar and willow in arid, stony hill country, we rose, gradually at first, then sharply on scores of hairpin bends and over the Fotu La, a pass at 13,432 feet (4,094 m). On a fine road surface most of the way we made good speed, and Kargil was reached before noon. This small, dull town of 3,000 inhabitants had been more important by reason of it being at an intersection of old trading routes between Russia and India, and China and the West. Now Kargil has a few hotels, mostly scruffy, and markets like rows of wooden lock-up garages raised two feet above the ground and occupied by grocers, ironmongers, tailors, butchers, bakers and other traders. The population is predominently of the Muslim faith, and apparently the practice of 'muta', limited duration marriages of as little as one day, still goes on. Houses are one or two-storied, and mostly built of mud bricks. Streets and homes are illuminated by means of a large diesel electricity generator, which roars like a helicopter during the hours of darkness until about 11 p.m., when the lights go out. Kargil is completely cut off from the outside world for several months in winter, and inhabitants must then rely on stockpiled food. During the summer barley, wheat, peas, tomatoes and potatoes are grown on the outskirts, and extra food comes in by lorry.

Shortly after our arrival in Kargil for an overnight stop the jeep drivers turned nasty, saying we had agreed to employ them to go further, which was not so. Neelam found himself accused of accepting money to take our side (he received no payment as liaison officer, though his employers continued to pay him in his absence). A shouting match, complete with the usual local participatory audience, ensued; a judge whom we met by chance asked if he could help, and told the drivers they were getting the agreed official rate for the distance they had driven. And that was that.

The jolting truck journey next day along a long and deep and fertile valley took us to Sanko village, where we had to sign the register at the local police station before proceeding; amongst those who had travelled up the valley before us, according to that register, was one Mickey Mouse. At the end of six hours following the valley road which deteriorated to a rough track, we were stuck in a cleft carved through old snow as high as the sides of the truck. The gap shovelled clear some days before by local people was wide enough but the back wheels spun impotently in mud and the vehicle leaned over a few degrees to lie on the snow as if resting after its hard journey. And that was the end of about a week of travel by one form of transport or another.

We were perhaps half a day's walking short of where we had hoped we might be, but that was not important for we were not pressed for time. Having unloaded the equipment we camped where we were on a meadow at about 10,000 feet, and within half an hour a deal had been struck with local villagers for eighteen ponies and nine porters for the next day. They duly arrived, and under a hot sun our caravan set out to walk eleven miles (18 km) on a rough road through beautiful rocky countryside where the last of the year's pink roses grew on high ledges. At first the valley floors were taken over by a patchwork of agriculture with poor villages of mud brick houses here and there, but both fields and human shelters grew less and less common the further we progressed. Most of our porters dwelt in these or similar buildings and worked these fields, undertaking porterage only occasionally, when the ties of the land permitted. They were simple men, and might have suffered considerable imperiousness from sahibs, but they set about their work readily. Without a trace of subservience, and with pride but no arrogance, they clearly wished to give fair service for their pay. I took to them right away, though others of our party could not regard them without suspicion, based perhaps on the expectation that porters, almost as if by tradition, would give trouble. Mostly they huddled without complaint at night, thinly clad and under blankets in the open, except for one night so cold that they asked to share tents with us; we managed to find space.

With bronchitis not over, and breaking in a new pair of legs, it was for me an awful struggle towards the end of the day.

'Norm took a battering,' said Barry Needle when we arrived at our camp that evening. He had walked with me all day. A thirty-eight-year-old engineer who had resigned from his job to be on the expedition, he was our medical officer, and also took charge of rations. (The wisdom behind this was if he poisoned you he was responsible for curing you.) Barry was very strong, industrious both in the preparatory stages and while on the expedition, and his judgement was good. He had broad mountaineering and rescue experience, was calm, and while not possessed of a great sense of humour was not the sort of person who puts a damper on the fun of others.

Steve Berry was thirty-two, and like everyone else but me, single. He had given up his job to go to the Himalayas, and had formerly been an estate agent, a profession which gives some clue to his personality; for instance, estate agents are neither known for shyness nor noted for having sleepness nights worrying about what people think of them. Steve had worked extremely hard to organise the expedition, and he earned the right to lead it by initiating the project and by sheer hard work. He had a bad climbing fall several years ago and as a result of his injuries, which were extensive and included damage to his head, he sleeps with one eye partly open; this had earned him the nickname 'Cyclops'. He had been on one previous Himalayan expedition, and had climbed in the Alps and the U S A.

Richard Berry, Steve's younger brother, and known to Steve as 'Titch', was twenty-eight, a surveyor who also had given up his employment to be on the expedition. Good-humoured (sometimes like a naughty boy) and generally constructive and buoyant in his attitude, he had a talent for mechanical repairs, which came in handy putting stoves right; at high altitude, where not only cooking but also the availability of precious drinking water depend on the stoves functioning, this skill is far more critical than might be assumed lightly.

Steve Monks was twenty-two, amongst the top few of Britain's rock climbers and determined to get as much as he could out of his sport; to this end he took only temporary jobs so he had plenty of time off for climbing. He had done many hard ascents in the Alps and Norway. He was easy to get on with.

Damian Carroll was a twenty-five-year-old teacher who had resigned his post on a remote Scottish island in order to go to Kashmir. His red hair went with the usual pale skin, which forced him to protect himself carefully against the sun's rays when high up; the method he chose with a large piece of cloth made him look from a distance like an Arab. He was quick-witted and had a good sense of humour, though his puns were as bad as mine. He was a hard climber who had been on two expeditions to Norway.

John Margesson, aged thirty, had been three years an army officer before becoming a land agent. He had very extensive expedition experience which included a year in Africa, and he had trekked or climbed in Nepal, the High Atlas, Arctic Norway and Central America. He admitted he had little sense of humour and was very serious. I found him to be as he said, and also precise, physically strong, and a very hard worker.

The next stage of the trek, up the left of a steep-sided gorge and along a wide valley, was longer than the previous day's; seventeen and a half miles (28 km) was the estimate of one of the locals, though I felt his reckoning to be on the high side. Whatever the case, we arrived at the ancient camping place of Gulamantongus, having passed over rock avalanches and snow drifts which blocked the crude road to wheeled traffic. With skin rubbed off in various places by the new legs, in the groin, from both buttocks and from both stumps, and with blistered hands into the bargain, the relatively minor but simultaneous pains from several regions were wearing. The pain entered my consciousness in two ways, at different times as component parts from each area of injury, and sometimes as a whole; so now and then I would recognise that a stump was sore at a particular spot, or a palm was telling me it was being rubbed, and when I was not conscious of one or other individual hurt I just felt myself to be generally in pain.

Early next day the liaison officer of a Japanese expedition to Kun (a close neighbour of Nun) passed by, hurrying on his way down to summon a helicopter for a sick climber stuck high up on the mountain.

'Won't take much to lift off a Jap who hasn't eaten for three days,' somebody said, and the liaison officer, understandably, was upset by this unthinking remark. Such a comment may go almost unnoticed in some expeditions, but once overheard by an outsider its nature is transformed from one of resigned, morbid humour to one of insensitive crudity.

Now loomed a river crossing, by pony. Memories of Argentina flooded back as I clambered on the back of a small beast; its size caused me to ponder whether it could carry me, or I should carry it. Having both my legs on this time was a mixed blessing; it was an advantage as far as balancing on the pony was concerned, but they were bound to drag me down if I went in the water. The Suru river spread wide to a quarter of a mile where we aimed to ford it, in two broad channels of sixty and one hundred yards and two smaller ones, separated by pebble banks. The water turned out to be not much over three feet at the deepest, so some waded across; Steve Berry nearly got swept over in so doing. In an hour and a quarter all equipment and personnel were across.

Springy turf interspersed with muddy, rocky ground then took us by early afternoon to a camp at 12,500 feet, and next day the porters urged their ponies up very difficult moraine and boulder fields, and across an easy river. On a particularly steep jumble of moraine bank one pony fell and rolled over a couple of times, but still they all kept going. Another intermediate camp at about 13,500 feet was the limit for the beasts, and then we and the porters took everything on our backs for two days to base camp in a snow bowl, at about 16,000 feet. On the first of those days a helicopter arrived to pick up the Japanese casualty but as far as we could tell from the sound and intermittent sightings it did not hover or land to take anyone off from above. It returned early the next day, though, thus adding to the suspicion that no one had been evacuated the previous day; soon after the departure of the helicopter I met the leader of the Japanese expedition descending a snow slope, saying, 'Happy day! Happy day!' and, 'We want you good ruck.' They had had enough and were pulling out speedily, and who could blame them? Their man had almost died, and was saved, and they were hurrying off home.

Not infrequently, expeditions have problems with porters. Our Muslim men from Panikar village neither went on strike nor complained, and worked for what is by local standards a fair rate, and by European standards a pittance. On one day of man-carrying equipment they even made a second carry late in the cold afternoon with inadequately shod feet already wet from being on the snow earlier. The porters were paid and, in keeping with the practice of that area, notes which had been even slightly torn were politely rejected; they had to be near perfect, even if grubby. When the porters left, saluting formally, smiling and waving to us, our liaison officer departed too. He said he would go trekking and would return in two weeks, but he did not come back. It is unusual, to say the least, for a liaison officer to leave an expedition in this way, but Neelam felt unwelcome. There had been a certain amount of personality conflict between Neelam and at least two expedition members; it would be difficult, if not impossible, to properly apportion blame in this, but certainly the fault was not all Neelam's. Having said that, his subsequent behaviour in not returning to the expedition was foolish. He went back to Srinagar, where his wife joined him for a holiday, and this confused his case somewhat as he said he was going trekking. I am sure the whole experience, beginning with a feeling of alienation and ending in a failure to carry out all his duties as a liaison officer, must have been very painful for him.

For three days, in the manner of ants, back and forth we went, carrying to a dump at about 17,000 feet (5,180 m), and on to an advanced base camp at 18,000 (5,486 m), before the weather closed in and imprisoned us in a snow and wind blasted base camp for four days. As is natural under such circumstances our interest turned to food we did not have, such as steak and kidney pie, raspberry tart, fish and chips and Cornish pasties. We were also intensely interested in what we *did* have, and our diet of freeze-dried and dehydrated foods higher up, with fresh vegetables and tinned stuff at base camp, was not bad. Powdered milk, intended for babies, proved to be particularly popular, and our eggs, several dozen of them, had survived the journey in. Tinned meat had been scarce in Srinagar, and we missed it. Custard and onions (separately, I should add) were favourites too. We consumed, also, a fair amount of rice, chapatis and dahl (lentils), more from necessity than stoic deference to the local diet. A pressure cooker at base camp helped us to save fuel by cutting down the lengthy period normally required to cook in cold conditions and at high altitude, where water boils at a lower temperature and cooking consequently takes longer. Though we all cooked, Barry did much more than his share.

'Just goin' for a tiddle an' then I'll get t'stove goin',' he would say, or something similar, and he must have cooked twice as often as anyone else. During bad weather in our dug-out snow kitchen this was a lot more work than it may sound, because the kitchen was only partially roofed and therefore rather open to the elements.

As soon as the weather released us on 3 June we all recommenced carrying food and equipment to advanced base camp, known to us simply as A B C, and for a further five days puffing people were tramping up and down ferrying essentials to A B C and Camp 1. The latter camp had been established by Steve Monks and Damian on 6 June, at about 19,000 feet (5,790 m). Apart from 250 feet of snow at forty degrees or more, which is a stiff pull when you are heavily laden and above 17,000 feet, the going to A B C was fairly straightforward. Still, several hours at a time toiling in the heat on soft snow at high altitude was tough work. As Steve Berry put it, 'No words can convey the agony of high altitude exertion.' Those words we did use are best not repeated. On one occasion poor Richard made a carry from base to A B C, forgot to unload everything from his rucksack on arrival there, and gave part of his load a return trip back down to base!

Pressure on a bone at the end of the left stump gave me an intermittent and awful pain when I climbed, and I was worried that this might stop me. Then something else happened which looked as if it would be severely limiting: one of the metal crutch spikes had started to crack. The spikes were slotted on to the crutches like spearheads or arrowheads on shafts, and were clamped there by a metal band which tightened with a screw. Metal fatigue had me again. Under Richard's guidance I removed the flanges which were cracking, and as luck would have it the spikes minus flanges fitted flush inside the hollow crutches. Purely by luck, too, the spikes had holes drilled for split pins, to hold ski baskets (rounds) in place, and the crutches had corresponding holes made to take screws to hold rubber tips in place on boggy ground. And I had spare split pins. Soon I possessed a set of spikes fitted firmly and of far greater strength than before.

'Jammy,' Richard said.

From base camp White Needle was a long way away, but even at a great distance the mountain looked very elegant, and I wanted to climb it very much. As we saw it the mountain, all snow and ice, arched up on the left in a huge gracefully curved back to a corniced summit, from which it fell away steeply on the right side. White Needle had a great simplicity and purity of line. The view we had of Nun, though it was huge, was less impressive than from the west. I knew I should try to resist White Needle's charms, because we were supposed to be suitors of Nun, but it was not easy. Much to my delight, it gradually became clear that it was most unlikely a safe route to Nun would be discovered except by going over White Needle. A reconnaisance was required and John and I jumped at the chance to go. We made our way up to ABC, in my case on snowshoes, which imparted a big-footed Donald Duck appearance.

Although an avalanche of a few tons had come within a hundred feet of ABC, it still appeared to be a safe camp, near a big rock cliff.

Steve Monks and Damian had gone down to base for a rest, Richard and Barry were above Camp 1, conveying equipment and supplies part way to Camp 2, and Steve Berry was with John and me at ABC. On 8 June Steve's first words were, 'Don't think we'll get much done today,' and we spent the morning unzipping the tent and looking out. But hope does not influence the weather.

On the morning of 9 June the three of us were able to go up the gentle glacier between ABC and Camp 1. Though we roped up to cross a couple of crevasses, mostly it was a safe plod. Camp 1 consisted of two small tents pitched on an airy ridge, with a gigantic rock cliff on one side and a crevasse on the other, into which Steve Berry and John dropped up to their waists at different times. Being at 19,000 feet put us in a good position to try White Needle.

John and I, sharing a tent, both woke at 4 a.m., and though the wind was forceful, at 5.15 a.m. we started melting snow for water, in case the weather let us go. But no, a high wind persisted all day and even made us wonder if the tent would blow off the ridge or be torn to shreds, for the material drummed and the little shelter rattled violently and shivered and trembled in furious gusts; the tent survived, however, and we did too, thanks to that. During a brief lull Steve descended to ABC because of a headache.

The subsequent stormy night wailed and howled itself through, and shortly after 5 a.m. we again drove ourselves to prepare. Muesli and tea made up breakfast and not long after 8 a.m., though visibility was not good, the wind had dropped to an acceptable level. Having crossed a crevasse or two, we tackled a short, forty-five degree slope of soft snow, on which Steve Monks and Damian had left a fixed rope. After that rope length we were on the very crest of the narrow, snowy, south-east ridge of White Needle, with a rock cliff of several hundred feet on the left and steep ice and snow and crevasses to the right. With fresh snow everywhere, soft and insecure, it was quite dangerous, though not difficult. The ridge did steepen twice into short steps like a steep house roof, but generally we just had to walk carefully on an uphill gangplank on the long ridge leading towards White Needle. Slithering off to the left was the real danger; in many places the snow cover was such that crampons could not go sufficiently deep to bite the ice. Even where the ridge sloped at as little as twenty-five to thirty degrees on the left we had to beware of sliding over the cliff. There was little chance of preparing safe belays to stop anyone who slipped, and for this reason, as well as for speed, we moved unroped most of the way. Barry, coming this way two days later, slipped, and for a little while Steve Berry watched him slide and expected him to go over the cliff edge. However, Barry stopped himself.

Mist hung over the white ridge most of the time and by two in the afternoon a moderately strong wind had sprung up and light snow drifted down.

'If it doesn't get better soon we should turn back,' John said.

'We could bivi.'

We said no more on the subject, both of us avoiding facing up to the unwelcome prospect of a cold bivouac, but the weather got worse and an hour later we did as suggested, digging a pit for shelter on a large snow plateau and laying out a bivouac bag. At an altitude of about 20,500 feet (6,250 m) we found ourselves in a good location from which either to retreat next day if the weather remained bad, or to head for the summit if it was reasonable. In good weather we might have made the summit that day; even in the weather as it was it might have been possible to press on and get there, but time was on our side so we played it cautiously.

The night was cold, minus 20°C (-4°F) at ABC and more like minus 25°C (-13°F) where we were, but at 6.15 a.m. the weather was reasonably clear, though it was still windy; Nun and White Needle were visible now and then. I woke John, who had suffered a fidgety, restless night through the cold, and who now proceeded to have a paddy at not being able to light the stove in the wind. It can get you that way high up, in dangerous territory, after a less than comfortable night, and I was not immune from feeling ratty either. In the end I managed to get the stove going inside my rucksack. We put some hot milk and muesli inside ourselves.

Soon Nun and White Needle had been swallowed in cloud again. As a precaution against crevasses we roped up and within five minutes

John had gone to the top of his thighs in one; he went in twice more soon after.

'I'm going to be desperately slow,' he said when he got out. 'It's killingly hard.'

He was breaking trail on soft snow so had more work to do.

The weather deteriorated again quite soon. Surrounding peaks disappeared in mist and snow, and the wind picked up snow to blow hard at us.

The left stump gave a sharp pain every so often and I was not sure how things would work out in that respect.

The slope increased to a steady thirty- to forty-degree slog. We would have needed half the time had the snow been firm, but we sank to the knee and cursed again and again. So it was not until just after noon that we came upon the equipment left by Barry and Richard three days before. A bivouac bag, a snow shovel, a stove and fuel were added to the little pile on the snow slope.

The elements were not with us and visibility decreased. It had been bad enough, but soon deteriorated even more to a 'white-out', when no division can be discerned between falling snow and the slope you stand on; it is then almost impossible to judge angles or to see if the slope ends in a chasm, so you are close to blind.

'If it doesn't improve we'd better go down,' John said.

'I think so.'

This was an unwelcome conclusion, obviously, but we had to weigh everything up, and weigh it again if circumstances changed, and weigh it again and again. We delayed, stopping to eat a little, and in half an hour had witnessed only slight improvements in the weather. The dimly-seen slope ahead looked like it reached a tiring forty-five degrees for a short while, then dropped back to thirty-five. Down at A B C the others waited in vain for the weather to clear, and speculated about what John and I were doing. They doubted that we were trying for the summit of White Needle.

'All right, let's give it a try,' John said.

He may have known that was what I tended to favour, though not strongly; I would not have argued if he had said otherwise, for we had time to try in better weather. And from our clear weather sightings we thought we had to go over White Needle to Nun because lower routes were too dangerous.

Though only a few yards ahead John was just a misty figure in the drifting feathers, but the wind did not rise sufficiently to insist that we stop.

The slope eased back, and very vaguely, up and to the left, we saw a greenish overhanging ice nose which could have been part of the summit cornice; we headed for it. The summit ridge was at right angles to our path as we came up White Needle's steep back, and we turned left along the slightly rising ridge before reaching what we judged to be the highest point at 2.20 p.m.

Attaining the summit of this elegant white peak was all I wanted. One month to the day after leaving England, I was satisfied with the outcome of my first Himalayan venture, having reached 21,500 feet (6,553 m). (Later Richard and John made a survey of the area and came up with a figure of 22,043 feet (6,719 m), but the survey was based on the only known altitude, that of Nun, when a sighting of that mountain was impeded by cloud. A conservative estimate would put the altitude at 21,800–21,900 feet, so I may just have been on the highest summit I had reached, but I could not be sure.) It was a peak of modest height by Himalayan standards, but a cautious introduction suited me.

The weather cleared for a short while, sufficiently for us to conclude, on the basis of this sighting and what we had seen earlier of the slopes below White Needle, that the way to Nun's summit should be over White Needle. So as well as giving us the ascent itself the reconnaisance had been worthwhile, and a little more essential equipment had been left high up. No matter what happened next, I would not go home with an empty heart.

'White Needle, especially the steep slopes near the top – desperate,' Steve Berry wrote. 'Such a struggle getting up ... it was pretty scary moving along the summit ridge with massive cornices on the right and mind-bogglingly big drops on the other.' 'The last stretch up the steep slopes was very strenuous. Knackered!' was Damian's version.

In poor weather again, we did not linger long on the summit, but began the descent of ground which was more dangerous on the way down, but less of an agony. Three times I went groin-deep in a crevasse and John admonished me for carelessness; then he walked into one himself (giggle, giggle). By evening we were back at ABC, to find no one else had done anything that day because of the weather. Now, if we could just get someone up Nun ...

Over the few days after we climbed White Needle it was verified that the route over that mountain was the way because any lower variations were too dangerous. Steve Berry and Barry had tried to cut out the tiring ascent of White Needle by keeping low, and had come back very scared, having passed beneath insecure ice pillars, on avalanche-prone slopes, on steep and rotten snow and ice, where Barry fell in a large crevasse.

Everyone carried towards White Needle and Damian, in company with Steve Monks, descended 400 feet westwards from the summit to establish Camp 2 on a col there, between Nun and White Needle.

On 15 June Damian and Steve left Camp 2 '... and immediately found it very hard going,' Steve said. 'We were only able to take ten steps or so before having to rest and catch our breath. After several hours we had covered only four rope lengths – 600 feet.' They climbed all day on steep, soft snow to bivouac at 22,000 feet in a bergschrund, which is a large transverse crevasse formed between two snow slopes lying one above the other, where gravity forces the lower slope to part company with the one above purely by reason of mass. Next day they crossed from the lower lip to the upper of the bergschrund, with difficulty, climbed 600 feet of fifty-degree snow and ice to get on to the east ridge, then followed a long, steep snow ramp, and more snow, to reach the summit of Nun at 5.20 p.m. They descended the same day to their bergschrund bivouac.

'We were totally exhausted and simply crawled into our sleeping bags and went to sleep,' Steve wrote.

The next day was hard too. 'Last section up to Camp 2 is desperate,' Damian wrote. 'Steve almost out on his feet. I'm not much better. Down to five steps at a time; exhaustion, misery. Never again.'

The expedition was successful, and there was the bonus of White Needle. On 19 June, Richard and Steve Berry dragged themselves on to the summit of Nun.

Immediately after going up White Needle for the first time I had told Steve Berry, Barry and John that I was content just to carry loads for them; the appetite was sated for a while, and the left stump was still troubling me. Even so, I tagged along to Camp 2 with Barry and John on my own condition, that I would turn back if the need arose.

In biting early morning cold we roped together and descended fifty-five degree snow and ice from the col for 150 feet, crossed a bergschrund and lost 300 feet or more while traversing forty degree snow to reach Nun's flank below the east ridge. Then began the wearying height gain on soft snow and under threat from avalanches all the time.

'I feel bloody weak as a kitten,' Barry commented at one halt.

At 11.15 a.m. we met Steve and Richard, victorious and elated on their way down.

'I was like a zombie,' Steve said. 'Titch did all the leading. Hey, Norm, didn't expect you to get this far. It's bloody hard.'

We parted company, with those who had the slope in their favour able to move three times as quickly as the unfortunates who had to go uphill on snow which collapsed underfoot and took them in thigh deep. In eight hours we covered the route to the bergschrund, which had taken Richard and Steve nine hours. So, we were not going too badly.

Our bivouac at about 22,000 feet lay under ten foot icicles hanging from the bergschrund's upper lip; the lower lip rose like four feet of parapet, giving the feeling we were on a balcony. Good weather was what we needed now, all we needed now.

We did not get it, however. Barry went up over the bergschrund next day and stood in heavy hail on the snow and ice slope, while I had a tremendous struggle to get over the big gap which ran like a horizontal groove gouged along the whole south face by some giant with a V-shaped chisel. I made it after expending an enormous amount of energy.

I recover quickly from exertion, and had worked out what to do next to get further up the ice; but as I rested I knew there was a decision to be faced. We were walking an extremely fine line with the weather so bad, us so high, the route so serious and retreat so difficult. We stood at the junction where daring and recklessness took different paths, it seemed. A violent inner battle took place, for in the prevailing conditions it was debatable whether two should try for the summit, let alone three – moving one at a time on ice and steep snow it was obvious that three would take half as long again as two. A party of three would be sticking their necks out and risking two bivouacs above where we were, and real problems if worse weather caught us out higher up. We knew that well enough, for even with tents and adequate food and fuel, the storm at base camp had been a reminder of what the mountains can do to a group which did not even have to go anywhere. We were out on a limb where a shortage of fuel or rations could be a real danger. The overriding argument of all was that though I was self-sufficient I was unable to carry much in the way of the extra fuel and food and equipment which were required; I did not deserve the ascent because the route was too serious. I had known all along that it would almost certainly turn out that way, and all those who had gone before had been extremely hard pressed to make it.

I must quote an outside view, to show that excuses were not creeping in but reasons were being weighed.

'I thought after his supreme effort on White Needle that he would be content with that,' Steve Berry wrote afterwards. '. . . His thoughts were for his companions, and his attitude throughout was that if he felt he was impairing anybody's chances he would bow out gracefully.'

By now the glimmer of hope I had nourished of reaching the summit was almost extinguished, though the ice and snow climbing ahead was likely to be less trouble than the soft snows of the previous day; with the right equipment, medium-angled snow and ice gave me the best possible chance of moving quickly.

In the end I made my decision coldly, as if someone outside was looking at it all objectively. I did what I felt I should, and accepted the responsibility as a member of a team and as the hitch-hiker of the group. Having climbed White Needle, it was easier than it might have been, to do as I should.

'I'm going back down,' I said to John, and called the same to Barry.

The two of them hesitated for some time, debating whether they should go on, even as a faster two-man party. Eventually they went.

Alone on the bergschrund balcony I waited, half expecting the weather to chase them back, but they did not reappear.

I began to wonder if I could have carried on if the expedition had not commenced with bronchitis, and if the left stump had been less troublesome. Would I have gone a bit better, sufficiently to make a difference?

During the night spindrift showered like a waterfall into the crevasse, burying me three feet deep, and with the advent of morning I found the stove defunct.

Over twenty-four hours after I had last seen them, Barry and John puffed in, having reached the summit at 8 a.m. There they said a prayer for a climber who would have been with us but who disappeared while climbing the previous summer, in the Alps.

Six out of seven on top, and a double leg amputee to 22,000 feet; we had not done so badly by comparison with the team before us.

Could I have got up Nun if I had carried on? Quite likely, I think, for there was no technical difficulty to stop me, but judging from the state of exhaustion of those who got there, if I had been successful it would have been at the cost of speed through being a larger party, and further slowed in all probability by my pace. As the weather turned out better, the actual, hindsight risk was not as much as it might have been, but we could not know it would go that way. If it had worsened, three might have died, and the east ridge of Nun was not worth that.

In the afternoon the descent began on snow so soft we went unroped, for no one could have stopped anyone who slipped on that treacherous cover. Above, the snow was poised, ready to slip. The slopes beneath fell away from hundreds and hundreds of feet, interrupted in places by ice cliffs which would have been a terrible hazard if anyone went. Visibility was poor and small avalanches slid down with great frequency, obliterating tracks made a minute before.

A 'never again' feeling seized me several times, but that is common enough amongst climbers. Twenty minutes away from the steepest slope leading back up to Camp 2 on the col, John, who was in front at the time, fell in a crevasse. Dropping up to his armpits, he could feel nothing beneath his boots. He managed to get himself out before we reached him but he was very shaken by the experience.

Next day we gasped over White Needle and down to Camp 1. The following day we were reunited with our contented companions at ABC, and descended together to base camp where, to our great annoyance, we discovered several items had been taken: a passport or two, some money, chocolate bars, a jacket, exposed and unexposed film, a plastic bucket and, most serious of all to a group bent on celebration, two bottles of whisky. Brown bears have been known to raid base camps in the area (one Czech report says, 'In the time of their unpresence the Himalayan bears visited their camp and destroyed it.') but we found it difficult to picture a bear wandering off with a bottle of whisky in one paw and a bucket of film and passports in the other. The culprits, it transpired, were members of a thirteen-strong Austrian expedition from near Salzburg, attempting Kun, and camped well below us. Suspecting our base camp to be abandoned, they had searched through and come across Steve Monk's diary, in which the last entry was one month old and said he was about to go off to set up ABC. Since four weeks had elapsed the Austrians reached the wrong conclusion that the camp was abandoned, and their leader explained that apart from the whisky and confectionery all items had been removed for forwarding to the British Embassy in Delhi. Once having reached the wrong conclusion many expeditions might have tucked into the consumables rather than transport them all the way to Delhi; these items were paid for, and most or all of the other property was returned. In a further attempt to make amends the leader lent us a stove, as several of ours were not working properly.

There was one other objective left, a peak of 21,000 feet (6,400 m) called Zaska 1, which had had only one previous ascent, in 1980. Steve Monks, Damian and I thought the risk from avalanche was too great. Steve Berry, Richard, Barry and John wanted to try it, though. I agreed to carry a load towards the mountain for them, as they would not change their minds, and a morning passed in carrying with them and getting back to base camp.

Damian and Steve Monks had descended so I was alone, but not for long; in the late afternoon John appeared, on his own.

'We got caught in an avalanche,' were his first words. 'Tell you about it when I've had something to drink.'

I waited to hear whether anyone had been injured or killed. One sentence would be enough. He related what had happened. Not long after I had left them they had stopped to eat and were just commenting on how nice it was to be there when they heard a crashing noise above; it went on for some time, the obvious roar of an avalanche. A massive cornice had collapsed and fallen 400 feet down a steep slope towards them, where they sat beneath an ice cliff. The cliff cut them off from a view of the deadly threat which was headed towards them, and someone had remarked without any concern, 'That's a big one.' But suddenly the avalanche reached the lip of the cliff and spewed over, hard ice spreading out in a wide fan and showering down towards them. Somebody shouted, 'Run!' Steve wrote, 'Instantly I got up and started running down the slope. I thought sickeningly, "I am a dead man, this is it, there's no chance." I fell on my face and thought, "I'll be flattened any second," got up and ran again. The crampons I'd just put on were sticking in the snow, threatening to make me fall again. I looked round, chaos, the avalanche coming towards me. Blocks of snow and ice flying past me, two of the others off on the left, it looked safer so I ran left. Then I was out of it and stopped, looking round for the others. Two safe, a third (was it Richard?) in the middle being tossed up and then out of view. Oh no, he's buried! I shouted something like, "Oh my God, not Richard," and immediately saw he was O K and yelled, "Barry!" Then miracles, he sat up and we got him out.'

It had been a near thing. Barry escaped with bad bruising of one leg. They dug out most of their buried equipment.

'What had made me unclip from the rope at lunchtime?' Steve wrote. 'Richard was on the other end of it and running in a different direction.'

If I had been there, I could not have run as fast as they. The likelihood of being killed or injured would have been high.

Laboriously, we hauled everything lower by carrying and dragging. Some of the equipment taken part way and left to be collected the next day was inspected first by a brown bear or two; one cooking pan had a tooth or claw hole right through it, and other things were strewn about.

At the arrival of our porters and two skinny ponies we withdrew to the valley. On the way down the porters treated us to freshly caught trout cooked over their little stick fire. We crossed the river by means of a yellow rubber dinghy belonging to the Austrians – pulled back and forth by rope – and took a belly-shaking, bone-rattling, dust-swallowing ride by truck to Kargil. Then on to Srinagar by way of an exceptional 'My God, look at that drop!' road over the Himalayas.

Judy joined me there for a holiday. The surrounding natural beauty was the main attraction, and in particular the adjacent lake area was extremely pretty; there we saw swallows and ducks and ducklings in abundance, bright kingfishers, bold hoopoes, geese and goslings and dragonflies, massed water lilies and bright pink roses, poplar and plump willow, reflected green mountains, yellow-green reeds, flat islands supporting little thatched houses a mere foot and a half above the clear water, floating island vegetable gardens, tourist houseboats galore, dugout boats, and shikaras, which look like brightly painted gondolas and perform the same taxi function.

It was on my mind to go back to Nun, but I could not get on the expedition I had hoped to join, and I was lucky not to have been accepted for I had already contracted salmonella and shigella, very unpleasant and occasionally fatal forms of dysentery. Had I stayed in India I would not have been well enough to climb, anyway.

The Jammu and Kashmir Mountaineering and Hiking Club put on a reception for us, and in Delhi we had a press conference at the Gymkhana Club, with representatives of the Indian Mountaineering Foundation and Air India. They had all reacted very helpfully towards us; we were befriended, too, by Ghafoor Wahid, an almost blind young man who ran an orchard. He put us up in his bungalow in Srinagar and his kindness added a great deal to our enjoyment of the holiday. Back in Delhi, Renee Chandola, a befriender of foreign and native expeditions alike, put us up and helped in many, many ways.

Thanks to Steve Berry most newspapers described the decision to turn back on Nun as 'sporting' and 'in a spirit of sacrifice', and a few assumed wrongly that I must be 'heartbroken'. They failed to understand what pleasure can be derived from making a sound decision.

The expedition began for me with bronchitis and ended with salmonella and shigella but no illness could lessen the pleasure of what had come about in one year: the east summit of Ameghino on one leg, taking part in a successful expedition on a hard route, getting up White Needle, and the right decision, the most valid of my climbing life, at 22,000 feet. How much more could I expect from this splendid sport? Would not the time soon come when I would have to abandon the more ambitious projects, which brought such joy? Increasingly, friends told me that time was here. But to my mind it was far away.

In April of the following year we held a reunion of the team at Richard's home in London, where we met the senior Berry who started it off so many years before by attempting Nun and climbing White Needle. Richard was not well mentally, and was heavily under the influence of drugs he had been prescribed. Next day he amused those who had stayed on after our celebration meal by writing to the Prime Minister, Margaret Thatcher, about how to solve the Falkland Islands crisis, which had just come to a head. His naughty boy streak came out, and there was a funny side to what he wrote, in a way. He began his letter with, 'This little incident with Argentina has caught you with your knickers down,' and went on to propose a solution which included kidnapping the Argentinian football team. But behind anything which might have been interpreted as amusing there lay a deep, impending tragedy, for shortly afterwards Richard was admitted to hospital suffering from depression and suicidal feelings. He wrote a letter explaining that he thought he had an incurable mental illness, and, typically, that he did not wish to be a burden on anyone. Then he killed himself by jumping from a very high building.

He had always seemed so resilient. I believe it possible that the salmonella and shigella which he caught at the same time as I was a trigger of his depression. If that is so, then as we stood at a scruffy roadside café in Kashmir, craving meat and deciding whether to take the risk, we were unwittingly treading ground far more dangerous than we imagined. Did he say, 'How about it?' and I, 'Well, I'm not sure. It's a risk, but then we've faced a lot of risk lately.'? Or was it the other way round? I cannot remember, but neither of us would have been so foolish without the company of the other in this silliness. There would be no point in recrimination nor guilt feelings, but I do regret that such an innocent indiscretion may have triggered a chain of events which led to the death of a likeable man.

7

Aconcagua, Argentina
22,834 feet

With regard to employment, uneasiness crept insidiously over me. After a near two-year stint raising money which was spent largely on segregated sports for disabled people, I had to ask myself what the hell I was doing. And I had to accept that my heart was not in it.

The strongest of my reservations was that it was all too separate, a backwater, and I wanted to take part in the real world. I did not want the top 2,000 feet chopped off any mountain for my benefit. I was not a blind disciple of the principle of integration, but preferred to lean away from segregation whenever practical options for integration existed.

Sport for disabled people had gone wrong way back through too much emphasis being placed on mimicking prestige athletics. When some of us started looking into the possibilities in outdoor pursuits, there was a great resistance from one or two of the leaders of segregated sport, perhaps because outdoor pursuits were seen as a threat to their empire if they were a means of integration. People were expected to fit in with certain sporting categories and rituals, decided for them.

Integrated, segregated, competitive, non-competitive – it was not for me to say one form of sport is invariably preferable to another, but fulfilment is more likely to lie in a wide choice. Opposition came more from those supposedly concerned with the interests of disabled people than from those who understood adventure sports. From some of the former, but by no means all, there were scare-mongering and faint-hearted tales based on nothing but prejudice and poorly-founded guess-work. There was, too, a certain amount of trying to hide behind a shield of medical 'authority'. Amongst those who were well-informed about adventure sports, reactions were varied: enthusiastic cooperation and encouragement, cautious consideration of the possibilities, reluctance, some of this based on genuine concern about safety. All these reactions helped us to go forward on the right and careful path between over-protection and foolhardiness. I had no intention of encouraging any disabled person to indulge in unsuitable activities, nor see them need-lessly barred from something which, if it gave them a tenth of the fulfilment I'd found in climbing, could greatly enrich their lives. The campaign was complicated, not just because there are many adventure sports, several of which require a great deal of knowledge if participation is to be acceptably safe, but also because there are so many types and degrees of handicap. I can only think that the opposition failed to understand the subject but were still prepared to give negative opinions. So, if they could not be converted they were best left alone.

They have had to come round, or look foolish, because at the end of the campaign anyone who said that outdoor pursuits were unsuitable was choosing to ignore a vast amount of evidence to the contrary. In a few years the face of sport for disabled people in Britain, and as a result in many areas of the world, changed a great deal. The position, parti-cularly with regard to integration, had improved somewhat, but I could compromise no longer. I resigned my job.

Then, too, 1981, the International Year of Disabled People (IYDP) came to an end. What a relief, after a tidal wave of voluntary commit-ments.

'It was wonderful, a fantastic success,' said ninety-five per cent of those asked about IYDP in a street poll, according to a newsletter published in early 1982. However, I must admit that according to the newsletter the question asked was, 'Was IYDP wonderful or do you want a knuckle sandwich?' The author of the spoof newsletter had worked very hard for IYDP and was one of a small group of us who found some relief from the serious side of the work in irreverent humour.

Opinions about IYDP were mixed; there would be no point in saying otherwise. Such a campaign cannot be quantified, but my impression, gained from those whose opinions I would respect, was very favourable. Discounting perpetual malcontents and moaners, and ignoring those who did not comprehend what it was all about, it had gone well. In my view there had been too many stunts, too much exhibitionism, which did nothing to foster the image that disabled people were normal human beings with normal needs and hopes and a few bits missing or not working in the way one might expect, but on the whole it was a successful campaign.

We ended the year with access improved in scores of places, with schools having made very special efforts to help children to understand, with information services having sprung up, with useful publications being brought out, with more volunteers involved, with advances in relevant technology, prevention of disability and work in the third world, with hundreds of fund-raising efforts, scores of conferences on important topics, with increased attention paid to integrated housing for disabled people, with improvements in transport. Special attention was given to religion, leisure, employment, family life, residential care, sport, and several other aspects of life which are of particular importance to disabled people. Scores of youth, women's, religious and philan-thropic organisations paid particular attention to disabled adults and children. And no one who was involved was complacent, for we realised it was a beginning, not an end.

I had enjoyed the privilege of having worthwhile things to do for so long that I seemed to be taking that privilege for granted; or was it simply that I was spiritually tired? The dilemma all along had been this: to get the outdoor pursuits campaign going with sufficient momen-tum my commitment had to be deep. There were no half measures. So, for a decade, one or two days voluntary work a week would not have been enough; at least half my time was spent working for nothing, and that was the only way to get the job done. That is not said in any way as a boast, for I was doing what I wanted to do and brought much on myself by encouraging demands on my time when it suited me. But when I began to feel resentful sometimes about those demands, it was time to take stock; I learned that I did not have it in me to give like that any more, at least for the time being.

1982 heralded two major climbing objectives. Time was running out and the mountains had to be taken soon. And how was all this to be afforded when it would cost more than I earned in a year? To begin with, the deposit saved for a flat on which Judy had set her heart was commandeered. She moped and made me feel shameful for only a couple of days, then encouraged me to carry on with my pursuit of dreams. What a woman! 'The time is ripe, cherry ripe,' I told her, and once she had got used to the idea she said, 'Yes dear,' and was affable again.

I began to wonder if I could be sane, for climbing weighed so heavily on my mind and was almost all I wanted in life; mountaineering was my destiny and my delight. The prospect of more adventure was both temptation and trap, and could not be resisted. How could my response be that of a rational person? Well, though now I seemed more like an impatient, greedy gourmand than the gourmet of earlier years, this was only a continuation of that behaviour which had so far brought sublime rewards, and there was not the slightest doubt that so far my course had been proper. Nothing had changed except my limits, which had ex-panded with experience and, particularly, because of the crutches. If earlier climbs had been within the bounds of sanity, then so were those to come.

The first of 1982's expeditions was a return match with Aconcagua. The expedition was scheduled for mid-January 1982. In December 1981 a letter arrived telling me it had been cancelled because too few people had shown an interest in joining the team. There I was back at square one, by now not an unfamiliar position. Fortunately Pete Cummings (the doctor on the first Aconcagua expedition) was able to give me the addresses of leaders of two other expeditions aiming for the same route. At his suggestion I wrote to them and in late December was accepted on one, once more an American expedition.

By stages Judy and I negotiated away from spending a few days over the Christmas period training on Dartmoor. We had bivouacked in snow a couple of thousand feet up in the Lake District the previous Christmas night. Non-climbers felt this to be somewhat eccentric.

'It'll be easier this time because I'll get a tent,' I coaxed.

'How kind,' she remarked. Over a few days her resistance grew, and she jumped at the alternative suggestion that I would stay home for Christmas, then go to the Alps alone for a couple of weeks. Then it seemed even better to go to Argentina three weeks early, instead of to the Alps, so three days on Dartmoor turned into three extra weeks in the Andes.

There were, of course, plenty of people who said it was not fair to impose such separations on Judy, though at the same time they accepted that men and women might be absent from home for business and career reasons or when involved seriously in sport. I can only say that climbing was in a way part of a vocation. And though she had in some ways enjoyed being in Kashmir, Judy was very much a home bird. She showed little interest in travel, and did not wish to visit remote areas, primitive villages, or base camps amidst boulders or on snow. Though it might have been pleasant, we saw no reason why we should share identical interests. Any Olympic athlete, round-the-world sailor or less ambitious athlete or sailor, or golfer or musician or tennis player, amateur or professional, male or female, is open to the accusation that frequent absences are not fair to the spouse; but what is the alternative? Many a marriage of constant companions is bland, claustrophobic, and death to any freedom of expression, for one or both partners. Men and women may have deep needs which cannot be contained within the constraints of someone else's concept of ideal or proper behaviour.

For those first three weeks in Argentina there might be no one to climb with. Yet it seemed the best way to go about things, so I booked a flight and resigned myself to the tide of events which would carry me to whatever mystery lay ahead.

Last minute purchases were made, and equipment sorted, in the first two weeks of 1982. At the limb centre a second pair of strengthened legs was ready.

'They fit very well,' I told Dr Fletcher.

'Must be somebody else's,' he remarked wryly.

An icy 15 January 1982. I had felt like asking, 'Aconcagua return, please,' at the underground station. The destination was Buenos Aires via Paris and Rio de Janiero. Rio was half a day away from Paris. Apprehension about failure and the fluttery excitement of going by 'plane to a foreign land, to climb, thrilled me and at the same time made me nervous, and I felt alive. As the doors of the aircraft swung closed in Paris I felt even better, for I had a row of three seats to myself, room to stretch out and sleep the night away.

Setting off on the march to the base camp below the Polish Route at about the time I left England were six climbers whom I was destined to meet, and though I would not climb with them they were to have an influence on the outcome of my trip. They were Jim Wickwire, George Dunn, Marty Hoey, Frank Wells, Chuck Goldmark and Dick Bass.

Buenos Aires. That slight fear: would we land safely? We did. Then the next little anxiety: will my baggage appear on the conveyor belt? Yes, we were reunited. The customs officer was perplexed when the Englishman with the worn climber's rucksack on his back opened his cardboard box for inspection; he was perplexed because he found a pair of legs in the box, and he looked from legs to rucksack to Englishman and back to legs again. It did not tie up, but he waved me on.

I have never seen so many friends and relations hugging and kissing and weeping as when we got through the barrier; it was very moving. At least half the people there, men and women, had tears streaming down their faces. There more than anywhere I felt alone, and wondered if the lack of a friend, or at least a companion, would lead to three wasted weeks. Well, I could do a bit of lower altitude walking, I supposed.

In my notebook was the address of an Argentinian climber who had introduced himself during the mule ride beneath Aconcagua; at the time he had invited me to stay at his place if ever I happened to be in Buenos Aires, but hasty arrangements had not allowed sufficient time to confirm that he had room, or even that he still lived in Buenos Aires. I telephoned. He was there. 'Come here,' he said, and put me up in a room off a courtyard complete with palm tree, and close to the small factory where he made sleeping bags and down jackets. Thus Hector Vieytes, his family, friends and staff became the first of many Argentinians to help me out on this visit, and Hector in particular started off a chain of events aimed at ensuring my three weeks of training would be well spent. We were in the land of mañana, where Hector and his friends might well choose to have half a day off to cook asado (meat done over an open fire) and drink wine, but on the issue of finding me a climbing partner Hector wasted no time. He telephoned Ulises Silas Vitale several hundred miles away in Mendoza, and the latter rang the president of the local climbing club to ask him to make some enquiries on my behalf. Ulises invited me to stay meanwhile at his home, simply because we were both climbers. He was very experienced, having climbed three times in the Himalayas as well as in his local Andes.

I flew almost the width of Argentina in one and a half hours to Mendoza, to stay with Ulises and his family, who lavished upon me typical Argentinian hospitality, and soon his efforts to find a climbing partner brought to his home Miguel Angel Sanchez. Miguel was twenty-four years old, swarthy, dark-haired and bearded, of medium height, and known affectionately and accurately to his mother as 'Flaco', which means 'Skinny'. He was unemployed, a condition he accepted with resignation rather than distress as unemployment was quite high in his country and he was a member of a fairly large family who had a reasonable income between them; formerly he had been a carpenter and a cashier, amongst other things. His formal education had ended at the earliest age the law allowed him to escape from school, when he was twelve. His interests lay mostly in pop music, jazz, the opposite sex, his family and climbing. He had the Argentinian passion for soccer, but only as a spectator since climbing had displaced this sport some years earlier as far as participation was concerned. Miguel was eager to climb right away, and it was soon settled that we would spend about two weeks in the mountains. It looked as if taking a risk had paid off.

As I would later be joining an expedition with communal tents, ropes and stoves I had not brought such items with me, but had an address from which they could be hired in Mendoza. However, Ulises insisted on lending us these things; climbing equipment is very expensive in Argentina, and suffers a good deal of wear and tear in two weeks, so this was a particularly generous gesture. Ulises' wife, Christina, drove me to the centre of Mendoza to buy fuel and to change some money. When I left the bureau de change it was as a peso millionaire, for there were over 17,000 pesos to the pound. It was a strange experience to see menu prices, complete with the same sign as used in the USA for the dollar,

Above Aconcagua

Below Ramon tackles a river crossing on the way to Aconcagua.

Right Ted Mayer

Below Muztagh Ata

Facing page
top Nun (left) and White
Needle.
below John Margesson on
the ridge leading towards
White Needle.

Above The first thousand
feet of the north face of
the Tour Ronde. The
route follows snow and
ice up the centre.

Right Dennis Morrod
approaches the
bergschrund on the Tour
Ronde.

Left The author nearing the top of the Tour Ronde.

Below Dennis Morrod descending from the Tour Ronde.

Above Left to right – Bob Braun, Brian Weedon, Glenn Albrecht.

Above left Tocllaraju

Below The final 250 ft on Tocllaraju.

Facing page The author crossing the bergschrund on Tocllaraju.

Left The author on Tocllaraju.

Below On Tocllaraju. Bob Weedon (left) and an Australian climber.

when sandwiches were 7,000; and if you got a taxi there would be 5,500 on the clock before you started.

Ulises drove me several miles to stay the night with Miguel's family on the outskirts of Mendoza: father, mother and four sons in all. From the hospitality of one family I was enveloped warmly within the next. Of course, it could not have occurred to me at that time that before long some would regard all the people of this country as enemies, but I must record what happened to me. Father was a watchmaker, a kindly man who made a big effort to use the few English words he knew, and the brothers, aged from twelve to close to thirty, said, 'Now this is your home.' Not having learned Spanish at school, and having only a few days' exposure to the language in Peru and Argentina, I had only 'struggle-by' Spanish. As well as a dictionary I resorted to a phrase-book. At Miguel's we were greatly helped by the dictionary and the place resounded with laughter at a television comedy sketch involving two robbers; they were unable to communicate to an English-speaking lady victim that they wanted her money, so she lent them her dictionary. Mama, a bouncy, rounded, ample lady laughed and laughed and laughed, and said, 'See, he understands! Mistair Norman understands!' each time I grasped the meaning of something one of the family said.

Next morning a neighbour gave us a lift to the modern bus station which, like all South American bus stations, is a place of bustle. We, however, drew a blank; we were there at 10 a.m., but Miguel had got the times wrong and our bus had left four hours earlier. Back to Mama.

'Quick ascent,' I said.

'Supersonic,' she said, and laughed and shook, and put the kettle on for tea.

Our lift next day was on schedule, and we took to the road for 106 miles (170 km) by bus to a hostel at a ski resort called Los Penitentes. In this summertime season no snow lay in the deep mountain-hemmed valley at 8,530 feet (2,600 m), but the hostel warden, Fernando Grajales, and his wife, looked after the many climbers who came to tackle Aconcagua. At Los Penitentes Miguel and I met six Americans who had just descended from that mountain. Jim Wickwire, who was the first American to climb K2, the world's second highest mountain, had climbed the Polish route with Dick Bass, and they gave a serious account of the difficulties created by long stretches of hard, steep ice where in most years lay easier snow. Marty Hoey and George Dunn, who were both professional climbing guides, had started up the Polish route but traversed right to escape the ice, and had reached the summit. Frank Wells, who was President of Warner Brothers, and Chuck Goldmark, had not continued to the summit on the advice of their more experienced companions. This was not a good year to try the route, and what they said put me in a gloomy mood. There was worse to come, when George asked with whom I would be climbing after training with Miguel.

'With an expedition that Eric Simonson's leading.'

'That surprises me, because I don't think Eric's coming. He's never mentioned it to me, anyway.'

'I had a letter three or four weeks ago saying he was.'

'Eric's one of my best friends, and I can't see him not telling me he was coming when he knew I was.'

Training to climb a route which was much more serious than usual, with an expedition which was not coming! I went into the lavatory and pulled a pained, grimacing smile at myself in the mirror, the sort of smile which made Judy laugh at times like this when fate seemed to be conspiring to play a peculiar joke. It had happened all too often in work and climbing, largely because I often trod where there was an absence of precedents, I suppose, and we needed to laugh for relief, and she would say, 'You poor thing.'

However, it was not necessarily all black, for if the expedition had been cancelled perhaps Miguel and I could do the normal route, or climb something else. Even if the expedition did turn up, it was wise for me to bear in mind the option of the traverse to the right to which George and Marty had alerted me. Not for the first time, flexibility, a change of objective, might be the answer; meeting those Americans put this notion firmly in my mind so the encounter had certain positive aspects. As well as that they let me join them to listen to their story, about how Frank had gone under twice trying to cross the river; about how they had been overwhelmed by the military hospitality at a tented camp on the way down and Jim had given a lieutenant two tents and his down jacket; about how the soldiers fed them guanaco ('Probably tortured it first,' Chuck said) and about how the lieutenant had presented Marty with a pair of spurs. They told of how army mules brought some of the rucksacks down while two or three of the climbers ran a day's march in two hours. I was pleased to be listening to English again after a week of struggling by in Spanish, and it was good of them to share their experiences with an outsider. They told me something of the future too: George, Marty, Jim and Eric Simonson were soon off on another big adventure, attempting Everest from the Chinese side, in March. (They did not complete the ascent and Marty did not return from China because she died in a fall; she was the third person I knew to be killed on that mountain in a period of six weeks.)

Shortly before they dashed away to go home next day, George left us a large amount of freeze-dried and other lightweight food, and gave me his address in the USA in case I wanted to climb where he lived. Wherever I went to climb it was always the same, addresses, addresses changing hands all the time, opening up opportunities for further fun. That same day I received another invitation to climb in someone else's country when the last of a party of Basques arrived at the hostel, but what was more important at the time was that five or six of the group of nine had reached Aconcagua's summit by the Polish route; in other words, three or four with a proper pair of legs each had not. Soon after, I was to meet two more Americans who failed, then two who succeeded out of a party of five, then three Italians who failed. What brought home most that the route was not to be under-estimated, though, was the fact that Miguel had attempted it in 1980, and had seen his twenty-year-old companion slip and fall several hundred feet to his death. His body was never found.

Miguel and I set out over rolling hillocks, wave after wave, where big hares bobbed away in fast uphill slaloms. Not far past the blue Horcones Lake we came upon the cocoa river chasing down, sufficiently strong to sweep us away or prevent us crossing. It was full, and we decided not to try to cross yet but to keep to our more difficult scree left bank, as we looked uphill.

In looking for a climbing companion for me, my friends had borne in mind my poor Spanish and sought someone who spoke English. It transpired that Miguel's English was little better than my Spanish, but between us we were able to find sufficient real or made-up words. For instance, Miguel invented 'glug, glug' for boiling water, and when stuck for 'hen' I used 'senora pollo' (lady chicken). We mimed and finger-spelt in the air, and eventually managed so well we stashed the diction-ary behind a rock for collection on our descent. 'OK?' he asked fre-quently, watching me closely all the time.

'Si,' I would say, even if it was a bit of a struggle on loose ground.

We OK'd and Si'd our way up, with eroded peaklets, folded and layered in geological origin and split by extremes of climate, to right and left. Four hours elapsed before the bank we followed refused to let us by a steep and very loose section. A long detour might be a waste of effort, so we decided to halt; we would cross the river in the early morning when the night freeze would have reduced the river's danger-ous volume. Rigging a flysheet for shade from the intense afternoon sun, we settled down like desert dwellers, on a sandy bank. There was no lack of time; we had not picked an objective so were not subject to the pressure of a timetable. We would walk up the first part of the normal route of Aconcagua and pick one of the lower peaks, of the order of 17,000 feet. Approaches to the normal and Polish routes both began from the south of the mountain, from a road running roughly on an east/west line. The former approach started further westward along the road and passed under the west face, while the other approach brought one in on the east.

At first light next day we got the rope out and Miguel crossed thirty feet of water, up to crotch deep; that may not sound deep but the force made it difficult to maintain a footing. I followed without mishap, and while he lit our little gas stove to warm his chilled feet I drained the water from my legs.

We took two and a half days to walk to Plaza de Mulas, 13,120 feet (4,000 m). Here was a stone military outpost which doubled as a climbers' refuge. We put our tent up nearby.

Two of Miguel's climbing friends turned up next day, intent on Aconcagua's normal route. We followed them to a hut only 600 feet higher, where amongst the names written on the wooden walls and beams were those of Ulises Vitale, Hector Vieytes and Cesar Morales-Arnao. All had been helpful to me at one time or another, the last of them having assisted my 1978 expedition in Peru.

Wisdom triumphed over impatience, so we rested at the hut until the next day, before aiming for about 17,000 feet (5,100 m). It was just a breathless slog on a faint, narrow track up dust and scree, producing exclamations from Miguel such as 'Bastard!' and 'Sonofabitch!' Yet five hours for that stretch was satisfactory. Three Spaniards descended, forced to retreat from Aconcagua through the illness of one.

After enduring a fiercely windy night we set out for the chosen summit, Cerro Manso, 18,231 feet (5,557 m). Manso means mild, and that certainly characterised this gentle hump. We put on crampons to cross easy, deceptively innocent-looking ice. There followed scree and easy snow, and we were on the top.

We were away from the tent less than three hours. In its own right the ascent of Cerro Manso seemed hardly worth the effort, but as an acclimatisation and fitness exercise it was just what I had come for. Four small postage stamp patches of skin had been rubbed from my stumps and would be healed before the next climb, with any luck, and then the legs would be as comfortable as I could expect.

The descent was uneventful, except we covered about twenty-two miles (35 km) in one day, and though this was mostly downhill, on rough terrain and laden with rucksacks it was a long, long way for me.

The river, coffee-coloured now in the early morning, was too full; even Miguel did not want to risk it. We waited in the hope that some mules might come by, and in not much over an hour half a dozen mules ridden by soldiers and one civilian appeared, going up the trail. They crossed the river to us, and the civilian greeted Miguel warmly with the customary hugs of Argentina. We forded the river on one of the animals and the mules departed up the trail.

'Flaco! Mistair Norman!' Mama shouted as she saw us getting out of a taxi outside their simple, one-storey concrete house. She hugged us tight and giggled, and everyone had a look at my trouser belt, pulled in two holes. Mama said if that was how much weight you lost she would come too next time. However, she did not want me to attempt the Polish route.

'No Polacos,' she said many times, shaking her head and pouting.

Nine days of training felt just right, so the first stage was completed satisfactorily. Now I had to find my expedition, if they were coming. There was time for one day of relaxation before I set out to patrol the coach terminus, observing passengers alighting from buses from Chile. According to my information this was the day they should leave Santiago for Mendoza, having arrived by air the night before. Late in the afternoon several dusty coaches groaned in, but there was no group resembling an American expedition. Miguel, who had been helping, left at 6 p.m. to meet his girlfriend. He had not been gone long when nine people climbed from a coach and started unloading rucksacks. I had found my expedition.

There was a simple explanation for George Dunn's suspicion that they were not coming: Eric Simonson was no longer the leader because the date of his Everest expedition had been advanced and various commitments meant he could not come to Argentina. John Smolich had taken his place.

Contrary to all we had been told, it took only an hour or so next day to obtain official permission to attempt the climb, and with final purchases such as fuel completed, we were free to take the bus next day to Los Penitentes. Not until we were there was it noticed that a kit-bag was missing so we were short of a tent, a stove and two days' food. We borrowed a stove, hired a tent, and bought a day's food, all from Fernando.

The three-day march of near forty miles to base camp revealed much about the characters of my nine companions, whom I found to be very easy to get on with. John Smolich, the soft-spoken leader, was good at seeking opinions on how the expedition should go, without in any way giving up his responsibility for decision-making. He was adamant that everyone should stay together, and though he had the usual share of early greyhounds, others whose pace varied (in two cases because of illness) and me in the party, he coped firmly and pleasantly on this issue. John had been a guide for three or four years, having abandoned a career as a surveyor.

The other John in the party, John Perone, was thin and looked older than his twenty-eight years on account of his semi-bald head. He was single, a chemical engineer who lived in California. What stood out most about him was that he was very funny. Beset by diarrhoea and dragging himself wearily up the long trail, he could still manage to come out with, 'You know, I'm more of a lover than a climber.' And when someone remarked that the presence of our one lady member, Mary, must affect the behaviour of the men, John stood there looking ill, with white glacier cream smeared on his lips and through the five-day black bristles surrounding them, with dust stuck to his face, with black fingernails, with dirty trousers and an old anorak, and said, 'Yes, it makes us all take more trouble over our appearance.'

The lady in question, Mary Michel, was an assistant manager in a climbing equipment shop, and had been introduced to wilderness hiking at a very young age by her father. She had acquired a great deal of hiking, climbing and skiing experience, and was sensitive about doing as well as the males. She was of average height and weight, and much stronger than appearances might have suggested.

Someone else who proved to be stronger than a cursory glance might have conveyed was Ramon Rodriguez Rocca, a Chilean engineering student who in addition to carrying more than his fair share of communal equipment took on board three big honeydew melons for us. He did not reach European or American average male height and lacked any obvious bulges of muscle, but that is often the way with good mountaineers. In consequence of his abilities, Ramon was a leading candidate for a Chilean expedition attempting Everest the following year. His English was about as good as Miguel's.

Mr Muscle of the group was Todd Marlatt, a boisterous ex-marine who worked in the oil business in Saudi Arabia. He could easily have been taken to be too full of himself, but, though he *was* pretty full of himself ('What is the name of the one who talks a lot?' an Italian had asked), his anecdotes were always interesting and his jokes funny, and he was bright. He had a dogmatic streak, and when, in describing his work he said his firm had been looking for somebody who was not opinionated and was a good listener, John P. stepped in neatly with, 'And that's the guy you work for?'

The oldest person in the group, Ted Mayer, was forty-six, originally from Germany but now, like all but Ramon and me, living in the USA, where he owned a small printing business.

Dan Montague was a soft-drawling, easy-going hospital medical technologist who also ran a raisin farm in California; 'raisin' raisins', as someone expressed it. He was less ambitious than some, and said that unlike the other 'dudes' he would be content to reach 21,000 feet as he had not previously been quite that high.

Paul Slota was a grocery store manager whose interest in photography added a good deal to his enjoyment of the trip. He was a quiet person who blended in unobtrusively.

Vladimir Kovacevic, a Yugoslav doctor, worked as an anaesthetist in Wisconsin. Apart from me, he was the only one of us who was married at the time and he had two children. Vladimir was fast at the beginning of the expedition and emerged as the person who disliked most the constraints of being in a large group.

Ages ranged from Ramon, twenty-five, and Paul who reached twenty-six during the expedition, through John P., twenty-eight, Mary, twenty-nine, John S., thirty-two, Todd, somewhere around thirty-five, Dan, thirty-nine, Vladimir, about forty, me, forty-one, to Ted. Todd, Ted, Mary and Paul had climbed Alaska's McKinley (20,320 feet, 6,194 m), Dan had been up three peaks in excess of 19,000 feet (5,800 m) and Ramon had many high altitude ascents to his credit. John S., though not having climbed anywhere near as high as Aconcagua, had very extensive experience. Vladimir and John P's experience lay with peaks of alpine proportions rather than Andean.

The march involved a forty-feet-wide river crossing on the morning of the second day. Most of the others struggled through water up to mid-belly and though none slipped the seriousness of the crossing, even with a rope, was obvious. John S. crossed with me, much to my relief.

Facing upstream I entered the clutches of the water and shuffled sideways. As it became deeper I speared the crutches into mucky brown wavelets with dirty white crests, into water which tore even at those thin poles so hard it took all my strength to prevent them being pushed away. My feet conveyed no information as to the contours of the bouldery bottom, so, unlike the others, I had to chance each step and hope that I could remain in balance with the help of the crutches. If the water pulling at my crutches created a problem, what it did to my legs made the crossing the hardest I have ever attempted, for the river worked constantly to sweep me from my feet into rough water. I would sink if I went over, and the river would dash me against boulders, and if I could not get out the cold would soon finish me if drowning did not. The difficulty was reduced a little as the limbs filled with water and became heavier, but when only at knee-depth I thought I would not be able to handle deeper water. A further step to the right, and the water was at mid-thigh, and I fought to get the right leg moved again after its partner had joined it. The river dragged at it as soon as it came off the riverbed and I feared I would not get it down again. For second after long second I thrust as hard as I could, trying to get it on the bottom again while the river wanted to take it downstream, with or without me. I battled, and won a step, but each successive step took me further from the bank and into deeper water. Two, three, four more short steps with the water up to my stomach brought relief in one way: I was in the middle and it was as safe to go on as to go back. John was right behind me, holding my belt. Funny, I thought, I don't know if he's holding me down, lifting me up, or pulling me sideways; we had not worked out what we would do. Another step seemed to take me no further. Don't look at the water, I told myself; it moved so fast it would disturb any balance achieved through the eyes, and I relied more than most on my eyes for balance because my feet told me nothing. With eyes on the hills upstream, I got another step. People on the bank were shouting, 'Great man!' and, 'Go for it!' The water shallowed, it became easier and easier, and I bounded out.

'We got power!' Todd shouted, raising a clenched fist, and John P. reacted more quietly with 'We's funky.'

Much of the early walk took us through prickly, man-high bushes that smelt of castor oil. The river spread wide here, narrowed there, and carved high grit walls and forced us to rise 200 or 300 feet to find a way through on slippery grit slopes. There were places where there was nothing underfoot but dried mud and boulders, and other sandy areas, and grassy places, and frightening steep banks of grit. At the end of the second day the wind raged and blew dust at us as we trudged wearily up a half-mile-wide, flat, pebbly river bed.

'You may get a sight of Aconcagua's tip up through the next valley,' I said, playing down the reality.

Then, there was Aconcagua. When they saw the view, 'Wow! Man! Hooee!' they went, dropping rucksacks to rush ahead to a crest for a better view. It was a splendid sight.

The last day into base camp took us first high up the right bank of the Relinchos valley. My first impression was that it was better than the left bank, and I remembered the year before when that bank had made me concentrate on every step, had made me sweat, had made me fear a fall into the river. Now the right bank deteriorated into looseness too, and we were very, very careful.

The uninterrupted view of Aconcagua and Ameghino which was soon ours excited our hearts like nothing else could. We were fired up, and marched quickly. Mostly I was last; skin had been rubbed from the stumps again in several spots.

146

At Plaza Argentina we stopped to rest, and talked to two people who had attempted the Polish route but had not reached the summit. Their three companions were still up there trying.

The greyhounds pulled ahead, and I stayed with John P., who had what all the Americans knew as 'the trots'. He was weakened, and had to stop frequently to drop his trousers. 'Gonna get a sunburnt butt,' he said, 'with all these trips to the bathroom.'

The mules laden with our food and heavy equipment passed us in the mid-afternoon and I paced John P. for the last couple of hours. We had speculated on how much ribbing there might be when we trailed in an hour or more after everyone else. But as we approached base camp we saw three figures scurrying towards us across the vast flood plain ahead; they had overshot. Since one was our leader and the other a Chilean whose local knowledge we had to rely on, there was considerable banter aimed at John S. and Ramon when five of us came into camp together.

So, here I was again in the same base camp, close to where the river we had followed narrowed and its source hid under the ice. My stumps hurt a lot, but I felt well, and the mules had brought up an extra pair of legs this time. 'Have a slug of this,' John P. said, getting out a bottle of whisky. I had a half share in it but he kindly carried it. 'That's for pacing me. How're your wheels?'

'Both feel quite bad. Raw in a few small places.'

John S. heard this, and consequently I was left out of the team of seven who carried to Camp 1 after we had enjoyed a rest day at base camp. Dan and Paul, both of whom were unwell, stayed behind too, and we agreed it was better that we rested, and we felt terribly guilty at the same time. 'Not doing much for my ego,' Paul remarked.

Three Americans whose two friends we had met at Plaza Argentina descended; two of them had succeeded, of a total of five. It was serious, and they had passed by three bodies on the glacier, they said. As far as I could gather from various sources, one was of the Argentinian who had died when I was beneath the mountain the year before, and the other pair were Americans who had met their deaths a few weeks earlier.

We started slowly up the moraine where my leg had broken the year before, and up a loose V gully. Though above the gully the terrain was a jumble of boulders, up to house size, with little frozen lakes in between, and though above that the scree was very steep and loose in places, it was just a matter of slow pace and laboured breathing. Four hours was all we needed. Our next camp was positioned in a wide, grey-rock, barren valley between Ameghino's icy walls on the right as we looked upwards, and Aconcagua rising sharply to the left. My prediction that we would find food abandoned on the route had not proved true thus far, so as soon as the tents were up on our flat, stony spot at about 16,250 feet John S. and I went scavenging. We found chocolate, corned beef, sardines, bouillon cubes, sweetened milk, biscuits, tea bags and other commodities in fairly large quantities. Any slight anxiety we might have felt about food was over.

Another carry was executed and the following day we loaded all which remained and made ourselves undertake a purgatorial grind up scree, steep scree, steeper still, to Camp 2. Now the altitude really punished us for coming up there, encumbered by heavy packs; we were heading into what Paul often referred to as the 'death zone', above 18,000 feet. Reluctance, altitude and heavy loads were overcome by the positive, earnest desire to go up, and the balance in our minds and bodies was sufficient to produce the next step up, and the next.

As we rested at about 17,000 feet a ruby-throated hummingbird flew up the way we had come, landed for a few seconds on one of Dan's boots, and took off somewhat to the right of the way we would go.

Having missed out on two carries, and having been near the back or last on the march in, I had begun to wonder whether overall I would be a weak link. I was going well on this carry, amongst the leaders and, though it was not a race, I found no need to push myself as hard as I had thought might be necessary. So I allowed myself the hope that I would perform comparatively better the higher we went.

John P. began to lag a little; at each rest stop he flopped in that slumped attitude which told all and made us wonder whether he would get up again. He stopped more than the rest of us and time and time again got himself up. I dropped back to pace him, and having taken a rope from his pack offered to lighten his load further.

'If you take any more I'll blow away.'

Vladimir and Todd went ahead as we urged our bodies to zig-zag up scree which wanted to slide, so it was gasp and slide and rest and gasp and slide for another hour. The leading pair reached the site of our camp and Vladimir came down and took John P's burden. Todd called down to me, 'How about you, big boy? Take your pack?'

'No, I'm all right thanks, Todd.'

In the shelter of a fifty-foot-high amphitheatre above the steepest scree our three tents were well protected. Judging from our altitude relative to Ameghino, I thought we were at about 18,500 feet. At least one more camp would be necessary before we could try for the summit.

Altitude dictated that progress should be slow, so the next day sped by as we rested. John S. and Ramon scouted ahead a little and when they got back John looked serious and said, 'It's gonna be hard.'

On Aconcagua, the weather alone could reduce our chances a great deal; this mountain stood so high it was frequently swathed in bad weather cloud while the surrounding area enjoyed the sun. We had not had much in the way of serious climbing so far, though the river and loose banks were not to be treated too lightly. Now the altitude and potential bad weather were serious enough, and on top of that the ice would be difficult.

Our little group had been moving only fifteen minutes up steep stony ground on the way to Camp 3 when the altitude claimed its first victim: John P. could not carry on. His speech was a little slurred and his gait unsteady, and the decision to stop was entirely his own. Never have I felt so sorry to see someone descend alone towards the prospect of three or four days of idleness and loneliness at base camp.

The more difficult part of the route started for the rest of us, on the steep glacier. As we sat to put on crampons the body of the Argentinian was visible 200 yards to our left and only a few score feet higher up the glacier. It lay in the snow, a vague bundle, and was perhaps wrapped in a sleeping bag; the distance was too great for us to tell, and no one mentioned it.

Having started up a snow slope which turned icy higher up, we were in no doubt that from now on great caution would be called for. While load carrying, even short stretches of thirty degree ice are not only tiring but very dangerous too; every foot gained is one down which the fragile human could slide and bounce and tumble at an unbelievable speed, and a high proportion of accidents which occur on Aconcagua stem from slips on moderately steep ice. Two more bodies seen at a distance were evidence of this; these were the Americans.

Ted, impatient as ever, took the lead in his jerky, turkey-strut manner, as if every step was dragged out of himself by a distinct mental effort rather than as part of a slow rhythm. That was his way, and he preferred to take slopes in very gentle zig-zags. Before long John S. resumed the lead and Ted took the gradient more gently than John.

'Stay in my steps, Ted!' John shouted at him in tight words tinged by tension. No wonder; I would not like to have taken on the extra burden of leading nine people on a mountain like this. To keep yourself going was more than enough for one man.

To our relief, within two hours we were finding our way up easy angled rock and scree, and looking for somewhere to pitch the tents.

'Wouldn't want to do any snow and ice harder than that without a rope,' Dan commented in his temporarily husky voice (he had a cold), and Paul said, 'I didn't like it but at least I really felt like I was climbing.'

The essential plod of getting poised to climb was over; nine days from the road to the glacier had earned us an attempt at the summit. Yet I was troubled; I had joined the expedition because Camp 3 was planned at 20,500 feet (6,250 m) and I estimated we were a long way below that, leaving too ambitious a summit day for me. The original intention of ascending 2,300 feet had been reasonable, but we were too low by several hundred feet. Or were we? There was no landmark from which to judge accurately. I made a half-hearted attempt, half-hearted because I was uncertain of our precise altitude and because I was reluctant to question his decision or appear to be complaining, to get John S. to go higher that day. If we were too low, we all deserved to share the blame, for we had surrendered to that awful sluggishness of high altitude which flooded over us after not much more than four hours on the go. We would all pay for it.

It fell to Dan and me to prepare dinner that evening, and breakfast the next day, so we were obliged to start the big day much earlier than everyone else. At 3.30 a.m. the cold was intense but we had to get started on melting the snow. One stove which had been working the day before did not want to start at first, and took half an hour to coax into action; two more hours went in melting sufficient snow for nine people. Our 6.30 a.m. departure was made in the last remaining minutes of that night's darkness.

Once our crampons were put on at the glacier's edge, five minutes away over steep scree, we roped ourselves together in three groups of three. I followed John and Mary and we set off in front, traversing from the right to the left across and up the glacier ice, at angles of up to forty-five degrees. To the sound of crampon rasp and ice axe clunk and heavy breathing we made reasonably good progress, drawing gradually ahead. It would have been easier and safer climbing straight up, using two ice axes, but we had to cross using one axe on the higher right side. (Or in my case, a crutch.) For an hour, two, three we traversed with the icy slope to the left, a constant reminder that tragedy could be just one slip away.

Moving across steep snow John hammered in three snowstakes, to which the rope was clipped for safety. I had used spiked crutches up to that point, but found it better to use an ice axe and one crutch on a particularly steep bulge of snow above a crevasse.

By 10 a.m. we were nearing a shoulder which marked the beginning of a very long snow ridge to the summit, and we sat to wait for the others.

Half an hour went by as we watched them creep in funeral procession across the slope. There was a delay when someone had trouble with their crampon straps, and then someone else lost a crampon, which was

recovered from further down the slope where it had come to rest fortui-
tously on rough ice. Somebody else came to a halt, leaning his head on
his ice axe buried to half its shaft length in the slope, and behind him a
figure moved slowly with very long pauses between steps. Paul and
Ramon looked like the only ones making progress without problems of
one form or another. Eventually the group came together.

'It's clear not everyone in this party can make it,' John said, and we
all talked over what we should do. What with the waiting and the
talking, three-quarters of an hour was irretrievably lost; the stove which
worked had cost at least half an hour, and the other which failed to
function had set us back a further hour. Whatever the cumulative
factors to delay us had been, it was plainly too late to launch out from
this point. Boiling clouds higher up revealed the presence of high winds.
We had bivouac equipment for only two people. Everything was
weighed, and we descended. (Later I read an Argentinian description
of the route, in which an extra higher camp was suggested; there is
something to be said for dividing the route in that way.)

John, Mary and Ramon had gone well, with Paul and me next in
line. However, when it was decided back at Camp 3 that four or five
people might try again next day, I agreed with John that the route was
too ambitious for me from this low camp. Therefore, I volunteered with
Dan to cook again and to get the water ready very early next day. The
plan was to be awake by 3 a.m., or earlier.

What a gloomy night it was; thoughts stirred in my head more than
I wanted. Two trips to Argentina had left me with the one-legged ascent
to about 17,000 feet, and Cerro Manso; an ascent, even by the normal
route, of Aconcagua in addition would have put quiet that feeling of
dissatisfaction which now bothered me. If only I could have had Aconcagua as well, I would have been overjoyed. The normal route and the
one-legged jaunt together would please me as much as the Polish route
on its own. If only, if only, if only ... Enormous disappointment was
crowding in. Now I would get up early to send four or five of the others
on their way, and I would sincerely wish them good luck, and whether
they succeeded or not we would go down; they would want to descend
as soon and as fast as they could, and John would do his best to see that
the whole group stayed together. What possible relief could there be
from this disappointment? I could think of nothing which could ease it.
The imminent end of the climbing season precluded an attempt on the
normal route in Miguel's company.

No one got up that night. I shared a tent with Dan and was unaware
of what went on in the other tents, but it was reasonable to assume that
the weather was unfavourable. With that thought in mind I drifted

back into sleep, and slept till late. Imagine my surprise when I learned that their failure to get up had nothing to do with bad weather but was a result of the lethargy of high altitude; I could hardly believe they had come all this way only to give up when the odds of success were a good deal better for a smaller party sent on its way earlier and minus the slower members. Vicissitudes were to be expected in this high and wild place, and when the mountain shunned you that need not prevent you trying again. Still, for everyone, there are days when motivation has been taxed too much; they had taken a beating, spiritually as well as physically, and some of them had been taken aback at how they managed.

'We still have the resources to get three or four or five people up,' I said to John. 'Somebody's got to go even if others have to sacrifice their chances.'

The last bit of what I said he looked upon as an admirable gesture of self-sacrifice on my part, and I had to put him right.

'After the first three or four candidates I want to be considered too, by lottery if necessary, for the last one or two places.'

John went to his tent to talk it over with some of the others. There had been, and still might be, a risk of the trip slipping from our grasp just when we should not be letting go.

An hour passed and John came to see Dan and me. Putting his hands around my throat he said, 'Now everybody wants to go!'

Even the Bambi-legged men of the day before wanted to join the attempt. Only Dan had decided against. He and I were melting snow a little later when John came back to our tent. 'Dan, if we were to traverse over to the normal route would you come too?'

'Sure.'

Here was the answer; the antidote to disappointment was at hand, if we succeeded. I would have been a little reluctant to attempt the normal route if not for our sortie up the Polish glacier, which had added some quality to the expedition; taken as a whole the trip was more interesting for that. Now we would go on a gradual rise over scree and snow to the right of the glacier, the way Dan's ruby-throated hummingbird had flown. Only three and a half hours of traversing rotten scree and snow patches and a snowfield led us to the highest mountain hut in the world, the tiny Independencia, set at about 21,300 feet (6,500 m). (There are several different estimates of the altitude in various accounts concerning Aconcagua.) This wooden, wedge-shaped building looks like a piece of cheese left there with the thin end pointing at the sky. It was about five feet high, and became known to us as the chicken coop. Three tents were put up, and I chose to sleep in the coop, where we cooked.

Todd was soon bent over a stove and shouting, 'Come on bitch!' He and Vladimir would share the extra burden of getting breakfast next day. I was pleased the second summit attempt would not begin that way for me, but as it transpired I did not get it easy on this eve of expectation or in the first hours of the next day; my water bottle, kept inside my sleeping bag to prevent freezing, leaked. One and a half pints of water distributed itself through the down filling, resulting in frequent awakenings and a lot of shivering, huddle, huddle, all night long. This was hardly the start I had hoped for to a very hard day.

Vladimir crawled into the chicken coop at 5.30 a.m. and cursed a troublesome stove.

Oatmeal cereal, bland, unwelcome and unappetising, but necessary. Away at 7.30 a.m. Weather: cloudy, low wind. Up easy snow to a slightly rising crest of snow and stones. A traverse on scree, and across an easy snowfield for 200 yards.

Soon our pace was broken by boulders, loose boulders which made us wary that one of our number might set one rolling on to someone else, so we tried not to get in line below anyone. We were in a gully which gave loose scrambling like some of the harder routes on British mountains, but the extra 20,000 feet made any further comparison meaningless. The steepest snow was only thirty degrees; it felt more like sixty, and demanded considerable effort from us all, making every step a little battle against inertia. Effort, effort, effort, effort.

Following a fifteen-minute halt at 11 a.m. John and I went ahead, with Ramon well in advance of us. The top of the gully was not far away and it was likely that from there we would see where we had to go. I feared we might be faced with a distant and high summit which would lead John to say we would have to turn back. Not so far away was a storm. Still, I was in no mood for turning back.

At 11.45 John was twenty feet ahead as we weaved between boulders lying on steep ground. He stopped, and said, 'Come up here and take a look.'

His voice had betrayed nothing, neither elation nor dismay, but as I scrambled towards him he gave me the obvious clue by saying, 'You deserve this. You've worked hard enough for it.' Unless he turned out to be a surprise sadist, the news was going to be good.

I reached him, to discover that the gully ran at a right angle into the ridge which linked Aconcagua's twin summits, with the higher north one to our left and the south to our right as we came up. The south summit looked more interesting, snowier, and showed us a fine ridge, but it was the bigger one we were after, the highest of all the Andes.

The north summit was a rock chunk which I estimated to be 300 feet above us.

'Be there in an hour,' John said.

I felt good, with a belly full of warm hope.

'I was worried it might be further away and a lot higher and I might have to say it was too far,' John said.

Progress was slow but inexorable. Ramon was soon waving at us from the summit, while John and I waited a hundred feet short vertically for the others to catch up. Paul was right behind me, Dan going well behind him, and forty minutes separated him from our tail-ender, Todd. He was just behind Ted and Vladimir. So with the exception of Ramon and John, who were in a class of their own, the early greyhounds were finding it hard.

We must beware of seeing that as a judgement, rather than as the observation it is intended to be.

At 1.15 p.m. we dawdled like a single file, exhausted army patrol and flopped down on the summit, a flat brown rock area bigger than a tennis court and almost free of snow, presumably because of high winds. We took photographs of each other alongside a two-foot high tubular alloy cross.

'Congratulations,' Ramon said to several of us in turn. 'Congratulations.'

'Pity John Perone's not here too,' I said.

The training ascent, three weeks to the day before, had paid off. At 22,834 feet (6,960 m), or 23,028 feet, (7,019 m), if you accept the altitude claimed by many Argentinian sources, we were all at the highest altitude we had reached.

I felt not pride, but a splendid surge of satisfaction. That dissatisfaction which just over a day before had seemed beyond relief was now banished. I had risked much again, not just life and limb, and had won; I had sought inner serenity, and found it. And the Polish glacier had added some 'bite' to the experience. The results of the two expeditions to Argentina added together were so precious, so much more than I could have hoped for.

If ever the summits give me only a sense of relief from suffering, and permission to go down, without some feeling also of a sense of purpose, they I shall stop climbing. It is not a question of trying to prove anything; that time is long past, if indeed it ever existed. But there must be more to it than just a cessation of the physical and mental suffering brought about by pushing my limits to such an extreme that I need no coach to goad or encourage me further. I could think of Aconcagua and other ascents again and again and again, bringing them to mind at any time to relish the thoughts, fanning embers into flame as a never-ending source of spiritual warmth.

Twenty minutes on the summit of the lofty mountain seemed like no time at all.

'Touch it and get back down,' Todd had said, but like the rest of us he could not resist a break.

The storm which had been approaching enveloped us within minutes of our leaving the summit. Loose rocks rapidly became slippery too, plastered by an inch of snow. Now our minds turned more to survival than success; the summit was behind, courted, won, and abandoned. Reaching the uppermost snowfield we went silently down midst the dead cloth sounds of a place of snow. Fortunately, the wind did not rise much; for an hour and a half snow feathered down but visibility was always satisfactory and we had all retraced our steps to the chicken coop within plus or minus fifteen minutes of 4.15 p.m. And there we slumped.

Dan had several fingers frostbitten, and Ted and Ramon each had one finger affected; none of their injuries was serious.

Todd melted a little snow for us, but I was concerned that everyone should get more liquid inside them; lying inside the chicken coop I had plenty, for no one else came to get it and I drank a lot before it refroze. I called out that I would make some soup, or cook something more substantial if one person came to help but there were no takers. That was the measure of how tired everyone was. For a while the screech of argument sounded between tents, about someone neglecting to cook, I believe, and then everyone was asleep before dark. I would have made the effort to cook had the task been mine that day, because others had bothered when the going was not easy. But we were at the edges of exhaustion, and those who ate made do with a few nuts and 'candies'. It would be downhill all the way now, so this was not as serious as it might have been.

John was eager to get down and we did not melt any snow prior to departure next morning. During a grumbling, swearing, squabbling-like-starlings, muttering descent Ted had to stop to 'go to the bathroom' and Todd told him to hurry up, saying, 'This weather could kill us,' and 'Hey, man, we're all hurting.' The weather was intermittently quite bad, and everyone was tired and a bit anxious, and most of all keen to get off the mountain.

At Camp 2 Todd got the stove going in the early afternoon and we experienced the delight of quenching intense thirst simply with water. The finest wine in the world could not have given more pleasure. At Camp 1 a couple of hours down Ramon cooked a meal, and everyone but Paul and I hurried down to base camp, where they arrived in darkness. My stumps had grown extremely painful, most likely through the cumulative effects of several days on the go. When Paul got home he had infectious hepatitis, a disease which he might already have contracted at this stage, which would account for his feeling unwell.

After a good night's rest Paul and I descended to base camp, met up with the others, and went down the same day to the junction of Relinchos and Vacas valleys. My stumps felt even more painful, causing me to go slowly. Soon most of the others were just scurrying, coloured dots, mostly red and blue, and as the powerful words 'going home' drew them down they became black dots and then were too far away to be seen. The two Johns waited for me and accompanied me over the steep, loose and dangerous river banks; I was grateful for that, particularly because John P. had more reason than the rest of us to want to desert the mountain as fast as he could. He remained in good spirits and came out with a joke worthy of a mass groan when someone called out from a tent, 'Is it chilly outside?'

'No, it's Argentina you fool.'

Though I wished to go home too, I did not feel like many of the others, who resembled fugitives fleeing a plague area; no, I liked just to be there, and to look back and savour it all.

Next day the two Johns, Todd, Ted and Dan waited until I had completed the more dangerous section of the trail before all but John S. headed off quickly to the road. I did not like holding them up, but it could not be avoided; the stumps had had enough punishment, and now in the heat they let me know it. In the final stages I was so slow John S. went ahead several times to drop his rucksack and come back to take mine. It was an ignominious end to a highly satisfactory adventure, but I took comfort from the knowledge that I managed worst where speed was of no consequence.

Almost three days to get from Camp 1 down to the road. Pain was no stranger to me, and it was tough going, as ever when I covered long distances. This time will pass, was all I could tell myself; no, there was something else I could say, that it was worth it. Everyone felt the last stretch to be 'endless', but they could not have experienced the same enormous degree of relief which I did at the sight of the trees at the end of the valley. They waved in the wind like friends, and signalled, 'Here it all ends.'

Fernando waited with his pickup, and hugged me the way they do there, before driving the few miles back. We stank, of course, after all that time without a wash. Now we were back in civilisation the shower was a great attraction. We ate beef and salad at Fernando's, and drank beer and wine. We were bound together like other parties I had seen there, and we succeeded in capturing the sometimes elusive joy of life.

I bade goodbye to my new-found friends from the expedition, who travelled together to Santiago; I caught a bus to Mendoza and there was received warmly by the Sanchez family. I had for them a few small gifts and one of these, described by a stallholder as a mineral found high on a mountain near Aconcagua, caused an upset. I had given it to Mama, who proudly displayed it on a sideboard, when a heart surgeon friend of the family came to visit and Mama told him that the mineral came from a mountain.

'I think it came from a factory,' he said, and Mama looked close to tears. The substance may have been silicium, but I could not be sure, and a minute later it was pushed surreptitiously to the back of the sideboard, behind a framed picture. There was worse to follow, when one of the sons took a look at the mineral, which fell to bits as he handled it! I looked up the words for 'drop a bomb on the stall' and said them, and Mama laughed again. And next day some artificial flowers put matters completely right.

The surgeon had been to the Himalayas with an Argentinian expedition, and was interested in the exploits of others. He invited us across the street to his home for champagne with his family, so at about 11 p.m. we all trooped across there. He examined one of my fingers, affected by frostbite, and the lack of seriousness of the damage was summed up in the levity of his advice, which was, 'Three times a day dip it in a glass of wine. Then drink the wine.'

We returned to the Sanchez home at 1 a.m. and in the night-owl fashion of that country two more friends came to visit. It was one of those warm homes where friends and neighbours dropped in all the time.

Several letters from Judy had arrived while I was on Aconcagua. One told me that Sir Christopher Aston, who had worked extremely hard as the voluntary Chairman of the International Year of Disabled People, in England, had died of cancer. He had helped me to get to Argentina by arranging for a very generous grant from the Charities Aid Foundation to be used partly towards the various forms of work I did with disabled people and partly towards expeditions. He had died very shortly after I arrived in Argentina.

In Buenos Aires, Hector was genuinely pleased with my success. He invited some friends around and cooked asado, and a radio ham friend of his got me to talk to a lady in Colombia who wanted to hear about the climb. Later, hams called up from Canada, Antigua and Equador to send their congratulations.

Out of courtesy to the local people in Argentina, especially to those who had helped, I did an interview with a Mendoza journalist. At home I got away without any interviews; I was put off by inaccuracies, wrong interpretations and exaggeration, and on this occasion I was not promoting any charity so no one would derive any benefit from publicity. (Once a magazine credited me with an ascent of a peak of 50,000 feet in the Alps; Everest reaches a height of 29,000 feet. At the other end of the scale, after getting up one high mountain I was reported as having climbed to a summit of twenty-two feet!) Judy and I liked the feeling of keeping the climbing private; yet there was an uncomfortable reservation that this was selfish, for many people had contributed in various ways and over many years towards this success. They deserved the story too. I have never entirely come to terms with publicity, for I vacillate between tolerance and dislike, qualified by the knowledge that sometimes publicity can be usefully employed to someone else's benefit. Some years back there is no doubt I found a small bit of publicity to be exciting, but that feeling wore off. Even in those early days I regarded publicity as incidental, and I would never seek it.

Were it not for events originating from outside the narrow world of climbing, this sequel to my one-legged ascent would have been perfect. But about two weeks after I arrived home, Argentina's troops invaded the Falkland Islands. (There had been a lot of talk about the Islands this year, and the threat of invasion had been high, obviously.) Clearly, staying there was likely to lead to heavy bloodshed, and stay they did. We all know about the tragic loss of life and injuries which followed. But the issues were complicated and this is not the place for what could be no more than a cursory examination of the rights and wrongs.

The last word, almost, I leave to John Perone, who wrote to me and sent two photographs, one of Ted and me, the other of me on my own.

'I have enclosed two photos. One is the two ugliest people I have ever seen. The second is the ugliest person on earth. Hope someday we can climb together again. Keep in touch.'

People, places and the accomplishment of dreams. I was very, very fortunate. Life would not be frittered away on the mountains, it would be well spent; events had proved this to be so once more.

8

Muztagh Ata, China
24,757 feet

An American expedition led by John Cleare, an English photographer and mountaineer, was heading for Muztagh Ata in China in July and August 1982, so I wrote to see if I could be accepted, and received a favourable reply.

My opinion on publicity needed some revision, for a consultant to the Sony (UK) electronics organisation read a newspaper article about the International Year of Disabled People, noticed therein that I was hoping to climb Muztagh Ata, and suggested that Sony might come up with sponsorship. But first he wanted to meet and talk about the expedition in more detail. After a brief telephone conversation with him, I headed hastily to his office near the London Palladium. Being eager and twenty minutes early for our appointment, I waited in the Dog and Trumpet, and there a lavatory door jammed, leaving me hammering to attract rescue. The upshot was that I was late for the appointment, but this was not held against me and the interview went as I hoped it would. Shortly afterwards a cheque for over £4,000 arrived; this was sufficient to pay the high cost of my participation in the expedition. Various costly elements, of the order of a pound per kilometre for lorry transport, about £600 to insure a liaison officer and an interpreter, and long air flights within China, resulted in expenses being five times those of a similar venture in Nepal. Yet, despite my gratitude, it was only fair that I pointed out that I would not allow sponsorship to influence my mountaineering judgement; I would not climb one foot higher than I would have if I had paid for it all myself.

John Cleare did have some misgivings about my being on the trip, mostly because there were long distances to be covered on soft snow; we would need to ski, or accept a higher risk of failure through being on foot. Even for able-bodied people the walking option was considered gruelling; in 1947 Tilman and Shipton failed to make the summit on foot, and if two hard and proven expeditioners like them had failed, what chance did I have? In *Two Mountains and a River*, Tilman tells of the snow's 'vile consistency' and says that long hours of cold and fatigue led to their giving up. From his account they had not paid great attention to acclimatisation, either. Five earlier expeditions had failed on foot. John wanted everyone on his expedition to use skis and he was worried about my lack of experience in this respect. However, he was straight with me and was prepared to be flexible and to treat me as a special case who would work out his own best methods. For ascent, everyone else would have skins on their skis. Originally made from animal fur but nowadays artificial, skins grip the snow very effectively and prevent backward sliding, and the pile lies in such a way that the skis slide easily forward.

In order to augment my meagre skiing experience prior to the expedition, I went to the Dachstein glacier in Austria, in July 1982. Here one can ski year-round at about 9,000 feet. On a pair of hired skis I set off on the twisting cross-country track, and I learned quickly. What I learned I did not like, for it was soon evident that though on uphill slopes and on the level I could cope, going downhill was a different and wobbly matter. Downhill skiing on one real leg, assisted by small outrigger skis fixed to crutches, is easier than most people believe, but for the double leg amputee it is another matter. The single leg amputee discards the artificial limb and relies on the good leg but, obviously enough, if you have two artificial legs you can't follow suit. It is not a question of lack of determination. I reached the conclusion that after a great deal of training over many months or years a double leg amputee might cope on gentle to moderate slopes, but the risk of injury from downhill skiing on high mountains would be far too great, and the consequences of injury were likely to be dire. Also, the victim might not be the only one to suffer, for companions might be forced to take extra risks and fail on their climb through having to divert their energies to a rescue. Even on the way up Muztagh Ata there would be much traversing to be done above cliffs and crevasses, perhaps on ice, and skiing competence was essential; no, I could not justify going on skis. So was this a reason why I should not join the expedition? Perhaps, but there might be a solution: how about snowshoes for ascent and a sledge made from skis and a rucksack frame for descent? I made a sledge and further strengthened the contraption with a crutch tied across as a strut and footrest, and from 200 feet up a slope which was beyond my skiing ability I launched myself off. I picked up speed very rapidly and dug my ice axe in the snow as an effective brake. It seemed a better method for me, but I knew the proof of the pudding could only be in the eating, on the mountain, under expedition conditions.

*   *   *

Nearly twenty-four hours of air travel put us on 23 July 1982 in China's capital, Peking (known also as Beijing). The concrete buildings of the airport might have been any modern airport anywhere in the world, and we went through the typical sausage-machine of baggage reclaim carousels, immigration and customs. Then John held up a card bearing characters saying Chinese Mountaineering Association (was he holding it upside-down, we wondered?) and their two representatives stepped forward and greeted us. They had laid on transport for the one-hour drive into the city, the first of many acts which cocooned us in this land where lack of the language could have been a great bother. The rest of the team, nine of them, arrived two days later, and we were all taken under the wing of the Chinese Mountaineering Association, who provided an interpreter and a liaison officer, and made hotel and transport arrangements for us, amongst many other things.

Our accommodation was always satisfactory, in large and comfortably furnished, air-conditioned rooms, usually with a settee, armchairs, two or four beds, a table or desk, and always there was a big, brightly-painted thermos flask of hot water, cups, and a tin of tea leaves. Though knives and forks were available in dining-rooms, we mastered the use of chopsticks to tuck into course after course of fish, mutton, kebabs, duck and many cold meats, nuts, mushrooms, boiled eggs, fried cabbage, egg plant, bamboo shoots, rice, peppers, green beans, steamed bread and lobster. There was no shortage of beer, and most meals were rounded off with melon.

What we saw in and around Peking accorded with photographs and descriptions, as if the country had been showered with traditional symbols of Chinese style: straw hats and sunflowers, pony carts of melons, sedate cyclists on three and a half million seemingly identical black bicycles for a city population not greatly in excess of twice that number, (in Holland there is one bicycle per eleven people and in Britain the ratio is about one to thirty-three); brown, blue and grey trousers and jackets, but bright skirts and dresses too, paddy fields, tall, straight trees, pagodas, chopsticks, rice and noodles and hundreds of varieties of food, modern and simple four-to-ten-storey apartment blocks, wooden scaffolding, a few packed buses, many drab green lorries, the red star, portraits of Chairman Mao, posters exhorting good behaviour and very small families, and even some advertising consumer goods such as radios and television sets. People are placid and civil, and, as everyone knows, there are lots of people. Yet Peking has none of the teeming feel of many cities because the streets are wide and there are few cars, and though China's enormous total of about one thousand million souls amounts to one quarter of the Earth's population they do have the third biggest country in which to spread out. I've heard tales of overcrowded homes and poverty but saw no evidence of this myself. Standards of living are clearly much lower than in the western world, but there seemed to be no slum areas like those in India or Peru. My short stay in civilised areas was sufficient to give me only a cursory impression, however, and leaves me unable to comment in any depth on life in China. Prices everywhere are fixed, so there is no haggling, nor any tipping in restaurants or elsewhere, as this practice is looked upon as corrupt, and close to what we term bribery.

Anyone who travelled from the USA or Britain to Peking without visiting the Great Wall would be regarded locally as somewhat weird, even rude, and the Chinese Mountaineering Association had left time in our itinerary for a visit. Built two centuries before the birth of Christ (sections were constructed as early as 770 BC) the 3,600-mile (5,800 km) construction stands about twenty-six feet (7.9 m) high and nineteen feet (5.8 m) wide at the top. Its purpose was to keep out nomadic marauders from the north but the Wall was not entirely effective since no height could prevent bribery of guards. We were not disappointed with what we saw; when you remember the length of the Wall, rising and dipping and weaving over green mountains (I pictured it as four times the distance I walked from John O'Groats to Land's End) it is impossible not to be impressed.

There was time, too, to see the Imperial Palace, known commonly to Westerners as the Forbidden City because ordinary people were not formerly permitted entry. Graceful names themselves convey something of the elegance of the great buildings there: Gate of Supreme Harmony, Palace of Heavenly Purity, Palace of Earthly Tranquillity, Gate of Divine Prowess.

But we were here to climb. Peking airport, from which we flew westwards on 27 July, had recently witnessed its first hijacking, perpetrated by four men armed with knives. Their cause I do not know, but they were overpowered by angry passengers on the 'plane, and a few weeks later were executed.

Our progress westwards took place on two consecutive days on two flights of about three hours each, the first in a jet and the next in a rattling twin-engined prop 'plane, over brown desert. On the second flight the air-conditioning system was simple: everyone was given a fan. Between flights at the city of Urumchi, at the airport we happened to meet some of an expedition of eleven Austrians who had attempted Muztagh Ata by a route which was a little easier than our proposed line. Three of them (or was it five, as stated in a later newspaper report?) had reached the top, and several had been halted by the altitude. One had become very ill and was in hospital. The Austrians were not the only expeditioners we met at the oasis, factory city of Urumchi, for we also came across an unfortunate group of rafters who had come all the way from the USA to discover that the river they intended descending was dry!

The second flight brought us to ancient Kashgar city, by which time we had flown about 2,250 miles (c. 3,620 km) from Peking back towards England; John and I had back-tracked almost the width of this huge country and our companions from the USA had completed a journey almost half-way round the world. We stepped from the aircraft into a hot early afternoon in a land which in some ways seemed a thousand years behind the times. Adults and children in Muslim dress rode two-wheeled carts drawn by diminutive yet strong and resigned-looking donkeys, between mud-walled houses set along irrigation ditches lined by poplar. In other ways progress had touched the place, bringing in good roads and a few motor vehicles, including tractors, lots of bicycles and concrete buildings.

Casual tourists are not permitted in Kashgar, so our rare-bird presence created great interest amongst the local inhabitants. They clustered around in polite, curious, smiling hundreds whenever we stopped in the city. Whether we were in a vehicle or not, we were mobbed in a respectful, orderly way as knots of where-the-hell-did-all-these-people-appear-from? spectators grew tight and vast. Yet when we were on foot they never pushed in on us, and our eager audience would swarm around, a step or two away, as we rich strangers moved. When in our stationary minibus there was a slightly menacing undercurrent as dozens of faces were pressed to the windows, like we were Martians on display in a glass cage and they were not entirely sure of us. Nor we of them.

We toured the city in a minibus which was driven in the customary horn-blaring fashion of all vehicles there. Cyclists, pedestrians and donkey-cart drivers took no notice, because the horns are always blaring, but we never came across a driver who saw the ineffectiveness of the method as any reason to desist. The abject poverty of India is absent, and the place looked quite well-off as far as the basic necessities of life are concerned. There was no shortage of vegetables, fruit, grains, bread, cakes, spices, cloth, shoes, boots, lamps, knives and other ironmongery, and there was quite a lot of meat available. Most of the trading took place from the shelter of little roadside and marketplace stalls; and scribes sat outside the post office to assist those who could not write, or who could not cope with Chinese characters. There was less of the uniform Chinese dress in evidence, for the Kirghiz and Uighur people there have retained traditional dress of bright skirts and blouses and headscarves for the women, and more sombre trousers, jackets and shirts for men. In Kashgar, as in Urumchi, our accommodation consisted of guest house rooms inside a compound, and meals were always rich and satisfying. Bathrooms were shared with local residents: large frogs which hopped around the floors.

From Kashgar we set off on an early-morning chartered bus ride to try our fortunes on Muztagh Ata. The gravel road soon left behind the trees, mud buildings and sunflowers, and took us out into flat desert spotted with occasional oases, before running us along parallel to and in sight of the Silk Road. This formerly important trade route stretched about 4,350 miles (7,000 km) from eastern China to the Mediterranean and was used to transport the products of silkworm cocoons to Greece before the birth of Christ.

For hours we bumped up a deep canyon road, where gangs of men and women worked to counter the ravages of sliding rubble, rockfall and river. A hundred and more miles and nine hours went by, and rock walls, rock walls, rock walls, and high snowy peaks, and a huge, shallow, silted lake surrounded by sand dunes, in a broad valley. We were drowsy from the heat. Then someone shouted. 'There she is!'

Our view across flat green pastures was of a massive domed mountain with a benign appearance, but no mountain of close to 25,000 feet – Muztagh Ata is 24,757 feet high – can be climbed easily, as we were to discover. For all of us, bar John, this would be the highest summit we had attempted, and it was nearly 2,000 feet higher than Aconcagua. Soft snow and altitude would make it hard, crevasses and bad weather and altitude sickness would be the biggest risks.

We drove on for a while and pitched camp on a meadow at 12,500 feet, in sight of Muztagh Ata, the Ice Mountain Father. The full name is probably incorrect, as it is likely that the mountain was known simply as Muztagh, or Ice Mountain. The longer name is said to have originated when an explorer asked a local resident the name of this lofty peak and was told, 'Muztagh Ata,' the 'Ata', or 'Father', being appended as a term of respect to the explorer himself. But he got it wrong in his account so from shortly before the twentieth century the wrong name was reported, and perpetuated in subsequent documents. The mountain's isolation in treeless grassland succeeded by almost barren foothills made it look huge, as indeed it was, and it appeared every bit as awesome as Kongur, twenty-five miles away and 568 feet (173 m) higher.

Several dozen Kirghiz people lived locally in tents and rectangular flat-roofed, mud-brick houses in the vicinity of two large lakes, the Karakol Lakes. Large audiences congregated to watch us.

164

On the evening of our first full day at the meadow camp, a day occupied with sorting and packing food and equipment, the leader of a five-man expedition from Colorado appeared with his interpreter. They were attempting Muztagh Ata.

'Got two missing,' he said. 'They went for the summit three days ago. Should have got back the same day.'

Being unacclimatised, there was nothing we could do but offer qualified optimism and sympathy, some food and beer, before the two men went on their way in a truck flagged down on the nearby road. They would report what had happened, to the authorities. They had talked of hiring a 'plane for a search, and someone had voiced our scepticism about the possibility and practicality of such a proposal in this remote corner of China. It would have been preferable for at least two of them to have remained high and searched, weather and rations permitting, but the altitude really had drained them and I could to some extent understand how they felt. Next day we met the remainder of their expedition and learned that one of the missing pair had turned up, with considerable frostbite injuries after two bivouacs. The companion who had reached the summit with him, he said, had disappeared in bad visibility on the descent, and was presumed to have fallen over a cliff or into a crevasse. They achieved two out of five on the summit and lost one of them. So much for Muztagh Ata's benign look; it was just like any other big mountain. From a diary we found later it was clear that on setting up a camp at 21,000 feet the Coloradans had not been in good shape physically, and in consequence their morale was low. Three of the five said they could not go on, and two made the questionable decision to try to climb 4,000 feet to the summit in one push. In the Alps that height gain is commonly made in a day, but there are few climbers who can manage it safely above 20,000 feet, and they should be acclimatised and feel strong before setting out.

A week later, back at home in the flat we had bought recently (a nice place which Judy loved and had waited for a long time) someone told her about a newspaper report concerning a man who had died on Muztagh Ata. His age was put at forty-one years, which was my age, and though the name reported was not mine she had a slight nagging doubt that the name was wrong. I had always impressed on her that she should not put too much trust in newspaper versions concerned with climbing, and that it was highly improbable that any newspaper would fail to mention my lack of legs if an accident befell me. Though she knew this to be true the death report reminded her that we were undertaking a serious venture. She had three worrying weeks to face.

On 2 August we laid out our luggage before sixteen ruminant, reeking, twin-humped Bactrian camels which continued grazing from a kneeling position while loading went on. A wide-nostrilled, looking-down-the-nose attitude gave them a haughty appearance. After loading, they ambled a sure-footed way through areas of grass, then dusty sand, then rocky slopes, to our base camp at 14,500 feet (4,440 m). The beasts groaned and snorted and squeaked complaints, but went obediently where they were led; small wonder, for each had a piece of rope attached to a hole in the nose and tied to the camel in front or held by the man at the head of a three or four camel column. Capable of carrying over 300 pounds (135 kg) each, they were a valuable link in the chain intended to get us to the summit, and saved us several days of carrying.

We settled in a grassy, stony depression by a stream, at the foot of the west flank of Muztagh Ata. In a day we could have walked into the USSR. Fourteen black or black and white yaks grazed quietly there by our camp. Yak: 'Long-haired humped grunting ox' says one dictionary descriptively. Tilman and Shipton planned to use one such animal to carry equipment and food to base camp, and Tilman extolled their virtues at some length; he even listed as an advantage the fact that the yak's short legs and rapid steps give the rider the comfortable though false impression of getting somewhere quickly! He went on to say that their particular animal must have been the exception which proved the rule, or like all mountaineers yaks have their off days, for he 'very sensibly struck and sat down at the very first hint of what was expected of him.'

One other animal inhabited the environs of the camp, a shaggy, black-coated sheep which had walked up with the camels. Like another of its kind which had gone the same way a day or two earlier, it was destined for the stewpot; at least, that's what we thought, but the creature had other ideas, got loose from its tether, and escaped for ever in land where the grazing was good.

After the first six failed attempts on Muztagh Ata, a combined Russian and Chinese expedition made the first ascent in 1956. The second success went to the Chinese in 1960, and one of the participants in it was Mr Qui Yin-Hua, who later joined a successful Everest expedition; he was our liaison officer. Mr Qui had no toes as a result of his climb on Everest, but gave the impression that he felt he had received good value in exchange for his extremities. Since the Chinese ascent Muztagh Ata had received no more human attentions until an American ascent in 1980, when foreign climbers were permitted into the area for the first time since 1949. In 1981 two expeditions, one American and one Canadian, put members on the top, and the Austrians I mentioned had three (or five) there. No Briton had succeeded.

The performances of the Austrians and the Coloradans had influenced our thinking and brought about a revision of our opinion of the mountain. It was not going to be as easy as the earlier American and Canadian reports had portrayed, and the sense of John's plan to have four camps above base had been reinforced by what we had heard recently. The trend is towards alpine-style ascents in which climbers do not follow the up-and-down, up-and-down pattern of establishing camps at intervals, but instead carry everything and gain altitude without ever dropping back. There is a lot to be said for this approach of breaking new ground every day, but on a very big peak it may allow insufficient time for acclimatisation. Storms rage in climbing teacups about the two methods; there need be no bitter argument for the different philosophies of style can co-exist. On our first evening at base camp John emphasised that to put just one person on top was success; that was not what most of us had in mind, for each carried strong summit ambitions in his or her heart.

Next day. We must carry to Camp 1. Loads had been prepared the night before. My load, a tent, food and skis. Straight forward going on a steep slope of stones and dirt, but oh, the altitude! And the sun sucking the liquid out of us. Janet Jensen, one of the two women on the trip, carried on for a long time despite frequent vomiting, but was eventually persuaded to turn back. The rest of us dumped our loads as planned at 16,700 feet (5,100 m), after a climb of between three and four hours, then set about laying out flat stones in a crazy paving base for tents. With a couple of tents up, we scurried down to base to eat and relax. The early days are hard at altitude; then it gets worse as you go higher.

Next day was similar: the haul amidst small five-petalled flowers like primroses, others that might have been buttercups, then the pull up loose dirt and stones. Three carries to Camp 1 were required, but vomiting and stomach pains and back pains and diarrhoea disqualified me from the third. This was worrying because we were due to go up and occupy Camp 1 that day. From there the others would make three more excursions upwards, the last of these to occupy Camp 2. Two or three days of sickness could leave me weakened and, worse, I would fall behind in our acclimatisation programme. Our interpreter, Mr Su, fell ill too with a similar ailment to mine. He was a tall, slim and remarkable man aged thirty who, wishing to visit Urumchi from his home in Hanchow, had decided to equip his bicycle with a large water container and pedal his way there. The fact that he had over 3,000 miles to cover did not deter him, and in fifty-seven days he cycled across fertile plain and desert to Urumchi. There he soon found himself employment as an English interpreter with the Chinese Mountaineering Association, and this in itself was no mean feat because, during the cultural Revolution, he had been sentenced to 'primitive work' rather than study and his English was largely self-taught. He'd climbed his form of mountains against the odds, and we could not fail to respect this man. As well as the liaison officer and interpreter, the Chinese Mountaineering Association provided us with a cook for base camp.

The three Chinese personnel at base camp looked after me solicitously for two days. I dozed a lot, and dreamed that I had gone home for a rest and only when there did I realise that I could not travel back in time to join the others. The dream felt so real and the feeling of panic and disappointment hung over me when I awoke because in truth my chances were shrinking while the illness lasted. Two days with hardly any food was poor preparation for what might lie ahead.

Two days saw me right, and Mr Su insisted on coming with me to Camp I to carry my crampons, sleeping bag and water bottles. We had been going for an hour when a figure appeared on the skyline. It picked its way down the stones and turned into Don Brown, a doctor, our oldest member at the age of sixty-four, and still very fit. Within the previous few years he had climbed Aconcagua and Mt McKinley. Don was the only other person trying the mountain on snowshoes, and he had some devastating news for me.

'It's no good. It can't be done on snowshoes.'

'Why's that?'

'You just slip back on the slopes. It's too steep and too soft.'

'Good gracious me, what a shame,' I said – or words to that effect.

I stood on the stone slope with Don just three or four feet above as the news sank in, and I remembered that his snowshoes covered twice the area mine did and were therefore much more efficient. The Coloradan leader's verdict had been that it was virtually impossible without skis, owing to the soft going. After getting on the expedition and receiving Sony's generous sponsorship I was going to look silly, because I had been too ambitious. Any mountain of this altitude would force failure on to a large proportion of experienced, able-bodied climbers, and I was going to finish up with egg foo yong on my face because I had not researched the route sufficiently and had not paid enough attention to how I might get up the soft snows. Hope had been allowed to lead, where soundly based experience should have been my guide. Don had made a mistake too, or had been given the wrong guidance, had recognised this, and had reached his decision: he was going home.

My conduct was different because I wanted to salvage anything I could from this personal fiasco. I would at least carry as much as I could as high as possible, and share a little of the victory of anyone who reached our objective. So I headed up to Camp 1 and soon met another descending figure, this time a haggard Ted Mayer, with whom I had climbed Aconcagua earlier in the year. He was ill and was therefore descending to base camp, and it sounded like he had the same bug as I had had. He told us that of ten people who had set out the day before from Camp 1 to Camp 2 at 19,100 feet only six had made the full distance. The others had to leave their loads part way. (So what chance was there for me? I couldn't help wondering.) At base camp Ted became so ill he was unable to ingest even water, so Don put him on an intravenous drip.

At Camp 1 the others descended from their second carry to Camp 2. The following day they would occupy that camp, but I agreed with John that it would be premature for me to stay there because I would be gaining altitude too quickly and risking altitude sickness. After carrying next day I would have to return to sleep at Camp 1 before carrying again the next day. 'To be quite honest,' John said, 'if you get to Camp 2 I don't think you'll get any further.'

He was not being unnecessarily negative. He had seen what was ahead. John had supported my case for an attempt at the mountain even in the face of someone who had failed the year before and who had on the basis of that experience maintained it was absolutely beyond me. When I first planned to climb in the Alps, John had written me a very encouraging letter, and I knew he had an open mind.

It looked bad for me, but hope was not entirely extinguished. If the snow froze hard enough during the night and I started very early and reached Camp 2, I might still be in the running. I had been ill and was less well acclimatised and the ascent of the next 2,400 feet (730 m) had stopped four out of ten of them, including the only one on snowshoes, but if I did not make a good showing on the next carry it was clear that my hopes could be extinguished altogether.

Now I was committed to snowshoes because I had left my ski boots at base camp. Without them it was not possible to wear the skis, and I could not afford another day descending and re-ascending to and from base.

A three-quarter moon lit the chilly way and I was off two hours of more before the others. China has no times zones, just the same time throughout the whole vast country, but making an allowance of two and a half hours for our being so far west of Peking my departure was at the equivalent of 4 a.m. The early start up a rib of small, sharp rocks got me at dawn on to easy-angled ice where crampons were necessary; firm snow slopes followed. There was no more rock between here and the summit. By 10 a.m. the first sliver of sunlight flashed over the mountain which stood ahead of me; the orb appeared rapidly to banish blue shadows and soften the snow. Sun, you're softening *my* snow. Go and put on a cloak of cloud, there's a good sun.

An hour later I was sinking to the knee and forced to resort to the showshoes. With them strapped on all went well for a few minutes on level snow, and then came a gentle slope of thirty degrees. I went at it, but the front edges of the snowshoes broke through the crust and I floundered again at knee depth. The baskets (rounds, like those on ski sticks) on my crutches sank a foot, two feet, sometimes so deep that my hands were buried in the snow. Many a time a step up resulted in collapsed snow and I would drop back to where I had been. Don said it was impossible; for twenty minutes I fought to rise forty feet and I knew that at that rate I would have to give up and accept what he had said. On top of that, *if* I reached Camp 2 John doubted I would manage what followed. Was it worth this unequal struggle?

I stumbled on, up to the knees in snow, and dragged the big feet out, and went in up to the wrists and sank occasionally to the top of one thigh and battled to get that damned leg out and then went in to crotch level on both legs. Oh for a rock ridge or face, quite steep, so effort would be rewarded with height gain! Oh for some ice! When the crutches were laid parallel to the snow like they were skis they did not sink so deep, no more than a foot, and that helped a little, but the altitude would not let me fight all the way up in conditions like these. I was virtually crawling much of the time and that rate of progress was out of the question and in any case this would lead to frostbitten fingers. It was not the sort of thing that fighting could overcome; no amount of determination would bring success, unless I risked stepping from the firm land of judgement into the mire of foolhardiness. Only a man who could walk on water had any chance here without skis. It would be grossly wrong to jeopardise the lives of the others by becoming an exhausted, frostbitten, altitude sick casualty requiring rescue, and even if rescue proved safe it would be selfish to risk adversely affecting their chances of success.

Despair was close upon me, but had not yet seized an unbreakable hold. Try taking the slope at a gentler angle, I suggested to myself, and started on the first zig of what I hoped might be a lengthy series of zig-zags. The snowshoes sank only half as deeply. Oh joy! For the time being I could carry on. Soon the slope eased off to almost level ground and the snow became firm in most places.

There was a crevassed area which could not be avoided because the crevasses came in from the right towards a rock cliff falling away for 2,000 feet on the left, and I had to go up a snow ramp in between. This ramp not only sloped down towards me, but was also canted down from right to left, from crevasses towards cliff. The latter gradient was such that anyone who slipped might slide over the cliff edge. Where the ramp narrowed to a hundred feet between the crevasses and the cliff, some of the skiers had been quite scared, particularly on descent.

It was a true Scylla and Charybdis. The higher one went up the right side of the ramp, the greater the crevasse danger. Reducing the crevasse problems involved keeping closer to the big drop; my choice was to keep quite low there and trust to the ice axe pick on one crutch to brake me if I slipped. In some places it would have been preferable to wear crampons, for there were intermittent patches of ice or hard snow, but mostly it was so porridgy or fluffy that snowshoes reduced the possibility of breaking through into crevasses, of which there were some even low down the ramp near the cliff. Before venturing further I consciously rehearsed in my mind what I would do to hurl the pick into the snow or ice if I slipped: an unarrested slide would have me over the edge in five seconds. A high level of desire for the objective pushed fear to a great extent, to the back of my mind.

Spikes on my crutches gave considerable security and as long as I kept my eyes open the crevasses did not seem to be too much of a menace. By looking up the ramp rightwards, often I could see where the wider part of the split in the ice showed, being too wide to be bridged by snow, and this gave a clue to the line. On the lower side there was sometimes evidence of the horrible hole in the form of a slight concave trough in the snow. Seven or eight crevasses which were big enough to be dangerous were identified and I went further down towards the cliff to avoid them, or prodded with the crutches and found a firm place to cross, or took a big step-cum-leap across.

In fifteen minutes the snow ramp took me up to where I could rise rightwards and away from the cliff, and the crevasse hazards grew less. Having been going for seven hours I needed to get to Camp 2 soon in order to leave myself enough energy for the descent. Crevasses would be less well bridged then because of the sun's work, and I did not want to go doddering down in a weary state. My pace was falling rapidly through prolonged exertion at such an altitude. Several people had said the trudge to Camp 2 was exhausting, and indeed four had not completed the distance at the first try, so I had a very real fear that I might spot the camp at such a distance that a retreat was the only way. However, I topped a rise and there were the two tents, only fifteen minutes away. I knew then a slender chance still existed that I would go for the top.

Colin and Bob, two doctors who had teamed up and climbed together, arrived at Camp 2 shortly after me. I got the impression that they were very aware of the threat which hangs over all doctors on expeditions: that their chances might be destroyed if they had to attend to a patient over a prolonged period.

Having constructed my sledge I started down, meeting Steve McKinney, the deputy leader, then John, then Grim, Johan and Mary, toiling under huge loads in the heat of the day. Grim, whose real name was Jim Wilson, was a forty-four year old psychology and economics teacher, tall and very strong on his quite spindly legs. He proved to be a reliable and considerate companion, and his good manners caused him to draw apart if others of us became too riotous. Johan Hultin was fifty-seven years old, a runner who kept himself very fit, a wine-loving pathologist who came originally from Sweden before going to live in the USA. I did not have many opportunities to spend time in his company but he seemed to have hidden depths, and though he was slow he looked the sort of plodder who was a likely candidate to be by far the oldest person to climb Muztagh Ata. Mary Laucks was a physics student on the way to a PhD and at twenty-six was our youngest member. She was broad-shouldered and strong, but not so heavy as to prevent her being also a fast long-distance runner. The other woman in the party, Janet Jensen, was an easy-going, smiling accountant, a resident of Honolulu. She travelled extensively, was a pilot and sub-aqua diver, and was at ease with the world because she was at ease with herself.

The sledge worked quite well where the snow was steep, but would go only straight downhill. With no means of steering, this style of transport was of limited use because our route traversed a lot; straight downhill would only take me over the cliff in the upper section between Camps 1 and 2. Still, I managed half a dozen exhilarating runs of up to 200 yards. I regretted not having brought up my ski boots from base, but my boats were burnt now. Even if I did not risk downhill skiing, ascent on skis and descent by sledge and on foot was looking like the best procedure for me.

At one point as I dragged the sledge on a rope behind me across a slope one leg went all the way into a crevasse. With the crutches I was able to prod about and find its line, and roll clear.

Janet had been ill and had not carried to Camp 2 that day, but she intended to go with me next day. At 5 a.m. it was snowing, at 6 a.m. snowing still, and the sky did not become clearer until 10 a.m. The weather was unsettled and the snow would be soft, so we waited a further day and started out at 5.45 a.m. There followed over nine disgruntled hours of thrashing a way up a snow cover much worse than on the previous journey. Despite the early start there was only one short slope where crampons could be used. The rest was just slope after slope of grunts and misery and gasping. On skis, Janet managed much better than I.

At Camp 2 we learned that Bob, Colin and Steve had set up Camp 3 at 21,000 feet (6,400 m) the day before and returned for a day off, while John, Grim and Johan went up. The latter trio arrived back at 7.45 p.m. and one look at their drawn faces told all.

'It's very serious above here, man,' John said.

In poor visibility he had not found Camp 3 so the loads had been dumped (very near Camp 3, as it transpired) and the descent by compass had called for a lot of skill from John. There was talk of awful crevasses and steep ice, and though he did not say it I knew John felt I should not go higher.

'Looks like this may be as high as I go,' I offered, to make it easier for him.

'It would help to have someone in support here.'

I hardly needed to ask my next question.

'You think I shouldn't go any further?'

'Yes. It's serious.'

There was no argument. I had said all along that I would stop if we thought it wise. I could still help by getting breakfast and melting snow to fill water bottles for the six who had elected to go on, Bob, Colin, Johan, Grim, Steve and John. And it might prove useful to have someone rested and standing by at Camp 2, as John had suggested, in case someone was ill or injured.

So I mother-henned a few hours away next day, watched the lucky ones go, and wished I was going too. At the same time I knew if I went higher the soft snow would probably defeat me.

Mary had a bad headache, but her appetite had not failed. She and Janet planned to descend the next day, but their plans were about to be influenced by a third party; in the early evening Ted arrived, glazed-eyed.

'Oh, God, that was tough!' he said in a breaking voice, as he slumped into a tent. 'Janet, can you undo my laces?'

He had been unable to eat for three days and had had his fluids via an intravenous drip, so it was not surprising that he had found it hard between 1 and 2.

'You're not aiming to go higher, are you?' I asked him.

173

'I'm gonna do it!'

'We'll see. Right now I don't think you should.'

'I know when to turn back.'

'I think that time's come.'

Janet joined in and we tried to impress on Ted that he had been ill and was behind in acclimatisation, that he would have to cross crevasses alone, that we would not know if he met up with the others or not, that Camp 3 was not easily found, that there might be no tracks to follow because of the wind filling them in, that if he became ill some if not all of the others might have to descend with him, and that John had said Ted should not climb any higher. Throughout all this Ted was unbending in his resolution to carry on. He was certainly not short on determination.

Next day when I enquired how he was Ted said, 'I feel great. This will be a rest day. The altimeter shows bad weather.'

We all got together in one tent for a pow-wow. Janet, Mary and I repeated our concern about Ted climbing but he said he was going and why didn't we help by carrying part of his load for him? We said we would not do anything to encourage him and the debate heated up. Mary began to take on an angry, hawklike appearance and to me looked like she was going to give Ted a nasty pecking. Mary and Janet wanted to descend but Janet suggested they might wait one more day in case Ted got ill and needed to be helped down. He had hardly eaten, and vomited during the day. Janet's consideration for Ted was all the more admirable because she had herself vomited and brought up blood during the night. I favoured her going down that day, but she made her decision and stayed, as did Mary. In any case the wind got up.

'I'm frightened of the steep bit above the cliff,' Janet confided to me. 'I keep thinking about it, especially at night.'

When you are not well the character of any mountain changes for the worse in your eyes. Muztagh Ata, though in truth neutral, now appeared nasty to Janet.

'I can rope you down,' I said. 'No problem.'

'It's amusing,' Janet said. 'Here you have two helpless females and a sick man and you have to guide them down.'

'Helpless' was a bit strong, but as the day wore on Mary's condition gave greater cause for concern because her headache continued despite sleep and aspirin. That was a bad sign, and her appetite deteriorated.

After Ted had vomited I asked him again if he was going down the next day.

'I'll decide in the morning.'

Though he insisted he would climb, Ted didn't eat supper, and looked grey and ill when I took him a drink.

The night was very windy and I grew concerned that the opportunity for descent had not been grasped at the right time the day before, when there had been no doubt everyone could get along on their own two feet. Anyone who became worse through the altitude could deteriorate very rapidly towards a critical condition. But Ted's presence had complicated the issue.

Friday the thirteenth dawned.

'Have you got an oven in there?' Ted shouted to me above the wind, from his tent.

It took a while for it to sink in that this was not a joke, and he meant a stove. Only rarely did he get a word wrong like that and remind us of his German origins. I passed him the stove and he boiled some water for drinks and cereals. I felt better disposed towards him and asked if he was going down.

'I'm under no pressure.'

This non-committal reply swayed my decision towards seeing Janet and Mary down first. When the wind dropped, around noon, I set off a little ahead of them, down a gently sloping snowfield. Janet and Mary were worried about icy conditions and soon removed their skis, and Mary, troubled by cold feet, hurried on ahead without a rope. I waited where the crevasses lay close to the cliff edge.

'You want a rope here, Janet?'

'I'm scared shitless.'

I took that to mean yes, set up a belay with an anchor known as a 'dead-man' (a metal plate hammered into the snow), an ice axe and a crutch, tied the rope on her and fed it out as she descended a rope's length. After four or five more rope lengths she was on safe ground, half an hour below Camp 2. She joined Mary and they waved goodbye.

Now, what about Ted? I could not know, until I had almost completed the ascent back to Camp 2, that there was nothing to do about him. Just before that camp came into view I looked up and saw a dark figure moving slowly up a snow ridge, 300 feet above. Ted had 'summit fever', no mistake about that.

Should I follow? I came down on the side of no, because by the time I packed he would be an hour or so ahead. Deciding what to take would be a problem because I did not know what Ted had in the way of food and fuel and stove. The snow would be soft. I didn't like the look of the weather either, with dark cloud swelling in from the south west; it would help no one if we became separated. Above all, the others planned to go for the summit in two days and we could not acclimatise properly nor sensibly cover nearly 6,000 feet in that time. John had had a bad barking cough and it was quite likely that one or two of the six would be forced to descend and could report whether Ted had found Camp 3. If he had not, then someone would have to go to look for him, if enough fuel and rations remained. I would be fresh.

On Friday 13th and Saturday 14th I sat at the camp on the bottom edge of the huge, tilted snow bowl, and wondered what was going on high on the mountain. I tried to sort out in my mind how I would cope with the disappointment of my failure; if they all failed, too, it would be even worse. It was something I would have to face, though, if I kept pushing my limits on serious expeditions on mountains of this scale; to aim for the extreme of what you can achieve is to court disappointment at the same time. I could not complain about the results of previous expeditions, for on each occasion I had been successful in one way or another. Of course, I did now and then wonder if there was any twist of fate which might result in my having a shot at the summit, but it would need a miracle now. The dream recurred, about going home and being too late to get back, and with my hopes dashed the awakening was as forlorn as the dream itself.

The dead Coloradan's cassette player and some tapes had been left in one of the tents, and I played the theme music from *Chariots of Fire*, which finished with a resounding version of Jerusalem. At first, the words 'Bring me my chariot of fire!' had the deepest effect, for now there was no way I could reach the summit, save through that unforeseeable miracle. But my mood lifted, for the music had a profound effect in such high, beautiful and lonely surroundings. Now I knew better what people meant when they said sometimes that they were inspired, often in an unconnected area of life like work or health or grief, by a runner or a writer, a musician or a mountaineer. If my chance came, I felt able to draw on better reserves.

At 1 p.m. on 15 August Steve skied rapidly down, forth and back, forth and back, steeply across the slope above Camp 2. (He reckoned he did not exceed forty miles an hour!) Why would he descend? Was he ill? Had there been an accident? He drew to a halt by the tents.

'Hi, Steve. You seen Ted?'

'Yes. He missed Camp 3 and spent the night out. There was a big argument with John who said he should go down and Ted said he was going to solo it.'

Steve unfolded the story. While carrying from Camp 3 to Camp 4 they had come across Ted sleeping in the snow, 600 feet above Camp 3. At first they had thought him to be the missing Coloradan.

'Hello, Robert,' Ted had greeted Steve.

'I'm Steve. Camp 3 is 600 feet below here. Down there.' He pointed it out. 'You go down there and rest. We'll see you when we get back from this carry.'

'OK, Robert.'

On their return from Camp 4 Ted was still lying in the snow so he was escorted to Camp 3, where he was not made welcome. He had insisted he would solo the climb if no one else would go with him and the argument with John had followed. Steve had stepped in to say that as it was clear Ted was determined to climb he would wait for a day and attempt the summit with him. In opting to do this Steve showed an exceptional spirit of unselfishness, for if the weather turned bad his chance of reaching the summit could disappear. In any case Ted had not had so much time to acclimatise and might prove to be a slow companion. On top of that, as Ted's presence had strained food and fuel resources, Steve chose to descend to Camp 2 to replenish supplies while Ted rested. Steve had shown that there was more to the man than just the will, and the ability, to win.

'Conditions are firm above here,' he said to me. 'Why don't you come up to Camp 3? You could carry some fuel and food for us.'

I was packed in a shade over the time it takes fast runners to cover a mile. At that stage we planned no further ahead than that I should carry to Camp 3 and stay the night there. But did this change everything? It was unlikely, for it would take a long time to climb 6,000 feet at a pace which would avoid altitude sickness. But still, without being over-optimistic, I once more began to allow myself to toy with the idea that there was a possibility that I might be about to reach my highest summit. Perhaps my chariot of fire had arrived.

With four bottles of fuel and plenty of food, as well as my sleeping bag and other necessities, I set off ahead of Steve, up a steep snow ramp above an awful cliff of ice. Within twenty minutes I was breaking through the snow crust to the knee. For one, two, three, four, five, six steps I sank right in. It can't be done if there's much more of this, I told myself, but it became easier. By 3 p.m. I was starting up the steep back wall of an amphitheatre of snow and ice, and an hour and a half more put me nearly at the top of a second amphitheatre. The last hundred yards made me fight and pray for firmness in place of the featherbed stuff which yielded underfoot. Steve easily caught up near Camp 3 and showed me where it was, tucked away in a crevasse thirty feet wide and a hundred long, a navel in a vast snow belly. Four hours and twenty minutes to gain 2,000 feet was satisfactory at that altitude.

As I crawled into the tent Steve had a surprise to reveal.

'I have to tell you now, John asked me to tell you to go down. But things have changed.'

'You did right, taking the initiative when things changed,'

'Hope John thinks so.'

As he had taken the risk of ignoring John's instructions, we concocted several slightly altered versions of what had happened. We found it difficult, however, to settle on the best version, so in the end I said I would explain everything to John when the time was right.

Earlier differences with Ted were forgotten; Steve's action had poured oil on troubled waters. I had felt no ill will towards Ted, in any case, even though our judgement of what his behaviour should be did differ.

Steve and Ted planned to climb to Camp 4 next day and stay there for the night, then try for the summit. I knew it would be unwise for me to go with them, for that would mean a height rise of 4,000 feet in not much over twenty-four hours. At this altitude that would be asking for trouble, even death. The only comfort was that I had carried up enough food and fuel to give this pair a fighting chance.

Climbing is a game of vicissitudes and the door I thought had closed did open a little again, for next day's weather was bad and forced everyone on the mountain to rest. If it had been fine I would have been left behind.

Our five friends at Camp 4 were not able to make their move for the summit. 'What a storm!' Grim wrote. 'Tents securely fastened to huge blocks of snow and ice. I cannot help but think how the situation could become desperate if the storm really sets in; no way one would want to move up or down.'

Throughout that day we downed hot drinks and took many a swig of water, for this would aid acclimatisation. Our aim throughout the ascent was to pass copious quantities of clear urine, and we often had someone or other announcing happily, 'My pee's clear.'

A nine-and-a-half-hour test of strength next day started easily enough on firm snow which could be cramponed, but close to Camp 4 at 23,000 feet my happy world was transformed to one of torment as I plunged in to the knee and mid-thigh. With 500 feet still to gain I had started by trying to do forty steps without stopping, but soon it got so bad I was having to fight for one step at a time. Up to then I had been in front of or just behind Ted all the way, but now he and Steve drew far ahead. In half an hour they were at the tent on the level space hacked from a slope; I prepared myself for fifty minutes, but that time elapsed and I was still snowploughing a deep trench. There was still a long, long way to go.

Five people had been skiing slowly into sight above Camp 4 for some time. They made many, many turns to descend the slope very gradually. Three of them came down further past the camp, and I was able to congratulate each in turn: John, Grim and Johan. With Bob and Colin they had made it to the summit in four hours from Camp 4. In Grim's words, 'John's hands frostbitten; he was beat. Bob very cold – could not get camera out. Johan's camera frozen.' Now the pair of doctors were occupying one tent there while the trio was on the way to the next camp to leave a tent vacant for the new arrivals.

'I'm sorry plans have changed without an opportunity to communicate with you,' I told John.

'Changed for the better,' he said. 'Good luck for tomorrow, man.'

I looked at three exhausted men descending on their real legs, and wondered what I was doing there. Without skis, having been ill, and perhaps being behind with acclimatisation, what was I doing there? The collapsing snow was almost impossible to climb and I was gaining less than a hundred feet an hour. I considered stopping for three or four hours to get the freeze on my side, but if I was to have a chance the next day I had to get some rest, and lots of liquid. So I went on, taking the slope in the gentlest of zig-zags. I would raise the left leg and it would sink eighteen inches, then as soon as I lifted the right leg the left would go in even deeper, to be joined by the other one. I would pull the left one up with the assistance of the left hand and the motion would put the right one in even deeper. I would step up after dragging the right one out, but the snow would collapse and the right snowshoe would come down on top of the left, trapping it. The snow around the hole made by the legs would fall in, increasing the weight to be lifted at the next go, so I needed to pull with a hand again. I would prod with the crutches in an effort to find a firm spot, two firm spots, but as soon as I put any weight on them down would sink and crutches and both feet too, and the weight of my pack would bend me almost double. Oh, God! How could I gain nearly five hundred feet like this when it needed a rest after just *one* step up, when it was so hard to breathe, so hard to take *one* step? For *every* step I had to make up my mind and say, get ready, and now, go! And sometimes a step took me no higher because the snow was crushed underfoot.

This was one of the toughest days I've spent on a mountain. Forget about grades in the normal sense; grade 3 snow and ice would have been easier, even up there. People see the photographs afterwards, pictures of quite gentle slopes, and they say, 'Looks easy.' 'Fools,' you think, but no, they are right. It *looks* easy; no photograph can capture the agonies of altitude.

179

How long could I go on like this, approaching 23,000 feet? Hell, it was hard, it was hard, it was hard. In a state of utter frustration I muttered and shouted, 'Poxy bloody snow!' and a dozen profane variations. I bellowed, 'I'll be up to my tits in snow!' and was amused at suddenly hearing myself shouting at the unhearing white mantle up there. I calmed down and got on with it. It would have been possible to have deceived myself that I was close to the end of my tether, but experience told me I was not. There was enough 'keep-going' within me for a while.

The last 300 feet rise did not release me from its grip for over three hours. Steve had some hot food ready but I could not eat. My body shuddered with coughing and retching.

'How about tomorrow?' he asked.

'Day after,' I replied. 'I'm wiped out.'

'Can't. We'd miss the flights back to Peking.'

Our schedule was closing in.

'See how you feel tomorrow,' Steve went on. 'A night's rest can change everything.'

'Right. I recover quickly. If nothing else, this is the highest I've climbed, and I can add to that a bit.'

If I encountered snow like that just below Camp 4, I was doomed to failure. I think Ted was concerned about my holding him back, because he asked, 'Will we keep Norman in sight all the time?'

'Can't say. Depends on the terrain,' Steve replied.

'Don't worry, Ted. If I have to I'll turn back. I'm not going to get in your way,' I said.

We settled down in a very tired state, and Ted started groaning with the cold. It had been minus 10°F (−23°C) at Camp 3, and here it was much colder.

'To think we're all volunteers,' I said to Steve, and we giggled a bit, more than we would have done at sea level.

I thought back, about scores of letters to potential sponsors, and I remembered an airline, a newspaper and expedition members who had pulled out at a critical time. I remembered guides who sniggered in the early days; I remembered a broken leg and four days spent crawling in Argentina; I remembered organising and leading an expedition because up to that time I could not get on one; I remembered bronchitis while travelling to the Himalayas, salmonella, shigella. I remembered washing up in a hotel and waiting, waiting, waiting for the right weather; I remembered thirteen years in a bedsitter, and the insecurity of the sort of employment which allowed time for climbing; I remembered sore and bleeding stumps, tiredness, disappointment, wetness, cold, hunger, thirst; I remembered a frightening mule ride, dangerous river crossings, scary snowfields, crevasses and stonefall and fear, fear, fear; I remembered nausea for hours on end; I remembered a 900-mile training walk. Yes, I was a volunteer, and I am not complaining about a single moment of those years. During that time, the patches of skin rubbed from the stumps amounted to a square foot or two, but they hardened in the process. There was insufficient time and spare drive to properly follow a career, but a vocation emerged. Financially, it was costly in many ways; emotionally I was rewarded more than anyone could hope to be. The hours of tiredness and of pain added up to hundreds and hundreds; the feeling when success came wiped them all away. It was all worth it, for success sustains.

August 18 was Steve's twenty-ninth birthday. I wanted him to have the summit for a present, and I wanted to be there to see him get it. We were unsure about the weather at first, and made a late start at 1 p.m. Immediately above the tent I sank deep. Hell, this mountain was keeping me guessing to the end. Soon, however, I was walking a firm crust of up to two inches overlying powdery snow. If I sank at all it was only six inches. Steve went ahead and I hung on to Ted's tail, within forty yards.

In two and a half hours I reckoned we were at 24,000 feet. At least I had surpassed my previous altitude best by a wide margin; yet I took little comfort from this. Perhaps within my grasp at last, perhaps not, the very capriciousness of the attempt on this summit had increased the sense of challenge, and I opened my mind rather more to the option of a bivouac if the snow conditions demanded this. The snow remained firm; if only it was like that all the way to the summit . . .

After three and a half hours of uniform, gently-angled crusty snow that looked like slabs of polystyrene, I saw that Steve had stopped 200 yards ahead. His skis stood up in the snow. Could he be on the summit? Don't raise your hopes, I told myself. It is what it is.

He put his skis on and moved up again, and I was pleased not to have fallen victim to false hope.

The wind began to assert itself after Steve's brief halt. 'In early June on the North Col of Everest one could not experience such cold,' Tilman wrote of his mid-August attempt on Muztagh Ata.

We had been going for four hours when Steve approached a rock hump, big as a large whale, slightly to the right of the line we were taking. Two hundred yards to the left of that hump was another, to our left. First Steve climbed the right hump, then started traversing to the other, which looked higher. Yes, I thought, that's higher. It must be the summit, and I headed for it. Ted, who was a few yards ahead, wanted the nearer hump to be the summit, simply because it was nearer, and he went that way. Within a few minutes, I had joined Steve. He was crying.

'I've just thrown the bones off,' he said.

He had been carrying some of the ashes of a thirty-seven-year-old man who had died in his sleep, and whose brother had asked Steve to throw them from the summit. The successful ascent and this act together had a deep effect on us, for we were still alive, really alive.

'Well done, stormin' Norman,' Steve said.

Ted made it ten minutes later and I let out a Hee-ahh! warcry.

It was too cold for Steve to remove his mittens to operate my little camera, but though all the shots of me on the summit came out framed by wool, I treasure them.

There is a legend amongst the local nomadic people that an ancient city lies atop Muztagh Ata, dating back to times of peace and happiness. The city has had no contact with the rest of the world, and happiness and peace continue there, without death, cold, darkness or ageing, and fruit trees bear all year round. We felt old and cold, I can tell you, and death and darkness were not far from our thoughts, and we saw no fruit trees; yet it was true that none of the troubles of the lower earth had followed us up there, and none of them could later spoil the experience.

We returned to Camp 4 that day, and set off for Camp 2 or further down next day. However, we had descended no lower than Camp 3 when Ted had had enough for the day. We could not leave him there alone, partly because he had not been doing his share of cooking, and it was essential that he should be encouraged to keep up his liquid intake. Steve decided, and I agreed, that it was best for him to ski down to let the others know we back-markers should appear at base camp next day, and he went swiftly on his way. Since until a few weeks before he had held the world record for speed skiing at 125.7 miles per hour (201 km/hr) Steve was the man for the job. In three or four hours he would be at base camp. 'As time went on, we could see it was Steve coming down,' it said in Grim's diary. 'And with good news – whew!!! I really was expecting the worst – don't know why.' But for Ted and me things were not going to be straightforward; there was a little drama in store for us.

Grim's words tell what was going on at base camp: 'What a scene here tonight. After beer and shrimp cocktail, a huge dinner with about ten dishes. Ne (the cook) had worked all day on this – chicken, peanuts, rice, potatoes and mushrooms, soup, peppers, pork and melon, plus some wine Mr Qui had brought and served now he knew everyone was safe. And a birthday cake for Steve, which Mary and Jan and Ne had made from scratch. John at his best with mountain stories, tales, songs. All this in the middle of Asia. A setting to remember!'

The words 'everyone was safe' turned out to be premature. We were not all safe. Not yet. Not by a long way.

Throughout the night in our dome tent Ted had groaned and muttered, 'Oh, God!' I thought little of it, having heard him when he was cold at Camp 4. But this time it was not the cold which created his discomfort, but something much more serious, as I discovered in the morning.

'Norman, I'm snowblind.'

Snowblindness is a temporary, very painful condition. He was not totally without vision, but would have to be guided down.

'It may take a while but I'll get you down,' I said. 'Did you take your goggles off yesterday.'

'Yes. It was overcast.'

'Fool.'

The weather was not in our favour. Cloud created what we call a white-out, when it is impossible to distinguish between the snow and the cloud. Visibility was as low as three yards. Ted wanted to wait, but I preferred to avoid any delay which might cause others to come up to look for us. They had made the ascent with a few resultant minor frostbite injuries and had probably got down safely, and it was time to get away. Any attempts on their part to re-ascend to Camp 2 or Camp 3 would involve a certain amount of additional risk which could be avoided if we headed down. Ted was hardly in a strong position to argue.

Once we were packed and the tent down I moved out of the crevasse into thick whiteness. We had marked the upper part of the route with wands, bamboo sticks supporting thin orange flags, and though they were spaced 200 or 300 yards apart and therefore much too far apart for us to follow under prevailing conditions, they would give us reassurance every so often on our long and meandering descent of this white wilderness.

A brief gap in the cloud was enough; I drew an arrow in the snow towards the first wand below Camp 3, then waited for Ted to come towards me. He could not see well enough to pick out my tracks and spotting a wand was out of the question for him, but he could follow my vague outline if I did not get too far ahead. We reached the first wand, and the slope and memory told me which way to go to the next. There it was, and another, and another, but then the slope eased. Visibility was about four yards and it was essential that we maintained contact with the line of wands. Later it would become easier because John had

183

written the compass bearing from one wand to the next on each little flag, but this had not been done in the upper section.

'We'd better sit and wait for a while in case it clears, Ted.'

'How about spreading out?'

Had I heard right? 'There are only two of us, Ted, and you can't see.'

We sat on the slope.

'I can tell it's getting lighter,' Ted said.

The cloud thickened.

Ten minutes later he said, 'It's getting better,' and it got much worse.

After sitting on the slope for half an hour Ted said, 'It's getting worse, isn't it?' and the cloud cleared briefly. My head was going left, right, left, right, like it was on a swivel, and there, 200 yards away, was a wand. I took a compass bearing before it disappeared in a cloak of white.

'Right, Ted. Two seven five degrees. Let's go.'

'Can you help me up?'

The past few days had taken their toll and his pack was heavy. Pain is tiring too. His fatigue was not serious at this early stage and at our deliberately slow and cautious pace, but it would have to be borne in mind. Had I known the true cause of his tiredness I would have been more concerned: Ted had amoebic dysentery.

'I'm surprised he had the strength to accomplish what he did,' Don wrote to me. 'For he truly risked his life for that summit.' The ailment which had seized him, as it might have taken any of us, induced in him fever and fatigue, and could get worse, with abscesses on the liver and other complications.

So there I was, descending in a white-out from 21,000 feet, with a snowblind man who had amoebic dysentery. I opted to go unroped because it was highly unlikely that Ted, on skis, would break through into a crevasse if I had gone ahead on foot without doing so. Also, if I fell into a crevasse when roped to him it was quite likely I would pull him in after me.

'I guess we feel a little like warriors just home from battle, yet there is some anxiety about the others,' Grim wrote. 'Mr Qui perched on his rock, with John's binoculars, looking for signs of them. A storm brewing on the summit. I bet it's wild up there now. The mountain looks *so* big and majestic.'

We walked on a bearing, slid 200 feet down a slope, walked a bit further, and reached the wand.

'We're at the wand, Ted.'

'You son of a gun! You did it!'

'I know the approximate direction so we might as well go forward on two seven five and see if we come on to the next wand. If we don't we can follow our tracks back.'

We advanced for three or four long minutes but saw no wand. Visibility was at its worst by then. Six feet away, below on a gentle slope, I could just make out a slight trough in the snow.

'Stop there, Ted. Take a rest. I think there's a crevasse in front of us.'

My eyes played tricks in the everywhere whiteness and many times put an instant mirage wand where there was none. Another break in the cloud showed us we had done right by waiting, for there really was a dangerous crevasse just in front of us. We had to detour right, where a sharp change in the line of the wands showed how others had gone around the hazard. Having followed their example we slid easily for 300 feet, Ted on skis, me on my bottom. By then he was finding it difficult to side-slip down behind me, partly, I believe, because it is harder to balance when you cannot see properly, so he removed his skis and copied my method of descent.

We struck it lucky with brief breaks in the cloud and several times I was able to get a bearing on a wand and march towards it by compass. Then we came across the first of the bearings John had marked on the little flags, and those took us close to Camp 2 and out of the cloud. Bless you, John.

Picking a way between the crevasses below Camp 2 was a slow business. The ramp was much more icy than previously, and Ted was tired, but his vision seemed if anything improved, and he moved well and without any fuss. It was after 5 p.m. when John and Steve, who had been waiting anxiously, saw us from near base camp. A slide of 500 feet on a snow covered ice slope took us on to the stony rib which led to Camp 1. Mr Su waited for us there and took charge of Ted.

I was at base camp by 8.30 p.m., an hour and a half ahead of Ted, who looked fit to drop when he arrived. I had hurried down to let John and Steve know we were all right, but having seen we were safe they had already descended to our meadow camp. Considerately, they had left us each a bottle of beer, and three camels with a driver, so we too could go down to the meadow camp that night. At 10.30 p.m. Mr Su, Ted and I clambered on board the three animals and swayed forth and back for three hours in the near dark. As we picked a way through boulders, Muztagh Ata put on a ferocious thunderstorm, telling us we had been allowed up once, and down too, but not to take any ascent for granted. With the big emu-style head bobbing up and down ahead against the moonscape scenery I could sit back and reflect, and thank God for my good fortune. If John had opted for three camps instead of four, I would not have made it. If Ted had not forced his way up contrary to the judgement of the rest of us, Steve would not have descended to Camp 2 for supplies and would not have encouraged me to go up; Ted's determination had helped me. If I had accepted that as Don could not get by on snowshoes I would do even worse – not an unreasonable conclusion – I might have given up. If we had had good weather on one particular day at Camp 3 I would have been left behind. If Steve had been a lesser man neither Ted nor I would have had such an opportunity for success.

At 11.30 a.m. our little caravan reached the meadow. The docs took Ted to a tent, gave him something to kill his pain, and bandaged his eyes. Just about everybody turned out to shake hands or give us a slap on the back or a hug, and fetch a beer or some tea, and our camp was a happy place. There was such pleasure to be found then simply from a mug of hot tea, and from time to relax, to relish the past few days and the friendship of our tiny band which had worked so hard towards our objective, from the time to think about the beauty of where we had been. The sense of joy and well-being! And of relief!

'Well done, Norm,' John said. 'There are not many here who could have got him down in a white-out.'

I passed it off, saying, 'I was only trying to get myself down. Couldn't shake Ted off. Bugger kept following me,' and we laughed, but I did feel very pleased to have had something useful to do.

A bandaged and therefore sightless Ted, insisting on having a window seat, was led on to our bus, and we drove back to Kashgar. The rest is a happy blur; a visit to a market, a department store, gentle crowds around us again; an orchard where young men and women in bright costumes danced and sang and played musical instruments for us; a banquet, a craft shop, the flight to Urumchi, a jade factory, another three-hour flight to Peking, a second banquet with officials of the Chinese Mountaineering Association. At both banquets, apart from being served course after course of tasty food, we were introduced to 'mao-tai'. Served in glasses about right for egg-cups, if you like thrushes' eggs, neither the volume nor the appearance betrayed the power lying in this colourless spirit. The tradition is to call out 'Gan-bei', which as far as I could ascertain is the Chinese equivalent of 'Bottoms Up', and down the liquid dynamite in one go. We did. 'Gan-bei' followed 'Gan-bei' in rapid succession, as is the way. Leader, deputy leader, oldest gent, females and amputee received particularly attentive hospitality i.e. constantly topped-up glasses. I have it from reliable opinion that immediately after descent from high altitude the effect of alcohol is at least doubled, so we as the 'away team' were soon wrapped in the arms of 'mao-tai' and 'Gan-bei' and proclaiming deep friendships with the people of China; those friendships were sincere. And they were reciprocated. Some of the politics of this nation were at variance with those of our individual members, but as ordinary people we were friends.

Ted's bandages were removed and his sight was back to normal. We started putting back on the weight we had lost. John had shed twenty-eight lbs in three weeks and I fourteen lbs. Almost everyone had lost several pounds, but one exception I must mention: Colin reckoned he had gained three lbs. What on earth was his normal diet if he could put on three lbs while eating freeze-dried food at high altitude? John and I had both favoured being a little overweight to leave something to burn off, while the weight-watching Americans had a far more stoical approach and at each stopping point en route for Muztagh Ata had disappeared in all directions, running. Our respective performances proved nothing but the enigma of fitness for high altitude climbing.

Soon we were saying goodbye to our climbing friends who flew to the USA before John and I left Peking. Then we were saying goodbye to our Chinese friends, and embarking on sixteen and a half hours of flying to Paris, before taking the short Paris to London hop. Home.

We had been away for five weeks and two days. If it had not been for the paperwork John had to handle in Peking we could have lopped a few days off that time; not bad, considering we had climbrd a mountain of 24,757 feet.

For the first time in my climbing career I had, with John, achieved a British first, for no other Britons had succeeded in climbing Muztagh Ata. It was a climb of great quantity but little quality.

I suffered again the horrible dream that I had come home for a rest and could not return in time to join the others on the ascent. This time I awoke in a sweat, but in seconds I remembered what had come about, and I knew this magic could not be taken away. I had the ascent for ever, and was home too.

9

A Fine North Face

Fortunately Judy had a good Civil Service office job, but I had to pull my weight financially too. I had had some experience in lecturing about my climbing and from late 1982 I turned more to lectures as a source of income in fairly large dollops; lecture agencies relieved me of the need to haggle over fees. To make the lecture business work I had to obtain more slides, and it was quite a committing step to take, to enter the expensive arena of expeditions and to try at the same time to make a living from the results. Much time was spent travelling around the country by train, speaking at a library here, a public school there, at a ladies luncheon club somewhere else, at a sales conference, a literary society, a climbing club. Introductions by chairpersons, and votes of thanks, tended to be embarrassingly glowing, times to keep the eyes down, but there were funny moments too, such as the time when I stood in at short notice for someone who had died; an elderly lady paid me the weird compliment: 'I enjoyed your talk so much! I'm glad the other gentleman died.'

A new lifestyle permitted sufficient flexibility for some voluntary work, but I'm no Mother Teresa, and I found a level at which I was neither overworked nor resentful of the demands made. I had never been one to join committees unless I could see a very good reason for doing so, and once the outdoor pursuits campaign was well established there was no need for me to remain on more than two or three. Instead, working on an ad hoc basis with several projects concerned with disability suited me better than regular commitments. For too long I had done too much and it had all become a burden, and I lost sight of the people concerned. Whether selfishly or not, I was not going to let voluntary work get in the way of climbing, for in the long run the more climbing I did the more effective I would be in that work.

Partly because of the ascent of Muztagh Ata, there came upon me the deepest sense of urgency about attempting some climbs of quality, some smaller but diamond-bright routes, so in May 1983 I went to the Alps. Several years of rock climbing, a 900 mile walk, many visits to the Alps, and five expeditions in the Andes, the Himalayas and China, were preparation for what I hoped would be my golden years, when ascents would have more bite, when the attraction would be quality rather than quantity. It was not until 1982 that it became clear to me that this should be the way; I had to follow more dreams to reach El Dorado. Simultaneously I began to prepare myself mentally for the time when, through serious injury to a wrist, an elbow, a shoulder, a hip, my back, or through other injury or sickness or disability, my body would no longer endure the severe tests to which it was subjected; if the time came I would accept it, for I had had so much. Soon, a physical problem did loom: my left shoulder became painful when the arm on that side was moved. It hurt even to pick up a jacket. Though I joked about it ('Well, at least I have one good limb left') the seriousness of the injury did not escape me, and I feared my climbing future was threatened.

'We'd better fix you up with an appointment at a sports injuries clinic,' my doctor said.

The specialist there, Dr J. G. P. Williams, was no stranger to me because I had contributed a chapter to a sports medicine book which he edited. Less than ten minutes after walking into his surgery I was out again, having had an injection deep into the shoulder.

I bought an old bike to give myself more exercise and soon came to the conclusion that cycling on London's busy streets was as risky as climbing, so I stuck to back streets. Another element of my training produced some bewildered looks from a neighbour; I took to wearing a forty pound pack around the flat all day when working at home, and one day stepped out of our back door looking like I was headed for the hills, walked fifteen feet, scattered some food on a bird table, and went indoors again.

Remembering the experience of an acquaintance who forgot to post his insurance application form, lost all his fingers through frostbite, and incurred bills for several thousand pounds for medical and allied expenses, I made sure I was properly insured; an accident-free record resulted in my premium being the same as that paid by an able-bodied climber. Some of my insurances were arranged through the London Mountaineering Club, of which I was a member for several years. Though I used the club hut in North Wales occasionally, contributed articles to the newsletter and journal, and gave a couple of talks, I could hardly be described as an active club member. In fact the only record of my involvement during a three-year period concerned a one-day trip to the cliffs of the Avon Gorge near Bristol; a report which listed the many routes achieved that day concluded simply, 'Norman and Judy took some photographs and then went to the zoo.'

Since I needed material for lectures and writing, many acquaintances reacted differently to my going on expeditions; they no longer queried either my motives or the virtue of my actions, but now viewed the wanderings as acceptable. There were those, of course, who reacted enviously, on the theme of, 'All right for some. Gadding about all over the world. Lucky devil.' But though there had been some luck and many people had helped, it boiled down to continued application more than to luck. You *make* most opportunities happen, rather than wait for luck, and you take risks and opt for sacrifices and apply yourself hard. I have ceased to be surprised at the number of people who tell me they have a climbing or other adventurous ambition but they have never achieved it because no one would give them the money. I could advise them that getting there by stages and raising the finances are all part of the job and that securing the finance does not automatically bring the ambition about; anyone can dream up ambitions. Complaining that no one else will come up with the money is a feeble excuse, a sign of lack of commitment, and quite often they could afford to attempt what they had in mind provided they were prepared to make sacrifices. Though I do not mind if people lack ambitions (for there are some ambitious horrors around) I have no time for the windbags who say 'I wish I could' but always find excuses.

Immediately before climbing trips Judy and I seemed to live in different worlds inside our heads.

'I must put some more turf down in the middle of the garden,' she said one day.

'Fine. I'll need a new ice axe for the next trip.'

'Honeysuckle would look nice on that wall.'

'Mmm. Haven't decided whether to take my helmet yet.'

'Mary's given me some nice seeds.'

'Must get some more ice screws.'

'Could you move the trellis on to that wall?'

'Yes. Oh, would you get me another tube of glacier cream tomorrow? You'll be near the shop.'

'All right. Can you put the washing in the launderette and I'll collect it on the way back?'

'Yes. The pick on one of my axes is at the wrong angle.'

'I wonder if there's enough turf at the bottom of the garden that I can shift.'

It did not matter that our thoughts went about like two butterflies rarely alighting simultaneously on the same flower, for when it mattered we listened to each other. Her thoughts centred around her friends and closest relations, the little piece of garden which went with our flat, work and the people she worked with, and cooking, which she had studied for three years at a teacher training college. With the exception of infrequent walking excursions we had given up taking mountain holidays together, for the preparations for even the simplest venture assumed the proportions of mounting a crusade; this was because she was not truly enthusiastic about going, and once we stopped trying to fool ourselves about this we had no more problems. She was a home bird, without a doubt.

'A lot of people really do believe I must have deep frustrated ambitions,' she said one day. 'As if ambitions were inevitable and mine have been squashed. They assume everyone wants what they want. Couldn't be more wrong.'

It is only natural that foremost in my mind as I set out on my next climbing trip to the French Alps was a feeling of anxiety about how my left shoulder would perform. On the twenty-four-hour coach journey there, there was plenty of time to wonder about that, and about whether I would achieve another little ambition, to lead a grade 4 route.

Approaching Lyon, we came into a region of sodden fields and forests, flooded so deeply that fences running from high to low ground disappeared completely beneath the water. Farm lanes were submerged, leaving stranded buildings, pretty on their temporary islands. Trees of all sizes stood in the water or on islets, cornfields looked more like rice paddies, and in a sense it was beautiful, as if the water belonged there and had always been there. But of course behind the beauty, the seizure of land was an agricultural tragedy of half-submerged greenhouses and water-filled furrows. The whole scene portended conditions on the mountains around Chamonix: what had fallen as rain here would have left unusually heavy snow for late May on the heights. As we drew into town it was evident that soft snow was going to make the approach to most of the mountains impossible; my only hope was to rise above the fresh deposits by cable-car, to the cooler places. Things seemed stacked against me, for shortly after my arrival the only cable-car which had been operating was shut down owing to avalanche damage. The Brasserie National (known as the Bar Nat or Bar Nash), where English climbers congregate, was shut for several days' holiday, so my chances of finding a climbing partner were greatly reduced. The weather forecast was awful, too. The feeling of farce was reinforced when I went to book into a dormitory where Judy and I had stayed before I climbed Mont Blanc in 1971, almost a dozen years ago; the place was derelict.

The next dormitory I tried was shut, as was the next, so I booked into the cheapest hotel I could find, and began wandering the wet streets and bars, mooching about in pursuit of someone to climb with. The first day produced no results, nor the second, and more snow fell that day. Another day went by without any success, and I contracted a stomach upset. A few wet tourists came by coach, out-of-season animals who did not stay long.

At last I bumped into an English climber and we set out to climb the Dent du Geant (Giant's Tooth) at 13,166 feet (4,013 m). Though the weather forecast had been good we were caught in bad weather and spent two nights bivouacked at 12,500 feet on a ledge. We were forced to retreat from there without having reached the summit, but at least I was acclimatised and my shoulder had worked properly. My companion had to go home, so the hunt began again for a partner who would attempt the north face of the Tour Ronde, a grade 4 route on a mountain of 12,441 feet (3,792 m).

Temperatures in the town reached 30°C (86°F) and the place came alive. This was the Chamonix I had seen before, first in 1971. Now it was a Chamonix of busy bars and banks, suntan and sunburn and souvenir shops, postcards and pop music and pommes frites and pavement cafés, dogs and development, restaurants and hasty road repairs and tarmac tipped like black sugar from big lorries, tourists, tourists, tourists, young and old and all ages in between. Coaches, lots of coaches.

Ironically, the fine weather was not all good news, for, though no new snow fell and some cleared, the north face of the Tour Ronde was not frozen and was difficult and dangerous as a result. Two and a half weeks had gone by without results and the forecast was for equally hot weather over several days. I had planned to be there only three weeks and money was running low. To stay or not? Fate intervened when I went to change the last of my travellers cheques, when a bank clerk mistook dollars for sterling and paid out fifty per cent more than she should have; the unsolicited bank loan would tide me over for a few more days.

Three days later I met Dennis Morrod and Mike Dick at the Bar Nat. Mike, a former Harrow school pupil about to study for a degree in economics, was on his first visit to the Alps, whereas Dennis had been there many times and was clearly up to tackling the north face of the Tour Ronde. He was a forty-one-year-old motor mechanic who ran a small walking and climbing guiding business during the summer. He wanted to climb with me, not as a client, but as a friend.

Soon we were in the Torino hut (10,896 feet, 3,321 m) and reasonably confident that our chance would come. The night was chilly, just as we wanted it, and at 2.45 a.m. Dennis left the twenty-bed dormitory, of which we three were the only occupants, reappeared a couple of minutes later, switched on the dim electric light, and beckoned to me.

'Just take one rucksack,' he said. 'I'll carry it.'

I had never climbed a grade 4 route, but he was determined that I would, if conditions allowed the attempt. Mike was not going because the route was too serious for a relative beginner. We dressed, packed, drank some tea and followed our head torch beams out into the snow at 4 a.m. The wind was bitter, the sky clear (cloud would have kept the heat in, so a clear sky was what we needed) and underfoot the snow was acceptably firm. From the hut we gained height gradually, lost it and a little more in a vast white valley, and began to regain it all. Crevasses, contours and the need to follow the firmest snow forced us to leave behind a track like that of a drunken man.

Within an hour and a half we were hauling ourselves for 300 or 400 feet up a forty degree slope to our first obstacle near the bottom of the face; this was an unavoidable bergschrund (see Glossary), twenty feet high in places, which ran the full length of the bottom of the face. We headed for the only spot we could see where this natural dike narrowed and was bridged between the upper and lower lips by soft snow. While I paid out the rope Dennis struggled up the collapsing seventy degree snow above the gaping icicle-toothed mouth; I would not have been surprised if the mouth had swallowed him, but the bridge held. He disappeared from view over the top lip and the only clue to his movements was the way the rope ran out.

My turn came. The snow bridge took a second body, and held, and the snow above was firm, the right sort of stuff at fifty-five degrees, which gave support to kicked in, forward-pointing crampon spikes.

Dennis led the second pitch and I toyed with the idea of climbing second all of the way. But though this was my first grade 4 climb, the style of climbing suited me.

'Mind if I lead, Dennis?'

'On you go.'

An axe in one hand, a crutch with an axe pick clamped to it in the other. Four limbs shared the work. A hundred and forty feet of rope soon trailed out behind and I was belayed on rock. The leader of an Italian pair who had started just behind caught up; his second had had problems at the bergschrund, but had got up in the end.

The fourth pitch went to Dennis, fifty-five degree snow, finishing up a seventy degree rock V-chute for ten feet.

'It's half past nine,' he said. 'Could be on the summit by noon.'

Dennis led again, then I did, on snow which stayed at a little above or below fifty-five degrees. There was no rock belay within reach so I used three pieces of crutch tubing and an ice axe, then Dennis made a short lead of only twenty-five feet to reach a sound rock anchor. My turn again, to reach him and go past up the steep and now softening snow to the very limit of the rope. There was no adequate belay anchor, only the soft snow. Having whammed in three pieces of crutch again I called down, 'You'll need to go carefully, Dennis, the belays are not good.' But just before he started moving I spotted a yellow piton hammered into a crack just four feet above my head, and I clipped into it. So while Dennis climbed we were both safe, as he was when he went past me.

Just before he called for me to climb again, there was a noise which made me look rapidly up to the little rock platform where he stood. Something had dropped and was tumbling and making little jumps, end over end in the snow. Dennis could not see it.

'What's that, Norman?'

'One of my crutches.'

He had been using it to belay in the snow.

'I'm getting tired,' he said. 'It must have fallen out of the top of my rucksack.'

The tenth pitch was mine to lead. With a thousand steep and glistening snowdrop-white feet beneath my boots, I was aware of a feeling of seriousness, and told myself to keep cool and enjoy the experience I had waited for so long. I did feel fear, but it shrank in the face of the cause; this escapade was worthwhile. My first grade 4 and I was leading it! I remembered with a grin the headmaster, from a school quite close to where Dennis lived in North Cornwall, who said I was dragged up mountains. I suppose he suffered from what Judy calls 'small man's disease', which has nothing to do with physical size; out of all he might say concerning a varied climbing life his only comment was not only negative but erroneous too.

The rope had almost all run out behind when I found the next anchor, a boulder frozen in the snow. Dennis next, slowing down now but still not suggesting I should take the rucksack, and me hoping he would not. The twelfth pitch, mine. The thirteenth, Dennis's. The fourteenth, mine. We had kept to the right of the centre of the face, where protruding rocks provided anchors, so now, at the end of the fifteenth lead up snow, we had to traverse leftwards, because we had reached the top of the snow face which started at the bergschrund and ended abruptly here at a gully cutting straight across. That gully separated us from the final steep rocky summit tower, but by moving left we could reach the top end of the gully and a way to the top.

Dennis had belayed to a rock at the very top of the snowfield's upper lip. Before him, the whole north face, behind, the plunge of the gully. We joined two ropes together so I could move leftwards for nearly 300 feet to the next anchor; the sixty-five degree slope (at first) I had to edge along, keeping just below the gently rising crescent top, was by this time very soft, for it must have been after 5 p.m. Where had the time gone? It had been spent on care, because of soft snow; the Italians had gone similarly slowly and were only just ahead. We had spent much time sheltering from the ice they dislodged, too, while Dennis bellowed, 'Oi! Bloody watch it!'

A month later the steepest snow here would have gone, but it now provided a fine finish to the face; the short sixty-five degree section was the best bit. I crossed the first few feet 'a cheval', sitting astride the snow crescent with one leg above the gloomy gully on the right and the other above the face. Then, keeping a few feet below the thin lip I walked sideways.

A short, easy snow slope, a descent down loose rocks for a little way, a climb up awful snow, and there was a metal Madonna on the summit. Our height gain up the face was not great, about 1,200 feet, but the quality I had sought was there. And I had done my share of leading.

After 400 feet of descent to the south-east on the normal route's rocky ridge we took stock. A month later, in mid-July, there would not be much snow, but now it was deep, soft and dangerous. It would be soft all the way, and at the bottom walking with one crutch might be hard.

In 1979 this route was the scene of an accident in which someone slipped and carried away not only two people on the same rope but several others below. Eight people died, six of them from other parties. Soft snow was given as a reason for the slip. According to a reliable report one survivor, who slid about 1,000 feet (c. 300 m) was trapped halfway down an eighty-foot crevasse which was blocked by dead bodies. He was then charged with manslaughter, but the charges were dropped.

The weather forecast was excellent. We weighed it all and chose to bivouac. Digging a little cave in the snow beneath a boulder did not take long. We crawled in, but Dennis left the cramped space and passed the night amongst some boulders on a rock prow above a long and steep white slope. In order to keep weight down I had a bivouac bag but no sleeping bag, so spent a chilly night lying on the ropes for insulation. But what did it matter? There was no cause for concern about survival, and a little discomfort could be tolerated in exchange for the reward of this route. I slept or shivered, perhaps slept *and* shivered, the night away, and knew the cold was not so bad as to be serious. A few hours' sleep, a few hours' shivering, and the dawn came.

The bivouac earned us firm snow next morning. I led two traversing pitches on surprisingly steep snow for a grade 2 route which in this spot was normally described as 'the easy final slopes'. But conditions had driven us from the exact route, from snow and ice covered rocks on to serious slopes. This was June, not July nor August.

Dennis was leading the third pitch when a whistling, chattering sound made us look up; a red helicopter appeared from the opposite flank of the ridge we were on. It came from the Torino hut side, and passed within fifty yards, then rose and turned in a slow circle and came to look at us. I signalled that we did not require help: left arm like a clock hand at two o'clock, right had at eight o'clock. The aircraft went away. (When I climbed Mont Blanc so long before, one of my stumps was injured quite badly on the descent, and needed a day's rest. The guide with whom I was climbing said he had to get down because he had another client the next day. I agreed, therefore, to descend by the helicopter taxi service which operated in the area; the fare was not much more than paying the guide for another day. Unfortunately, however, a rescue helicopter was sent, entirely unnecessarily; I could have climbed down that day if there had been any real urgency. I survived the embarrassment, learned that at a suspicion of apparent difficulty there might be an over-reaction when I was involved, and came back.)

I was relieved to learn this time that the helicopter above the Tour Ronde was nothing to do with us. Someone had called it to look for the Italians, who had bivouacked a short way below us and descended this day to the Torino hut.

The fourth pitch, left to right across a slope as I faced it, and a little downwards, took us to a col which allowed access to 600 feet of firm, forty-five degree snow on the hut side of the ridge, and to an easy bergschrund crossing. Now it was just a walk.

We had a meal and plenty of wine, and there was a really excellent route to yarn about. We talked of climbing together again in the Alps, too.

I had a chat with the driver of a coach leaving soon for London, and though officially I could not book a seat until the following Wednesday, he let me board Saturday's coach.

Despite a warm welcome home, I was received with simultaneously slightly reproachful eyes, like those of a friends' dog when they packed for their holidays, and when they returned. Neither the dog nor Judy would have reacted that way if they had not cared, but they wanted us home with them, safe. That must not, however, be the only and final measure; there is more to life than longevity. There are higher values.

My shoulder was fine. There was only a tiny injury to the left stump, a small raw spot. I had learned that there would be quite hard north faces to suit me, probably for years to come. North faces which I could lead. After more than twenty years of climbing, horizons were still unfolding; the golden years had begun.

10

Tocllaraju – Trap Mountain

In November 1982 a letter had arrived to ask if I was interested in joining a US expedition to Peru the next summer. I said yes. John Perone, who had been on the second trip to Aconcagua, telephoned from the USA to say he was going too, and when the full list of the team arrived, there were the names of Dan Montague (the raisin-raiser, Aconcagua), Vladimir Kovacevic (from the second Aconcagua trip) and Ted Mayer (snowblindness and amoebic dysentery in China). The leader, Phil Ershler, and the Chilean deputy leader, Guillermo Beauchat, I had met in Argentina, so I knew all but three of the members.

Temperatures in England had been nudging the nineties (c. 32°C) for some days around the time I left for Peru. We were up early and Judy was excited because her first poppy, planted because I liked them, had blossomed into the special bright beauty of that flower.

Heathrow, Amsterdam, Zurich, Lisbon, Caracas, Curacao, Panama City, Lima. In twenty-four hours I was in another world, where the high altitude climbing had started; on the way we had passed close by the Eiger, the Mönch and the Jungfrau, where my alpine career had begun. Now fresh and unforeseeable adventures lay just around the corner, but though I tried to predict what they might be I was at a loss. Always, something interesting happened when we ventured into the mountains, but I could not begin to guess what it might be. Did I have a date with disappointment, or with delight?

Lima, cleaner than formerly and cleared of hundreds of thousands of shanty dwellings, was better than I remembered it, but I was in a hurry to reach Huaras.

Pepe had a new hotel in Huaras, close to his family's Hotel Barcelona. 'Come and stay in my new hotel,' he said. 'For you, a special rate.'

He had changed little, though at the age of thirty-three he had slowed down somewhat and, at least for the time being, his thoughts centred on only one woman.

In a nearby restaurant I saw something I had not witnessed on the first visit: children begging for leftovers. A boy of about eight, typically dark-skinned and brown-eyed, dressed in grubby grey trousers and shirt, stood silently on the opposite side of my small table as I ate alone. His eyes hardly left my plate. When it seemed I had finished the meal he looked hopefully at me, dropped his eyes to the plate, and back to me again. I nodded, and in small fistfulls he grabbed what remained, chicken bones with a little meat still on them, some lettuce and a few chips, and put them in a polythene bag. He smiled at me and left; most of them did it solemnly, unsmiling.

A man of about thirty crawled along the pavement outside, his legs dragging uselessly; in another country a wheelchair or crutches would have given him mobility. The scene reminded me of an aspect of the International Year of Disabled People which had made me uneasy: the predominant British emphasis had been one of self interest.

Four nights passed. I had chosen to arrive early to spend time acclimatising in Huaras, at an altitude of around 10,000 feet. We had no rendezvous point but I was confident I would meet the others in the town, which is what happened. We were ten in all, though two did not arrive until a day later, having spent the extra time in Lima replacing a stolen air ticket, travellers cheques and passport.

The boulder moraine approach to Pisco was even worse than I remembered.

'Some of the worst terrain I've ever crossed,' Dan said. 'Loose as a goose.'

Seven of them climbed Pisco. I opted out because my left foot came loose, but I climbed high enough to take the photographs I had been hoping for. More important, on the way to Pisco I met Bob Braun and Glenn Albrecht, two Americans whom I was to encounter again.

Next we headed for Huascaran. Having been up the north summit already, I could muster little motivation for the ascent, and from what I had seen from a distance the route was far more broken and dangerous than in 1978. However, the opportunity to take photographs at up to 17,500 feet, to replace some film stolen in 1978, was sufficient to draw me along with the others.

On a narrow moraine spine above base camp we passed the first of the mountain's victims, a small Japanese lady being carried down on the back of a local porter. We did not find out whether she was ill or injured. Then at around 17,000 feet we came across five Peruvian climbers descending with a blue bundle which they lowered ahead of them down the snow and ice, and dragged it on ropes across crevasses. A floppy leg sticking from the bundle at a funny angle, and a bare foot, were the first confirmation that this was a body. The foot, like the bloated face, was the colour of a red tan leather shoe, and the eyes were like glass. We heard it was a Canadian or American man who had died in a fall several days before.

The sight of the corpse cast a cold shadow on our spirits, yet the body did not influence me. Already I had a bad feeling about the route, and my decision to go no higher than 17,500 feet had been made. The dangerous way we had taken, weaving through crevasses and broken cliffs, had provided the long-awaited pictures, and considering the risks to be faced thereafter the reward was too small to tempt me on. Also, the replacement left leg had to be broken in, and was giving a great deal of pain where flesh was squeezed between the leather socket and a bone. Weight loss on expeditions often means that a perfectly fitting leg soon becomes uncomfortable because the whole body, including the stumps, must change shape and volume as fat disappears. The very long distances which must be covered on rough terrain can only aggravate the problems.

One of our team had already gone home after becoming ill and failing on Pisco, and now John, Dan and I had decided that the camp at 17,500 feet, a flat snow space reached at dusk, was as far as we were going.

John and I melted snow for water bottles and breakfast as the remaining six prepared for their early morning start. In an hour and a half they were strung out across a steep snow and ice ramp, and half an hour later they turned back. The place was too serious at that time for the combined abilities of this party.

Our descent through crevasses and ice cliffs, and down 500 feet of slabs threatened by falling ice, left everyone with a feeling of relief at getting back safely.

My deflated companions had been in Peru less than two weeks and though they had planned to stay three weeks they wanted no more to do with the mountains. Phil gave me a large quantity of leftover rations, and they all departed for the USA, or, in Guillermo's case, Chile. Guillermo had said he would stay and climb with me, but had changed his mind after seeing how slow my pace was, or because of the sense of danger we had all experienced on Huascaran.

'I'm just glad to be down safely,' he said, and Phil added, 'Much more serious than the west ridge of McKinley, and that glacier grumbled more than the Khumbu icefall.'

The year before, Phil had passed through the Khumbu icefall and, without resort to bottled oxygen, had reached over 27,000 feet on Everest.

The team's ardour had cooled too rapidly. There were many other relatively safe routes to try around Huaras. I sold some of the rations but retained sufficient to see two or three people through a climb. Alone again; not short of company but lacking a climbing partner.

There was no need to worry, for on the day the others went home, Bob Braun and Glenn Albrecht invited me to climb with them. A New Zealander, Brian Weedon, asked if he could come along, so the absconded US expedition was soon replaced. Bob and Glenn were biologists in their late twenties or early thirties and both had broad climbing experience. Bob was the quieter, more reserved of the two. Brian was twenty-five years old, had trained as a surveyor and worked in New Zealand as a climbing instructor. He had not been blessed with good fortune while in Peru; he had bought a watch which was wrapped for him and later he unfolded the paper to find a substituted bottle cap, and several low value coins which imitated the strap. Then someone had stolen his passport, money, travellers cheques and camera. By coincidence, one of his friends had lost both his legs below the knees through frostbite after two weeks trapped by bad weather on Mount Cook, in New Zealand.

Brian and I took a pickup truck cum bus a few miles northwards to our rendezvous with Bob and Glenn on the main road through the Rio Santa valley. Having met them on the outskirts of the village of Paltey we flagged down another pickup truck and bargained for a rough ride of about four miles to Collon, at 10,500 feet (3,200 m). It had been our intention to carry our rucksacks all the way from there, but a local woman approached us as we passed her mud-brick dwelling and told us her husband, Modesto, had a donkey and a horse which would take the loads from our backs for the next ten miles. At mid-day a deal was struck and we set off behind the two beasts. My left leg was extremely painful, so I lagged behind, and Modesto was soon telling my companions I would not make it to base camp; I had other ideas, of course.

We passed through the most beautiful pastoral scenes one can imagine; soft shades of green and cornfield yellow, and nice browns in mellow textures on gently undulating land where streams laid down lush ribbon borders; and patches of darker colour, where mud-brick, thatched dwellings and tall, dark trees and grazing cattle and sheep existed in harmony, and where the backdrop was of rounded, reddish-brown mountains behind us, distant white ones ahead. It was the kind of scene you can never properly describe. Though I limped painfully, trying to keep my companions in sight, I did not miss the quiet majesty of the place. It crossed my mind that from now on my work would involve putting up with pain, but oh, what views I would see!

Bob, Brian and Glenn were considerate companions, with one or other of them always staying back far enough for me to be in touch with the party. Through a deep U-shaped valley of steep rock walls we followed a river and its forest of quenual trees – thirty feet high and less, twisted branches, peeling papery bark – we approached base camp. Our objective started to show itself, and it was a fine looker. Tocllaraju, or Trap Mountain, is 19,796 feet (6,034 m) and was worth going to Peru for on its own.

Modesto, forty-nine years old, father of seven children, married to a woman of forty, made a half-hearted attempt to raise his price by about five per cent, but his will was weakened at being fed copious quantities of an excellent thickened soup concocted by Glenn and Bob, and he gave up. Wearing sandals made from old car tyres, and wrapped in a good poncho, he settled down on the sandy, football-pitch-sized beach where three of us slept in a tent and Brian spent the night out. During the night poor Modesto's animals departed, fortunately almost certainly downhill, but he would have to walk down now. Nibbling at a few biscuits, he padded off over the sand.

From base camp at 14,435 feet (4,400 m) we shared the vague path up a moraine crest with three Austrians. A little scrambling on easy cliffs, a short snow slope which called for crampons, an up-and-down walk on snow, seven hours gone by, and we were preparing to camp on a large, flat snowfield, close to the Austrians. We must have been above 17,000 feet by then.

6.15 a.m. Cold. My mind said my body did not want to move, but I knew the secret: make a small effort, like putting on a stump sock, then you feel a bit more like putting on one leg, which leads to another stump sock and to the other leg and to a jacket, and in three or four minutes you have almost forgotten that you did not want to move. It worked. Now I wanted to go, but there were too many crevasses for me even to begin to think about going alone. I needed the others. Glenn had decided against; like a lot of people, he had had a bad night at altitude. Bob had had an upset stomach the day before, and Brian had hardly slept, but they were going.

The necessary water was melted from snow and drunk as tea, and we started. Walking on easy angled snow up a snaking route, after an hour we roped up for a hundred feet where the way steepened and a crevasse waited at the bottom if we slipped. The Austrians were just ahead, and an Australian party of four, who had approached by way of a variation of our route, were some way in front of them. The south west glacier and the northwest shoulder, which we were on by now, was the way we should follow, according to a vague description we had read. Other than that, our hastily crystallised expedition had had little time for research except to talk to a Scotsman who said the route was straight-forward. Later it was rumoured that he had not reached the summit, and, considering how far his view began to diverge from ours, I can believe that.

The ascent was in constant doubt because of the weather. Though not the summer period, this was Peru's dry season, and the weather had been continually good, until now. On this morning dark clouds covered mountains of similar altitude all around us, but Tocllaraju was left alone, at least for the time being. We traversed steep slopes with big crevasses running their length at the bottom, 300 feet lower down, and moved carefully, unroped; to have belayed would have created too much delay, and we had one eye on the weather all the while.

'Probably just a walk to the top now,' Brian said at one stage, and afterwards we laughed about that.

At eleven in the morning a big decision confronted me. No more than 250 feet vertically below the summit the mountain reared up into a formidable last rampart and the real difficulties commenced. First there was a big bergschrund, fifteen feet of mouth, overhanging at the top lip and of considerable depth, running the full length of the mountain's final thrust. Above the bergschrund it looked as if some giant hand had placed a 250 feet high, layered, steep-sided meringue on the summit, and we had to climb the icy side which faced us. Amidst the large figures we talk of in the mountains, 250 feet does not sound much, but it equates with the height of a twenty-storey building. We stood and passed rude comments about the judgement of the Scotsman.

The Australians were already part way up, and the Austrians had resigned in the face of such serious territory at more than 19,500 feet.

'How about the last bit?' Brian asked me.

'I'll give it a try.'

'I was hoping you would.'

The trip to Peru needed a good ascent to complete it. Tocllaraju, Trap Mountain, was that ascent, and was worth some extra risk.

A steep ramp of snow and grey ice, like a precarious stepladder, could be reached by way of a very soft snow bridge which spanned the bergschrund; it looked the best (and only) way to tackle the gap. We roped up and set off one by one across uncertain snow. It held for Brian, held for Bob and held for me in turn. The stepladder led to an over-hanging lip of snow on which we did not linger, and the rope length of sharply inclined snow which came next was firm and enjoyable. The three of us congregated on a snow platform, wide as a single bed and half as long again, beneath an ice bulge. Looking upwards, we could escape to the right of the bulge. Brian went first and soon disappeared around it. Bob went the same way, up a steep chute of ice. When I followed, the hard ice fractured under my axe, and small chunks, each like a small discus in size and shape, were dislodged. A piece knocked out by one of the Australians, who were on the way down by now, hit me on the head; it could not be helped.

Had we known about this icy section I would have brought a second axe, but had to make do with the pick on one of my crutches. It worked well on snow but did not penetrate ice nearly so well as a proper axe, so I had to be very careful. If I had fallen it was possible that Brian's belay anchor, an aluminium stake, would have been pulled from the snow, and we would both have bounced down the ice into the bergschrund. Crampon points and ice axe picks bit only half an inch or less into the hardest ice, and quite often it shattered. Every move had to be made with caution; before moving a crampon I had to ensure that the other crampon and both picks were firmly planted. Arm muscles had to make up for a lack of leg strength and each move, performed as smoothly and carefully as possible, required both effort and concentration. Ten feet, twenty feet, thirty feet, forty, more.

'That friggin' Scotsman said this was easy,' one of the Australians remarked wryly as he descended past me.

The ice took us up to a narrow snow ridge which plunged ahead and behind. Turning right, we climbed, then walked, in a blasting wind for two or three minutes on gradually levelling snow to the summit. A gem of a climb.

A few days later we heard that four Austrians got into difficulties on the final section of Tocllaraju and had to be helped down by another party. I could believe that. Our descent was trouble-free, apart from Bob dropping my camera down a crevasse. It slid 200 feet at first, almost came to a halt, and popped over the edge. Bob had insisted on trying to get it back and I had said not if it involved any risk. He went, roped, about a hundred feet down a slope and into a dark hole, to recover the camera, which still worked. And some of the pictures already on the roll of film were the best of the trip.

Next day, for most of the way down the valley, we were able to look back at our gleaming prize. There was a small raw patch on the right stump, and a pressure point on the left stump hurt all the time. By the end of the day I was barely able to walk. No complaints. The approach had been excellent, the peak imposing, the final section exciting, and my companions considerate; the photographs were a bonus.

Climbing has brought in its wake friends and travel and wonderful times when emotions seemed as sweet as a human being could experience. Under the influence of a seemingly bizarre motivation we flirt with death and hope to come back alive, and sometimes climbers are said to have a death wish. That may be true of some but mostly, I think, the reverse is the case. It may at first seem anomalous, but they risk their lives to a greater or lesser extent because life is too precious to waste in appalling dreariness. Through climbing I have discovered my personal path to fulfilment, and feel extremely privileged to have done so. My appreciation of the blessings which have come my way is boundless. Sweet dreams have come true, rich memories spring back; dear God, let it go on and on and on.

Glossary

Aiguille
Steep, sharp rock peak (in French, 'needle').

Abseil
To slide down a rope.

Arête
A sharp rock ridge which may be at any angle between horizontal and vertical.

Belay
Noun: an anchor point which may be natural, such as a spike of rock, a tree or a thick icicle, or artificial, such as a piton or nut (see *nut*).
Verb: to make use of such an anchor or to hold the rope to safeguard a companion.

Bergschrund
A big crevasse (see *crevasse*) which forms between the upper snow and ice of a mountain and a glacier below.

Bivouac (bibi)
To sleep without a tent, usually in a waterproof bag.

Cairn
A pile of stones set up to mark a point such as a summit, or in a series to mark a route.

Chimney
A vertical or slanting crack of sufficient width to get your body in.

Col
A pass, saddle.

Cornice
Overhanging mass of snow formed by wind action.

Crampons
A framework of metal spikes, strapped to boots, to bite into ice and hard snow.

Crevasse
A crack in glacier ice. Some are very big.

Glacier
'A slowly moving mass of ice born from one or more perpetual snowfields.

Grades
For our purposes: Britain, on rock – Easy, Moderate, Difficult, Very Difficult, Severe, Very Severe, Extreme.
The Alps – 1 to 6, 1 being the easiest. (To assist the non-climber, in this book numbers have been substituted for the usual French alpine grades such as 'assez difficile'.)

Harness
A climbing harness is something like a parachute harness.

Karabiner (Krab)
A strong metal snaplink which closes on a similar principle to that of a safety pin. Used for attaching a rope to, for example, a piton (see *piton*) or climbing harness.

Moraine
Rock and dust rubble carried down by a glacier and deposited in huge mounds.

Nut
A metal chockstone which is inserted temporarily in a crack in such a way that it will not be pulled out (we hope!) when a load is put on it. Used for belays and runners (see *runners*).

Pack (backpack)
A modern type of framed rucksack.

Peg
See Piton.

Pitch
Section of a climb, the length of which is often dictated by the availability of belay anchors. Usually between sixty feet and 150 feet, the upper limit being the length of the climbing rope.

Piton
A metal peg which is hammered into a crack. The use of pitons is not generally popular nowadays because insertion and removal damage the rock; nuts (see *nuts*) are much more common.

Runner, running belay
See first the noun version of belay. In the case of a runner the climber does not attach himself or herself to the belay, but attaches a karabiner and lets the climbing rope run free through it. The karabiner then acts rather like a single pulley wheel. (See Climbing Technique.)

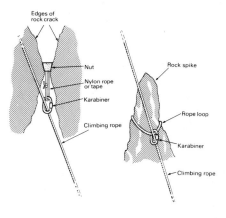

Edges of rock crack

Nut

Nylon rope or tape

Karabiner

Climbing rope

Rock spike

Rope loop

Karabiner

Climbing rope

Scree
Steep slopes of loose stones.

Second
Simply, to climb second. The word is also used as a noun to denote the second climber.

Snowshoes
The older type of snowshoe was often described as looking like a tennis racket. Modern types may be made of plastic, or metal frames with nylon strings, amongst other materials. When strapped to boots they distribute one's weight, thus reducing the depth to which the feet sink in soft snow.

Spindrift
Particles of wind-blown snow.

Traverse
Noun: a horizontal section of climbing. Also a verb meaning, obviously enough, to climb a horizontal section.

Wand
A light stick, possibly bamboo, usually with a small flag, left in the snow to mark a route which is complicated and/or in case of bad weather.

Climbing Technique

What follows is intended to teach those of you who know little about climbing just enough about the subject to understand this book. It is greatly simplified and should not be misconstrued as a guide to anyone who wishes to get on to rock, snow or ice.

On Rock

The first man to climb is called the leader. He is tied to one end of a rope which is usually between 120 feet and 150 feet in length. One other person, known as the second, is tied to the other end, or there may be two more people, one tied at the middle and one at the end. As the leader climbs, the rope trails behind, paid out by the second; the rope is too thin to climb but is there to save a partner who falls. If necessary and if possible the leader puts on runners (see Glossary) so the next climber can hold him or her in the event of a fall. If a leader falls from ten feet above a runner, the fall will amount to twenty feet before the rope goes tight. Provided the runner does not fail through a nut being pulled out or a karabiner breaking, for instance, the rope will then stretch and help to cushion the fall. The leader may collide with rock on the way down, and there may be long sections of rock devoid of places where runners can be fixed, so runners do not always reduce or eliminate risk.

The leader may climb until the full length of rope between him or her and the second has run out, or may stop earlier, depending on the distances between belays (see Pitch and Belay in Glossary). If possible the leader then sits or stands on a good ledge, and should be attached to some form of anchor (belay). The second climber starts up, to be held like a flying stage Peter Pan if a fall occurs. That may sound fairly safe, but belay anchors may fail, the second may be injured in a sudden fall of a few feet, or, if not climbing in a line directly beneath the leader, may swing about dangerously. On some traverses (see Glossary) the second may face as much risk as the leader. Also the leader may dislodge loose rock on to a second. Generally, however, the leader takes more risk, particularly where runners are widely spaced.

When climbing in a party of two or three, only one person moves at a time, the other two remaining attached to the rock.

As far as possible the legs rather than the arms are used to raise the body, because leg muscles are bigger and stronger. The climber looks for 'holds', which may be small protrusions, cracks of various sizes (which may be big enough to take a boot toe, fingers, a hand, a foot, a leg, an arm or the whole body), and at times will rely on the friction of boots on the rock.

On Snow and Ice

On steep snow and ice, in some ways the procedure is similar to rock climbing; the rope is used in the same way and a belay may be a thick icicle, a large, tubular screw driven into the ice, or a metal plate (like a pointed spade blade and called a 'dead-man') hammered into hard snow. If available, rock anchors, such as a rock spike on the wall of an icy gully, may be used too. But whereas on rock one often relies on natural holds for the hands and feet, on ice and steep snow one uses crampons (see Glossary) and various types of ice axes and ice hammers (which are shorter than an axe and have the weight concentrated more in the head), to bite in and give support. (The press often write about climbers using 'ice picks', which is incorrect.)

Mountaineering

High mountain ascents may require the rock and snow and ice techniques mentioned above, as well as the additional skills of being able to move safely over glaciers, to perform crevasse rescues, to judge where and when the avalanche risk is high, to assess the weather and to cross rivers. To put up with the sheer slog of carrying heavy loads for long distances, perhaps at great altitudes, requires determination. High altitude mountaineering does not always involve steep rock, snow or ice, but the risks of altitude sickness, bad weather, crevasses, long distances, soft snow, hypothermia, frostbite, loose rock (resulting in rock-falls and tricky climbing) and avalanches can mean that even the 'easiest' routes on big mountains are arduous and dangerous. The severe lack of oxygen distinguishes high Himalayan and Andean climbing from alpine climbing. Because of the differences in performance between people, and because of the need for speed, the rope and belay rules of rock and snow and ice climbing are not always followed; and a great many of the world's best mountaineers climb solo at times.

Conversion Table

Feet	Metres		Feet	Metres
10	3.05		4,000	1,219
			5,000	1,524
20	6.1		10,000	3,048
50	15.2			
100	30.5		15,000	4,572
			17,000	5,181
200	61		18,000	5,486
250	76			
300	91		19,000	5,790
			20,000	6,096
400	122		21,000	6,401
500	152			
600	183		22,000	6,706
			23,000	7,010
1,000	305		24,000	7,315
2,000	610			
3,000				

Major Ascents

Year	Mountain	Metres	Feet
1970	Mönch, Switzerland.	4,099	13,447
1970	Jungfrau, Switzerland.	4,158	13,641
1971	Mont Blanc, France.	4,807	15,770
1972	West Flank, Eiger, Switzerland.	3,970	13,024
1973	Wellenkuppe, Switzerland.	3,903	12,804
1974	Hörnli Ridge, Matterhorn, Switzerland.	4,478	14,681
1974	Breithorn, Switzerland.	4,165	13,664
1975	S.S.W. Ridge, Egginer, Switzerland.	3,366	11,043
1975	South Rib, Jagihorn, Switzerland.	3,206	10,518
1976	Arete des Cosmiques, Aiguille du Midi, France.	3,842	12,604
1976	Tete Blanche, France.	3,429	11,250
1976	L'Index, France.	2,595	8,514
1976	Aiguille, de L'M, France.	2,844	9,330
1978	Wallanaraju Sur, Peru.	5,120	16,798
1978	Pisco, Peru.	5,752	18,871
1978	North Summit, Huascaran, Peru.	6,654	21,830
1980	L'Eveque, Switzerland.	3,392	11,128
1980	La Luette, Switzerland.	3,548	11,640
1980	Point Kurz, Switzerland.	3,498	11,476
1981	E. Summit, Ameghino, Argentina.	5,115	16,781
1981	White Needle, Kashmir.	6,553	21,500
1982	Cerro Manso, Argentina.	5,557	18,231 (or more)
1982	Aconcagua, Argentina.	6,960	22,834
1982	Muztagh Ata, China.	7,546	24,757
1983	Gillman's Point, Kilimanjaro, Tanzania.	5,682	18,640
1983	North Face, Tour Ronde, France.	3,792	12,441
1983	Tocllaraju, Peru.	6,032	19,790

Acknowledgements

As well as all the people whose co-operation and helpfulness in many forms is recorded at various points in this book, there are a great many organisations and individuals who deserve thanks. I hope that between the text and the following list I have included everyone who deserves a mention; and what a lot there are!

W. Adams, Agfa-Gevaert Ltd., Air France, Air India, Alpine Club, Andean Society, Applied Chemicals Ltd., Senor Cesar Morales Arnao, M. Ashraf, Aston Containers Ltd., Sue Bailey, B.B.C., Berghaus, Michael Bentine, Major R. Berry F.R.I.C.S., Margaret Billings, Dick Boetius, Walter Bonatti, BP Oil, The Lord Mayor of Bristol, Bristol Evening Post, Bristol Round Table, Bristol and West Building Society, British Mountaineering Council, Buchanan Booth Agencies, The Burgess Twins, Brian Campbell, Canon Cameras, Caravan Ltd., Alok and Renee Chandola, Charities Aid Foundation, Chinese Mountaineering Association, John Cleare, Climbing Gear Ltd., Clogwyn Climbing and Safety Equipment, Collins (Norwich) Ltd., Colmans Foods, Diana Corbin, Mr & Mrs E. Croucher, Peter Cummings, Damart, Dingles (Bristol), Disabled Sports Foundation, Dixons Photographic (U.K.) Ltd., Phil Ershler, Europa Sport, Farillon, Mr & Mrs R. M. Feekery, Richard Fenton, Field and Trek (Equipment) Ltd., Alec Fish, Dr Fletcher, Dr K. Fowler, Fowlers of Bristol, Frenchay Hospital, Gallaghers Tobacco, Jim Galt, Mick Geddes, N. Gifford, Ginsters Cornish Pasties, Glenfiditch, Glorious Twelfth, Chris Grace, John Haig & Co. Ltd., J. E. Hanger & Co. Ltd., E. R. Hemmings, John Hinde, Honeywell Ltd., Bill Hornyak, Indian Mountaineering Foundation, Intermed, Jammu and Kashmir Mountaineering and Hiking Club, J. & K. Department of Tourism, Wanchuck Kaloon, Tourist Officer at Kargil, Karrimor International Ltd., Kellogg, Kingston-on-Thames Association for the Disabled, Bruce Klepinger, Kodak Ltd., Koflach Boots, Lima Tours, Steve McKinney, Mars, Senor Gonzales Mata, Dr John Minors, Dr P. Moffit, Mount Everest Foundation, Mountain Equipment Ltd., Mountain Travel, Mountain World, A. T. Needle, Nelsons of Aintree, Nicholas Laboratories, Nikon U.K. Ltd., N.R. Components, Crompton Parkinson, Pepe Espinoza, Eric Perlman, Peruvian Andean Club, Bob Pettigrew, Pindisports, Pocahontas Ltd., Joan Pralong, Mr Qui, Daniel Quiggin & Sons, Rainier Mountaineering, Ghulm Rasool, Jimmy Roberts, James Robertson & Sons, Roboserve Ltd., The Viscountess Rochdale CBE, JP, Roehampton Limb Centre, Rohan, Alan Rouse, Royal Geographical Society, St Joseph's School, Horwich, Miguel Sanchez, Gerhardt Schwartz, J. A. Sharwood, J. J. Silber, Gary Sillitoe, Smith & Nephew, Jim Smith, Rosie Smith, John Smolich, Sony (U.K.) Ltd., South American Explorers Club, Bill Sparkes, John, Claire, Jack and James Spedding, Dr Peter Steel, Arnis Strapcans, Mr Su, Tefal Ltd., Thornbury Rotary Club, Jens Toft, J. Toogood, Troll Safety Equipment Ltd., Tunbridge Wells Camera Centre, Twickenham Travel, Ultimate Equipment Ltd., Hector Vieytes, Viasa Airways, Ulises Vitale, Ghafoor Wahid, Warwick Productions, Jackie Welham, Norma Welsh, West-croft, Wexas International, Bill & Iris Marks and customers at the Wheatsheaf, Ealing, Dr J. G. P. Williams, Winston Churchill Memorial Trust, Wintergear Ltd., Women's Section of Southfields and Central Wandsworth British Legion, Woodhead Mountain Rescue Team, S. Wooller, Y.H.A., Yousuf Zaheer, Zero Point Nine.

Index

215